(Part III)
The Hymns and Hymn Melodies of the Organ Works

Charles Sanford Terry

Alpha Editions

This edition published in 2019

ISBN : 9789353899882

Design and Setting By
Alpha Editions
email - alphaedis@gmail.com

As per information held with us this book is in Public Domain. This book is a reproduction of an important historical work. Alpha Editions uses the best technology to reproduce historical work in the same manner it was first published to preserve its original nature. Any marks or number seen are left intentionally to preserve its true form.

BACH'S CHORALS

BY

CHARLES SANFORD TERRY
LITT.D. CANTAB.

PART III

THE HYMNS AND HYMN
MELODIES
OF THE
ORGAN WORKS

Cambridge:
at the University Press
1921

"No one who is familiar with the work of other centuries will contradict or hold my statement exaggerated, that Bach cannot be named except in tones of rapture, and even of devout awe, by those who have learnt to know him. We may discover and lay bare the secrets of his technique. But his power to inspire into it the breath of genius, the perfection of life and charm that moves us so powerfully, even in his slightest works, must always remain extraordinary and insoluble."

JOHANN NIKOLAUS FORKEL.

PREFATORY NOTE

"OF all Bach's works, the Organ Chorals are probably the least known, even to organists," Mr Newman remarks in Novello's edition of the *Orgelbüchlein*. "Until recently," another English writer[1] confesses, "not more than one organist in a hundred knew what Bach was driving at in the Choral Preludes as a whole. We were confronted with collections of pieces bearing German titles, with no hint as to pace, power, or registration. Sometimes the thematic basis could be identified and followed, but more often not. In many cases it was even impossible to say whether the music was intended to be joyful or sad. We need not be surprised that the puzzle was laid aside in favour of Preludes and Fugues that carried their message on their face."

In large measure English neglect of the Choral Preludes is due to unfamiliarity with the melodies and hymns on which they are founded, whereas, by reason of the intimate relation between them and Bach's music, a knowledge of both is imperative. No adequate attempt hitherto has been made to remove this serious impediment by placing the text of the hymns before English readers, systematically exploring them for guidance to Bach's treatment

[1] Mr Harvey Grace in *The Musical Times* for October 1920, p. 671.

of their melodies, and expounding the form and historical antecedents of the tunes. The author believes that the following pages will be found to provide the necessary apparatus for a neglected study.*

The author's discovery of Bach's early use of Christian Friedrich Witt's *Psalmodia sacra* (1715) opens a new field of exploration and has produced important results. It has at length forced the secret of its design and purpose from the *Orgelbüchlein*, a problem which German scholarship, persistently and minutely concentrated on Bach's art for more than sixty years, either neglected or found insoluble. It affords, moreover, with some approximation to accuracy, the means to date the Choral Preludes according as Bach's version of their melodies conforms to or differs from Witt's—*i.e.* Gotha-Weimar—use.

It is only necessary to add that the present volume repeats the method of its predecessors. The source of the hymns and melodies is stated: the tunes are given in their earliest published form: a translation of every hymn used by Bach is provided. Biographical and bibliographical information is furnished concerning such authors, composers, hymns, and tunes as do not occur in the earlier volumes of this work. In Part II an Appendix was provided disclosing the *locus* of the MS. and Autograph texts of the Oratorios, *Passions*, Masses, Cantatas, and Motetts. Similar information is provided here regarding the Choral Preludes.

References to the Choral Preludes are made throughout to Novello's Edition (Books xv–xix). Owners of other Editions can easily adapt these pages to their use by means of the comparative Table provided on pages 2–11. It would have been agreeable to collate the Schirmer Edition, prepared by C. M. Widor and Albert Schweitzer: its volumes VI–VIII are to contain the Choral Preludes, but are not yet published.

The present volume concludes an arduous labour. To those who have aided him by counsel and correction, and particularly his friends Sir Ivor Atkins and Dr W. G. Whittaker, the author makes his sincere acknowledgments. He cannot fail to add a note of warm gratitude to the Syndics of the Cambridge University Press for material aid towards the publication of this volume and for unfailing interest in an undertaking whose completion owes much to their encouragement.

C. S. T.

KING'S COLLEGE,
    OLD ABERDEEN.
        July 1921.

CONTENTS

	PAGE
PREFATORY NOTE	v
INTRODUCTION	
The Organ Chorals	1
The Texts	12
The *Orgelbüchlein*	18
The *Clavierübung*, Part III	66
Schübler's *Sechs Choräle*	70
The Canonic Variations on "Vom Himmel hoch"	75
The *Achtzehn Choräle*	78
MELODIES	83
INDEX	347

MELODIES

	PAGE
Ach bleib' bei uns, Herr Jesu Christ	83
Ach Gott und Herr	86
Ach wie flüchtig	89
Alle Menschen müssen sterben	93
Allein Gott in der Höh' sei Ehr'	96
An Wasserflüssen Babylon	101
Auf meinen lieben Gott, *or*, Wo soll ich fliehen hin	341
Aus tiefer Noth schrei ich zu dir	106
Christ, der du bist der helle Tag	109
Christ ist erstanden	113
Christ lag in Todesbanden	115
Christ unser Herr zum Jordan kam	120
Christe, du Lamm Gottes	124
Christum wir sollen loben schon	126
Christus, der uns selig macht	129
Da Jesus an dem Kreuze stund	133
Das alte Jahr vergangen ist	137
Das Jesulein soll doch mein Trost	140
Der Tag, der ist so freudenreich	143
Dies sind die heil'gen zehn Gebot'	146
Durch Adams Fall ist ganz verderbt	150
Ein' feste Burg ist unser Gott	153
Erbarm' dich mein, O Herre Gott	155
Erschienen ist der herrliche Tag	158
Erstanden ist der heil'ge Christ	160
Es ist das Heil uns kommen her	166
Es ist gewisslich an der Zeit, *or*, Nun freut euch, lieben Christen g'mein	266
Gelobet seist du, Jesu Christ	169
Gott, durch deine Güte, *or*, Gottes Sohn ist kommen	173
Gottes Sohn ist kommen, *or*, Gott, durch deine Güte	173

	PAGE
Helft mir Gott's Güte preisen	177
Herr Christ, der ein'ge Gottes-Sohn, *or*, Herr Gott, nun sei gepreiset	182
Herr Gott dich loben wir	185
Herr Gott, nun sei gepreiset, *or*, Herr Christ, der ein'ge Gottes-Sohn	182
Herr Gott, nun schleuss den Himmel auf	187
Herr Jesu Christ, dich zu uns wend'	191
Herzlich thut mich verlangen	195
Heut' triumphiret Gottes Sohn	198
Hilf Gott, dass mir's gelinge	201
Ich hab' mein Sach' Gott heimgestellt	205
Ich ruf' zu dir, Herr Jesu Christ	209
In dich hab' ich gehoffet, Herr	211
In dir ist Freude	215
In dulci jubilo	220
Jesu, meine Freude	224
Jesus Christus, unser Heiland, Der den Tod	227
Jesus Christus, unser Heiland, Der von uns	230
Jesus, meine Zuversicht	236
Komm, Gott, Schöpfer, heiliger Geist	239
Komm, heiliger Geist, Herre Gott	242
Kommst du nun, Jesu, vom Himmel herunter auf Erden?	246
Kyrie, Gott Vater in Ewigkeit	248
Liebster Jesu, wir sind hier	251
Lob sei dem allmächtigen Gott	255
Lobt Gott, ihr Christen alle gleich	258
Meine Seele erhebt den Herren	260
Mit Fried' und Freud' ich fahr' dahin	262
Nun danket alle Gott	264
Nun freut euch, lieben Christen g'mein, *or*, Es ist gewisslich an der Zeit	266
Nun komm, der Heiden Heiland	272
O Gott, du frommer Gott	275
O Lamm Gottes unschuldig	281

xi

	PAGE
O Mensch, bewein' dein' Sünde gross . . .	284
Puer natus in Bethlehem	286
Schmücke dich, O liebe Seele	289
Sei gegrüsset, Jesu gütig	292
Valet will ich dir geben	297
Vater unser im Himmelreich	300
Vom Himmel hoch da komm ich her . . .	304
Vom Himmel kam der Engel Schaar . . .	308
Von Gott will ich nicht lassen	310
Vor deinen Thron tret ich hiemit, *or*, Wenn wir in höchsten Nöthen sein	316
Wachet auf, ruft uns die Stimme	314
Wenn wir in höchsten Nöthen sein, *or*, Vor deinen Thron tret ich hiemit.	316
Wer nur den lieben Gott lässt walten . . .	324
Wie schön leuchtet der Morgenstern . . .	328
Wir Christenleut'	332
Wir danken dir, Herr Jesu Christ . . .	334
Wir glauben all' an einen Gott, Schöpfer . .	336
Wir glauben all' an einen Gott, Vater . . .	339
Wo soll ich fliehen hin, *or*, Auf meinen lieben Gott	341

PART II

ADDENDA AND ERRATA

PAGE

4. In Period I (1704–8) *add* No. 196.
    ,, II (1708–17) *delete* No. 196.
    ,, IV (1723–34) *add* Nos. 39, 53, 54, and *delete* Nos. 28, 107, U 3.
    ,, V (1735–50) *add* Nos. 28, 107, U 3, and *delete* Nos. 39, 53, 54.

5 ff. A fuller Analysis of the Cantata libretti is available in Forkel's (ed. Terry) *Johann Sebastian Bach* (Constable, 1920), pp. 187–224. Further information is afforded there also regarding their authorship.

27. In its revised and existing form Cantata No. 20 (O Ewigkeit, du Donnerwort) probably belongs to the later Leipzig period.

30 l. 18. Bach wrote four Choral Cantatas of earlier date than is here suggested: No. 4 in 1724, No. 8 *c*. 1725, No. 20 *c*. 1725, No. 93 in 1728 (?).

31 l. 12. Bach's dependence on Picander is probably exaggerated. See Forkel, *op. cit.* p. 178.

33 l. 16. Cantata No. 93 was composed in 1728 (?). Bach already had used the paraphrased hymn-stanza in Nos. 8 and (perhaps) 20.

53 l. 10. Bach's text of the Magnificat follows St Luke's Gospel and not Pollio's paraphrase.

62. Isaak's authorship of "O Welt, ich muss dich lassen" is doubtful.

63. To Rosenmüller may be attributed, but not positively, "Straf mich nicht in deinem Zorn" (see p. 66, l. 20).

74. Some of the melodies on pp. 74–126 are in the "English Hymnal," and, in Aria form (ed. Dr W. G. Whittaker), are published by Messrs Stainer and Bell.

96. The melody is included in the Moravian Hymn-book, ed. 1914 (No. 357).

xiii

PAGE	
111.	The melody "Nicht so traurig" is included in the Moravian Hymn-book, ed. 1914 (No. 655).
130.	A complete analysis of the melody is afforded at p. 330 of the present volume.
163.	Into the penultimate number (Tenor Solo "Sei getreu") of the Cantata Bach introduces the melody of "Jesu, meine Freude" as a Tromba *obbligato*.
181.	In its existing form the Cantata belongs to the later Leipzig period.
185 l. 7.	Bach's version of the last line of the melody is found in Witt's Hymn-book (1715).
199 l. 3.	*For c.* 1725 *read c.* 1736.
200.	The Introduction to Cantata 29 is the Prelude of the sixth Violin Sonata (E major).
215 l. 18.	*For c.* 1740 *read* 1732.
216.	Cantata 40 may be dated 1723 (?).
222.	Spitta III. 91 suggests January 1, 1736, as the date of the first performance of Cantata 41.
225.	The Cantata may be dated 1731.
234 l. 4.	Bach's version of the fourth and sixth lines is closely found in Witt (1715).
235 l. 3.	*For c.* 1720 *read* 1720 (?).
„ l. 4 from bottom.	Zahn (No. 1689*b*) quotes the tune as set *c.* 1560 to two secular songs.
260 l. 11 from bottom.	*Add* Cantata 12.
265.	The Cantata may be dated 1731.
268 bottom line.	Bach's version of the last line of the melody is found in Witt (1715).
279 l. 3.	*For* 1725 *read* 1726.
283 l. 3.	*For* 1735 *read* 1735 (?).
306 l. 17.	Bach's version of the final phrase in Cantata 112 is found in Witt (1715).
310.	Cantata 187 may be dated 1735 (?).
313.	Fr. Zelle (*Die Singweisen der ältesten Zeit*, p. 54) suggests that the melody derives from a "Bergmannslied."
336 l. 3.	*For* Georg *read* Martin.

PAGE	
343.	Pirro (*J.-S. Bach*, p. 87) suggests that the Cantata was composed for the funeral of Bach's uncle, Tobias Lämmerhirt, at Erfurt in September 1707.
346 l. 2.	*For* 1735 *read c.* 1735.
351.	Cantata 112 may be dated 1731.
354	in l. 3 of the second stanza *read* gebüssest.
359.	The tune is attributed to Johann Rosenmüller.
366 l. 3.	*For c.* 1730 *read* 1730.
389.	Wustmann dates the Cantata August 1707.
391.	Cantata 133 may be dated 1735 or 1737.
405.	For further notes on this melody see the present volume, p. 315.
425 l. 3.	*For* 1715 *read* 1716.
,,	Cantata 156 may be dated 1729 or 1730.
446.	Cantata 171 may be dated 1730 or 1731.
460.	A note on the score of Cantata 182 in Bach's hand indicates that it was also used for the Feast of the Annunciation.
474.	Spitta III. 77 dates Cantata 197 1737 (?).
477 n. 2.	*For* The work is *read* The Arias are.
478.	The Cantata belongs to the later (*post* 1734) Leipzig period.
494 (and Part I. 4).	Crüger's melody "Herzliebster Jesu" undoubtedly was suggested by Louis Bourgeois' setting of Psalm 23, which Crüger included in his 1640 Hymn-book. The last six bars are all but identical. See Zahn, No. 3199.

INTRODUCTION

The Organ Chorals

BACH'S lavish use of Lutheran hymnody has been pointed out in Part II of this work[1]. One hundred and thirty-two melodies are treated by him, either in his concerted Church music or in the Organ works, without taking into account hymn tunes of which there are four-part settings among the "Choralgesänge." Of the one hundred and thirty-two, seventy-seven are in the Organ works, twenty-eight[2] of which are not used in the Cantatas, Oratorios, or Motetts. On these seventy-seven tunes Bach constructed one hundred and forty-three authentic Organ movements, or sets of movements, distributed thus: in the *Orgelbüchlein* 46; in Part III of the *Clavierübung* 17; in the *Eighteen Chorals* 18; in the *Schübler Chorals* 6; Variations or Partite 4; miscellaneous or ungrouped Preludes 52.

The following Table names the seventy-seven melodies and the one hundred and forty-three

---

[1] Introduction, p. 60.
[2] In the Table the melodies are numbered 4, 6, 8, 15-18, 22, 24, 27, 31, 32, 34, 35, 38, 40, 41, 43, 44, 49, 50, 51, 58, 63, 70, 74-76.

movements built upon them[1]. The distinguishing capital letters have the following signification:

C. stands for the *Clavierübung*, Part III.
E. „ *Eighteen Chorals.*
M. „ Miscellaneous or ungrouped Preludes.
O. „ *Orgelbüchlein.*
S. „ *Schübler Chorals.*
V. „ Variations or Partite.

For convenience, page and volume references are given to the four Editions: B.G. stands for the Bachgesellschaft; B.H. for Breitkopf and Haertel; N. for Novello; P. for Peters. Elsewhere in this volume reference is given exclusively to the Novello Edition. A collation of the Peters and Novello Editions will be found at pp. 294–302 of the present writer's *Johann Sebastian Bach* (Constable: 1920).

1. ACH BLEIB' BEI UNS, HERR JESU CHRIST[2].
S. 1. N. xvi. 10. B.G. xxv. (2) 71. P. vi. 4. B.H. viii. 2.

2. ACH GOTT UND HERR.
M. 2. N. xviii. 1. B.G. xl. 4. P. ix. 38. B.H. viii. 5.
A variant of the movement is in B.G. xl. 152.
M. 3. N. xviii. 2. B.G. xl. 5. P. vi. 3. B.H. viii. 6.
M. 4. N. xviii. 3. B.G. xl. 43. P. ix. 39. B.H. viii. 7.

3. ACH WIE FLÜCHTIG[3].
O. 5. N. xv. 121. B.G. xxv. (2) 60. P. v. 2. B.H. vii. 3.

4. ALLE MENSCHEN MÜSSEN STERBEN.
O. 6. N. xv. 119. B.G. xxv. (2) 59. P. v. 2. B.H. vii. 4.

[1] Only those movements are admitted to the Table whose genuineness is beyond question. The existence of variant texts and of movements of doubtful authenticity is noted.

[2] Or "Danket dem Herrn, heut' und allzeit."

[3] Bach wrongly names the tune "Ach wie nichtig, ach wie flüchtig."

THE ORGAN CHORALS 3

5. ALLEIN GOTT IN DER HÖH' SEI EHR'.
C. 7. N. xvi. 39. B.G. iii. 197. P. vi. 10. B.H. viii. 8.
C. 8. N. xvi. 40*. B.G. iii. 199. P. vi. 12. B.H. viii. 18.
An older text is in B.G. xl. 208 and P. vi. 96.
C. 9. N. xvi. 41. B.G. iii. 205. P. vi. 29. B.H. viii. 29.
E. 10. N. xvii. 56. B.G. xxv. (2) 122. P. vi. 26. B.H. viii. 36.
E. 11. N. xvii. 60. B.G. xxv. (2) 125. P. vi. 22. B.H. viii. 24.
An older text is in B.G. xxv. (2) 180 and P. vi. 100.
E. 12. N. xvii. 66. B.G. xxv. (2) 130. P. vi. 17. B.H. viii. 30.
An older text is in B.G. xxv. (2) 183 and P. vi. 97.
M. 13. N. xviii. 4. B.G. xl. 44. B.H. viii. 11.
M. 14. N. xviii. 5. B.G. xl. 34. P. vi. 6. B.H. viii. 12.
M. 15. N. xviii. 7. B.G. xl. 45. P. vi. 30. B.H. viii. 14.
M. 16. N. xviii. 11. B.G. xl. 47. P. vi. 8. B.H. viii. 16.
A set of seventeen Variations, of doubtful genuineness, is
in B.G. xl. 195.

6. AN WASSERFLÜSSEN BABYLON.
E. 17. N. xvii. 18. B.G. xxv. (2) 92. P. vi. 34. B.H. viii. 40.
An older text is in B.G. xxv. (2) 157 and P. vi. 103.
M. 18. N. xviii. 13. B.G. xl. 49. P. vi. 32. B.H. viii. 43.

7. AUS TIEFER NOTH SCHREI ICH ZU DIR.
C. 19. N. xvi. 68. B.G. iii. 229. P. vi. 36. B.H. viii. 46.
C. 20. N. xvi. 72. B.G. iii. 232. P. vi. 38. B.H. viii. 48.

8. CHRIST, DER DU BIST DER HELLE TAG.
V. 21. N. xix. 36. B.G. xl. 107. P. v. 60. B.H. vii. 58.

9. CHRIST IST ERSTANDEN.
O. 22. N. xv. 83. B.G. xxv. (2) 40. P. v. 4. B.H. vii. 6.
A four-part setting is in B.G. xl. 173.

10. CHRIST LAG IN TODESBANDEN.
O. 23. N. xv. 79. B.G. xxv. (2) 38. P. v. 7. B.H. vii. 10.
M. 24. N. xviii. 16. B.G. xl. 10. P. vi. 43. B.H. viii. 51.
A variant reading is in B.G. xl. 153 and P. vi. 104.
M. 25. N. xviii. 19. B.G. xl. 52. P. vi. 40. B.H. viii. 54.
A movement of doubtful authenticity is in B.G. xl. 174 and
P. ix. 56.

11. Christ unser Herr zum Jordan kam.
C. 26. N. xvi. 62. B.G. iii. 224. P. vi. 46. B.H. viii. 58.
C. 27. N. xvi. 67. B.G. iii. 228. P. vi. 49. B.H. viii. 63.

12. Christe, du Lamm Gottes.
O. 28. N. xv. 61. B.G. xxv. (2) 30. P. v. 3. B.H. vii. 5.

13. Christum wir sollen loben schon.
O. 29. N. xv. 33. B.G. xxv. (2) 15. P. v. 8. B.H. vii. 11.
M. 30. N. xviii. 23. B.G. xl. 13. P. v. 9. B.H. viii. 58.
This movement has the alternative title, "Was fürcht'st du, Feind Herodes, sehr."

14. Christus, der uns selig macht.
O. 31. N. xv. 64. B.G. xxv. (2) 30. P. v. 10. B.H. vii. 12.
An older text is in B.G. xxv. (2) 149 and P. v. 108.

15. Da Jesus an dem Kreuze stund.
O. 32. N. xv. 67. B.G. xxv. (2) 32. P. v. 11. B.H. vii. 14.

16. Das alte Jahr vergangen ist.
O. 33. N. xv. 43. B.G. xxv. (2) 19. P. v. 12. B.H. vii. 15.

17. Das Jesulein soll doch mein Trost.
M. 34. N. xviii. 24. B.G. xl. 20. P. ix. 47. B.H. viii. 64.

18. Der Tag, der ist so freudenreich.
O. 35. N. xv. 18. B.G. xxv. (2) 8. P. v. 13. B.H. vii. 16.
M. 36. N. xviii. 26. B.G. xl. 55. B.H. viii. 66.

19. Dies sind die heil'gen zehn Gebot'.
O. 37. N. xv. 103. B.G. xxv. (2) 50. P. v. 14. B.H. vii. 18.
C. 38. N. xvi. 42. B.G. iii. 206. P. vi. 50. B.H. viii. 68.
C. 39. N. xvi. 47. B.G. iii. 210. P. vi. 54. B.H. viii. 72.

20. Durch Adams Fall ist ganz verderbt.
O. 40. N. xv. 107. B.G. xxv. (2) 53. P. v. 15. B.H. vii. 20.
M. 41. N. xviii. 28. B.G. xl. 23. P. vi. 56. B.H. viii. 74.

21. Ein' feste Burg ist unser Gott.
M. 42. N. xviii. 30. B.G. xl. 57. P. vi. 58. B.H. viii. 76.

THE ORGAN CHORALS 5

22. ERBARM' DICH MEIN, O HERRE GOTT.
M. 43. N. xviii. 35. B.G. xl. 60. B.H. viii. 80.

23. ERSCHIENEN IST DER HERRLICHE TAG.
O. 44. N. xv. 91. B.G. xxv. (2) 45. P. v. 17. B.H. vii. 21.

24. ERSTANDEN IST DER HEIL'GE CHRIST.
O. 45. N. xv. 89. B.G. xxv. (2) 44. P. v. 16. B.H. vii. 22.

25. ES IST DAS HEIL UNS KOMMEN HER.
O. 46. N. xv. 109. B.G. xxv. (2) 54. P. v. 18. B.H. vii. 23.

26. GELOBET SEIST DU, JESU CHRIST.
O. 47. N. xv. 15. B.G. xxv. (2) 7. P. v. 19. B.H. vii. 24.
M. 48. N. xviii. 37. B.G. xl. 62. P. v. 102. B.H. viii. 81.
A variant is in B.G. xl. 158.
M. 49. N. xviii. 38. B.G. xl. 14. P. v. 20. B.H. viii. 82.
M. 50. N. xviii. 39. B.G. xl. 63. P. vi. 61. B.H. viii. 83.

27. GOTTES SOHN IST KOMMEN.
O. 51. N. xv. 5. B.G. xxv. (2) 4. P. v. 20. B.H. vii. 24.
To this movement Bach gives the alternative title, "Gott, durch deine Güte."
M. 52. N. xviii. 41. B.G. xl. 21. P. v. 22. B.H. viii. 85.
M. 53. N. xviii. 42. B.G. xl. 65. P. vi. 64. B.H. viii. 86.

28. HELFT MIR GOTT'S GÜTE PREISEN.
O. 54. N. xv. 39. B.G. xxv. (2) 18. P. v. 23. B.H. vii. 26.

29. HERR CHRIST, DER EIN'GE GOTTES-SOHN.
O. 55. N. xv. 9. B.G. xxv. (2) 5. P. v. 24. B.H. vii. 27.
To this movement Bach gives the alternative title, "Herr Gott, nun sei gepreiset."
M. 56. N. xviii. 43. B.G. xl. 15. P. v. 25. B.H. viii. 87.
A simple four-part setting of the melody is in P. v. 107.

30. HERR GOTT DICH LOBEN WIR.
M. 57. N. xviii. 44. B.G. xl. 66. P. vi. 65. B.H. viii. 88.

31. HERR GOTT, NUN SCHLEUSS DEN HIMMEL AUF.
O. 58. N. xv. 53. B.G. xxv. (2) 26. P. v. 26. B.H. vii. 28.

32. HERR JESU CHRIST, DICH ZU UNS WEND'.

O. 59. N. xv. 99. B.G. xxv. (2) 48. P. v. 28. B.H. vii. 30.
M. 60. N. xviii. 50. B.G. xl. 30. P. v. 28. B.H. viii. 94.
E. 61. N. xvii. 26. B.G. xxv. (2) 98. P. vi. 70. B.H. viii. 96.
P. vi. 107–8 (B.G. xxv. (2) 159, 162) prints two older readings; B.G. xxv. (2) 160 a third.
M. 62. N. xviii. 52. B.G. xl. 72. B.H. viii. 100.

33. HERZLICH THUT MICH VERLANGEN[1].

M. 63. N. xviii. 53. B.G. xl. 73. P. v. 30. B.H. viii. 100.

34. HEUT' TRIUMPHIRET GOTTES SOHN.

O. 64. N. xv. 94. B.G. xxv. (2) 46. P. v. 30. B.H. vii. 31.

35. HILF GOTT, DASS MIR'S GELINGE.

O. 65. N. xv. 76. B.G. xxv. (2) 36. P. v. 32. B.H. vii. 32.

36. ICH HAB' MEIN SACH' GOTT HEIMGESTELLT.

M. 66. N. xviii. 54. B.G. xl. 26. P. vi. 74. B.H. viii. 102.
M. 67. N. xviii. 58. B.G. xl. 30, 152. B.H. viii. 106.

37. ICH RUF' ZU DIR, HERR JESU CHRIST.

O. 68. N. xv. 111. B.G. xxv. (2) 55. P. v. 33. B.H. vii. 34.

38, 39. IN DICH HAB' ICH GEHOFFET, HERR.

O. 69. N. xv. 113. B.G. xxv. (2) 56. P. v. 35. B.H. vii. 36.
On an anonymous melody dating from 1560.
M. 70. N. xviii. 59. B.G. xl. 36. P. vi. 94. B.H. viii. 107.
On a melody by Seth Calvisius, 1581.

40. IN DIR IST FREUDE.

O. 71. N. xv. 45. B.G. xxv. (2) 20. P. v. 36. B.H. vii. 37.

41. IN DULCI JUBILO.

O. 72. N. xv. 26. B.G. xxv. (2) 12. P. v. 38. B.H. vii. 40.
M. 73. N. xviii. 61. B.G. xl. 74. P. v. 103. B.H. viii. 109.
A so-called variant is in B.G. xl. 158.

---

[1] Also known as "O Haupt voll Blut und Wunden."

THE ORGAN CHORALS 7

42. JESU, MEINE FREUDE.
O. 74. N. xv. 31. B.G. xxv. (2) 14. P. v. 34. B.H. vii. 35.
M. 75. N. xviii. 64. B.G. xl. 38. P. vi. 78. B.H. viii. 111.
A variant text is in B.G. xl. 155 and P. vi. 110.
A fragment is in B.G. xl. 163 and P. v. 112.

43. JESUS CHRISTUS, UNSER HEILAND, DER DEN TOD.
O. 76. N. xv. 81. B.G. xxv. (2) 39. P. v. 34. B.H. vii. 36.

44. JESUS CHRISTUS, UNSER HEILAND, DER VON UNS.
C. 77. N. xvi. 74. B.G. iii. 234. P. vi. 82. B.H. viii. 116.
C. 78. N. xvi. 80. B.G. iii. 239. P. vi. 92. B.H. viii. 128.
E. 79. N. xvii. 74. B.G. xxv. (2) 136. P. vi. 87. B.H. viii. 122.
An older text is in B.G. xxv. (2) 188 and P. vi. 112.
E. 80. N. xvii. 79. B.G. xxv. (2) 140. P. vi. 90. B.H. viii. 126.

45. JESUS, MEINE ZUVERSICHT.
M. 81. N. xviii. 69. B.G. xl. 74. P. v. 103. B.H. viii. 130.

46. KOMM, GOTT, SCHÖPFER, HEILIGER GEIST.
O. 82. N. xv. 97. B.G. xxv. (2) 47. P. vii. 86 (B). B.H. vii. 41.
An older text is in B.G. xxv. (2) 150 and P. vii. 86 (A).
E. 83. N. xvii. 82. B.G. xxv. (2) 142. P. vii. 2. B.H. ix. 2.

47. KOMM, HEILIGER GEIST, HERRE GOTT.
E. 84. N. xvii. 1. B.G. xxv. (2) 79. P. vii. 4. B.H. ix. 5.
An older text is in B.G. xxv. (2) 151 and P. vii. 86.
E. 85. N. xvii. 10. B.G. xxv. (2) 86. P. vii. 10. B.H. ix. 12.
An older text is in B.G. xxv. (2) 153 and P. vii. 88.

48. KOMMST DU NUN, JESU, VOM HIMMEL HERUNTER[1].
S. 86. N. xvi. 14. B.G. xxv. (2) 74. P. vii. 16. B.H. ix. 18.

49. KYRIE, GOTT VATER IN EWIGKEIT.
C. 87. N. xvi. 28. B.G. iii. 184. P. vii. 18. B.H. ix. 26.
C. 88. N. xvi. 36. B.G. iii. 194. P. vii. 26. B.H. ix. 22.

[1] Or "Lobe den Herren, den mächtigen König der Ehren."

50. LIEBSTER JESU, WIR SIND HIER.
O. 89. B.G. xxv. (2) 49. P. v. 109. B.H. vii. 42 (31).
O. 90. N. xv. 101. B.G. xxv. (2) 50. P. v. 40. B.H. vii. 42(32).
M. 91. N. xviii. 70. B.G. xl. 76. P. v. 105. B.H. ix. 36.
M. 92. N. xviii. 71. B.G. xl. 77. P. v. 105. B.H. ix. 37.
M. 93. N. xviii. 72. B.G. xl. 25. P. v. 39. B.H. ix. 38 (part only).

51. LOB SEI DEM ALLMÄCHTIGEN GOTT.
O. 94. N. xv. 11. B.G. xxv. (2) 6. P. v. 40. B.H. vii. 42.
M. 95. N. xviii. 73. B.G. xl. 22. P. v. 41. B.H. ix. 38.

52. LOBT GOTT, IHR CHRISTEN, ALLE GLEICH.
O. 96. N. xv. 29. B.G. xxv. (2) 13. P. v. 42. B.H. vii. 43.
M. 97. N. xviii. 74. B.G. xl. 78. P. v. 106. B.H. ix. 39.
A variant is in B.G. xl. 159.

53. MEINE SEELE ERHEBT DEN HERREN.
S. 98. N. xvi. 8. B.G. xxv. (2) 70. P. vii. 33. B.H. ix. 44.
M. 99. N. xviii. 75. B.G. xl. 79. P. vii. 29. B.H. ix. 40.

54. MIT FRIED' UND FREUD' ICH FAHR' DAHIN.
O. 100. N. xv. 50. B.G. xxv. (2) 24. P. v. 42. B.H. vii. 44.

55. NUN DANKET ALLE GOTT.
E. 101. N. xvii. 40. B.G. xxv. (2) 108. P. vii. 34. B.H. ix. 46.

56. NUN FREUT EUCH, LIEBEN CHRISTEN G'MEIN.
M. 102. N. xviii. 80. B.G. xl. 84. P. vii. 36. B.H. ix. 50.
The movement bears the alternative title, "Es ist gewisslich an der Zeit."
A variant is in B.G. xl. 160 and P. vii. 91.

57. NUN KOMM, DER HEIDEN HEILAND.
O. 103. N. xv. 3. B.G. xxv. (2) 3. P. v. 44. B.H. vii. 45.
E. 104. N. xvii. 46. B.G. xxv. (2) 114. P. vii. 38. B.H. ix. 52.
An older text is in B.G. xxv. (2) 172 and P. vii. 92.
E. 105. N. xvii. 49. B.G. xxv. (2) 116. P. vii. 40. B.H. ix. 55.
Two older texts are in B.G. xxv. (2) 174, 176, and P. vii. 93, 94.
E. 106. N. xvii. 52. B.G. xxv. (2) 118. P. vii. 42. B.H. ix. 58.
An older text is in B.G. xxv. (2) 178 and P. vii. 96.
M. 107. N. xviii. 83. B.G. xl. 16. P. v. 45. B.H. ix. 61.

THE ORGAN CHORALS

58. O GOTT, DU FROMMER GOTT.
V. 108. N. xix. 44. B.G. xl. 114. P. v. 68. B.H. vii. 66.

59. O LAMM GOTTES UNSCHULDIG.
O. 109. N. xv. 58. B.G. xxv. (2) 28. P. v. 46. B.H. vii. 46.
E. 110. N. xvii. 32. B.G. xxv. (2) 102. P. vii. 45. B.H. ix. 62.
An older text is in B.G. xxv. (2) 166 and P. vii. 97.

60. O MENSCH, BEWEIN' DEIN' SÜNDE GROSS[1].
O. 111. N. xv. 69. B.G. xxv. (2) 33. P. v. 48. B.H. vii. 48.

61. PUER NATUS IN BETHLEHEM (EIN KIND GEBORN ZU BETHLEHEM).
O. 112. N. xv. 13. B.G. xxv. (2) 6. P. v. 50. B.H. vii. 50.

62. SCHMÜCKE DICH, O LIEBE SEELE.
E. 113. N. xvii. 22. B.G. xxv. (2) 95. P. vii. 50. B.H. ix. 68.
A movement of doubtful authenticity (attributed to G. A. Homilius) is in B.G. xl. 181.

63. SEI GEGRÜSSET, JESU GÜTIG.
V. 114. N. xix. 55. B.G. xl. 122. P. v. 76. B.H. vii. 75.

64. VALET WILL ICH DIR GEBEN.
M. 115. N. xix. 2. B.G. xl. 86. P. vii. 53. B.H. ix. 71.
An older text is in B.G. xl. 161 and P. vii. 100.
M. 116. N. xix. 7. B.G. xl. 90. P. vii. 56. B.H. ix. 76.

65. VATER UNSER IM HIMMELREICH.
O. 117. N. xv. 105. B.G. xxv. (2) 52. P. v. 52. B.H. vii. 51.
C. 118. N. xvi. 53. B.G. iii. 217. P. vii. 60. B.H. ix. 82.
C. 119. N. xvi. 61. B.G. ii. 223. P. v. 51. B.H. ix. 88.
A variant reading is in P. v. 109.
M. 120. N. xix. 12. B.G. xl. 96. P. vii. 66. B.H. ix. 80.
Two doubtfully authentic movements are in B.G. xl. 183, 184. They are both attributed to Georg Böhm.

[1] Or "Es sind doch selig alle."

66. VOM HIMMEL HOCH DA KOMM ICH HER.
O. 121. N. xv. 21. B.G. xxv. (2) 9. P. v. 53. B.H. vii. 52.
M. 122. N. xix. 14. B.G. xl. 19. P. vii. 67. B.H. ix. 88.
M. 123. N. xix. 16. B.G. xl. 17. P. vii. 68. B.H. ix. 90.
M. 124. N. xix. 19. B.G. xl. 97. P. v. 106. B.H. ix. 92.
A variant is in B.G. xl. 159.
V. 125. N. xix. 73. B.G. xl. 137. P. v. 92. B.H. vii. 92.

67. VOM HIMMEL KAM DER ENGEL SCHAAR.
O. 126. N. xv. 23. B.G. xxv. (2) 10. P. v. 54. B.H. vii. 52.

68. VON GOTT WILL ICH NICHT LASSEN.
E. 127. N. xvii. 43. B.G. xxv. (2) 112. P. vii. 70. B.H. ix. 94.
An older text is in B.G. xxv. (2) 170 and P. vii. 102.

69. WACHET AUF, RUFT UNS DIE STIMME.
S. 128. N. xvi. 1. B.G. xxv. (2) 63. P. vii. 72. B.H. ix. 96.

70. WENN WIR IN HÖCHSTEN NÖTHEN SEIN[1].
O. 129. N. xv. 115. B.G. xxv. (2) 57. P. v. 55. B.H. vii. 54.
E. 130. N. xvii. 85. B.G. xxv. (2) 145. P. vii. 74. B.H. ix. 98.
To the movement Bach gives the alternative title, "Vor deinen Thron tret' ich."

71. WER NUR DEN LIEBEN GOTT LÄSST WALTEN.
O. 131. N. xv. 117. B.G. xxv. (2) 58. P. v. 57. B.H. vii. 55.
S. 132. N. xvi. 6. B.G. xxv. (2) 68. P. vii. 76. B.H. ix. 100.
M. 133. N. xix. 21. B.G. xl. 3. P. v. 56 (53). B.H. ix. 102.
M. 134. N. xix. 22. B.G. xl. 4. P. v. 56 (52). B.H. ix. 103.
A variant is in B.G. xl. 151 and P. v. 111.

72. WIE SCHÖN LEUCHTET DER MORGENSTERN.
M. 135. N. xix. 23. B.G. xl. 99. B.H. ix. 103.
A fragment is in B.G. xl. 164.

73. WIR CHRISTENLEUT'.
O. 136. N. xv. 36. B.G. xxv. (2) 16. P. v. 58. B.H. vii. 56.
M. 137. N. xix. 28. B.G. xl. 32. P. ix. 52. B.H. ix. 108.

[1] Originally "Leve le cœur, ouvre l'oreille."

THE ORGAN CHORALS

74. WIR DANKEN DIR, HERR JESU CHRIST.
O. 138. N. xv. 73. B.G. xxv. (2) 35. P. v. 59. B.H. vii. 57.

75. WIR GLAUBEN ALL' AN EINEN GOTT, SCHÖPFER.
C. 139. N. xvi. 49. B.G. iii. 212. P. vii. 78. B.H. ix. 110.
C. 140. N. xvi. 52. B.G. iii. 216. P. vii. 81. B.H. ix. 113.
A movement confidently attributed to Bach is in B.G. xl. 187 and P. ix. 40.

76. WIR GLAUBEN ALL' AN EINEN GOTT, VATER.
M. 141. N. xix. 30. B.G. xl. 103. P. vii. 82. B.H. ix. 114.

77. WO SOLL ICH FLIEHEN HIN.
S. 142. N. xvi. 4. B.G. xxv. (2) 66. P. vii. 84. B.H. ix. 116.
This movement has the alternative title, "Auf meinen lieben Gott," the more correct style of the melody.
M. 143. N. xix. 32. B.G. xl. 6. P. ix. 48. B.H. ix. 118.
A movement of doubtful authenticity is in B.G. xl. 170 and P. ix. 39.

In addition to the foregoing, B.G. xl contains an Appendix of doubtful or incomplete movements (see page 346 *infra*). They are as follows:

ACH GOTT, VOM HIMMEL SIEH' DAREIN.
B.G. xl. 167 and P. ix. 44.
The basis of the movement appears to be Bach's work Completed by another hand.

ACH, WAS SOLL ICH SÜNDER MACHEN.
B.G. xl. 189.
A set of Variations, youthful if genuine.

AUS DER TIEFE RUFE ICH.
B.G. xl. 171 and P. ix. 54.
Possibly an early work.

GOTT DER VATER WOHN' UNS BEI.
B.G. xl. 177, N. xiii. 153, and P. vi. 62.
A variant is in P. vi. 106. Spitta attributes the movement to Johann Gottfried Walther.

O VATER, ALLMÄCHTIGER GOTT.
B.G. xl. 179.
Perhaps an early work.

JESU LEIDEN, PEIN UND TOD.
A movement on the melody is in P. ix. 52.

The Texts

Towards the end of his life Bach published the Catechism Chorals, Prelude and Fugue in E flat, and four *Duetti*, in Part III of the *Clavierübung*; the six *Schübler Chorals*; the *Art of Fugue*; the *Musical Offering*; and the Variations on "Vom Himmel hoch da komm ich her." The rest of his Organ works remained in MS. When he died, in 1750, presumably they were intact. To-day only about one-third of his Organ music survives in his handwriting[1]. The remainder has been printed from copies made by his pupils and others.

Bach's Autographs of the *Orgelbüchlein* and the *Eighteen Chorals* are in the Königliche Bibliothek, Berlin. The Schübler and *Clavierübung* Chorals and "Vom Himmel" Variations were in print before his death. It is therefore in regard to the miscellaneous or ungrouped Choral movements only that dubiety exists regarding the source of the published texts.

[1] Schweitzer, *J. S. Bach*, I. 266.

THE TEXTS

Bach's Organ Chorals were first edited by Friedrich Conrad Griepenkerl and Ferdinand Roitzsch for C. F. Peters, of Leipzig, who included them in his Edition of Bach's Organ Works (vols. v, vi, vii, ix) in 1846-47-81. In 1893 Ernst Naumann edited a larger collection of them for the Bachgesellschaft (Jahrgang xl). Nine years later (1902) the same editor included most of them in Breitkopf and Haertel's Edition. To the contents of the latter collection the Novello Edition (1916) makes no addition.

B.G. xl contains 52 miscellaneous (ungrouped) Preludes, 4 sets of Variations or Partite, 13 Variant texts or fragments, and 13 movements of doubtful authenticity, a total of 82 numbers. In the Peters Edition Griepenkerl already had printed 62 of them. Breitkopf and Haertel included 56 of them in their Edition. The Novello Edition contains the same number.

Of the 82 numbers printed in B.G. xl only four are in Bach's Autograph: "Wer nur den lieben Gott lässt walten" (N. xix. 22), " Wie schön leuchtet der Morgenstern" (N. xix. 23), a fragment on the latter melody (B.G. xl. 164), and the "Vom Himmel hoch" Variations. The remaining seventy-eight compositions come to us through MSS. written by other hands than Bach's[1].

[1] Bach's Autograph also exists of the early versions of two of the *Eighteen Chorals*. See *infra*, p. 80.

By far the greater number of the MSS. of Bach's miscellaneous Organ works are in public institutions. The richest in MSS. is the Königliche Bibliothek, Berlin, which, since Griepenkerl prepared the Peters Edition, has absorbed a good deal of the material then in private hands. The Amalienbibliothek (Princess Amalia Library) in the Joachimsthal Gymnasium, Berlin; Mozartstiftung (Mozart Institution), Frankfort a. Main; Stadtbibliothek (Municipal Library), Leipzig; and the Universitätsbibliothek (University Library), Königsberg, also contain valuable collections of Bach MSS.

In the **Königliche Bibliothek** are Bach's Autographs of the *Orgelbüchlein*, Anna Magdalena's *Clavierbüchlein* (1722), *Notenbuch* (1725), W. F. Bach's *Clavierbüchlein* (1720), the "Vom Himmel hoch" Variations, and the Eighteen "Great" Preludes. It possesses also the collection of *Count Voss* of Berlin, who purchased from Bach's eldest son, Wilhelm Friedemann Bach, a large number of his father's MSS.[1]; the collection of *Rudolf Westphal*, a well-known writer on Bach[2]; Professor *Fischhof's* Bequest[3]; an important collection made by *Johann Nikolaus Forkel* (1749–1818), Director of Music in the University of Göttingen, author of the first

---

[1] Schweitzer, I. 234.   [2] *Ibid.* 375.
[3] Spitta, *J. S. Bach*, III. 86 n.

THE TEXTS 15

"Life" of Bach (1802)[1]; the "Sammelbuch" or "Sammelband" of *Johann Ludwig Krebs* (b. 1713), a student at the Leipzig Thomasschule under Bach from 1726 to 1735[2]; a collection of Bach's Organ compositions made by his last pupil, *Johann Christian Kittel*, organist at Erfurt (d. 1809), in a copy made by *Herr Grasnick*[3]; copies of Bach's Organ works made by *Johann Peter Kellner*, a pupil of Bach's contemporary Johann Schmidt[4].

The **Amalienbibliothek** of Bach's works, made by Princess Anna Amalia, sister of Frederick the Great, passed, after her death in 1787, into the possession of the Joachimsthal Gymnasium, Berlin. It contains a collection of 24 Choralvorspiele of Bach's[5], made by *Johann Philipp Kirnberger*, who was born at Saalfeld in Thuringia in 1721, was Bach's pupil at Leipzig from 1739–41, and eventually became Court musician to Princess Amalia of Prussia[6].

In the **Mozartstiftung** at Frankfort a. Main is the *Schelble* collection of "140 variirte Choräle von Joh.

---

[1] Schweitzer, I. 235–36 n. See the present writer's translation of Forkel's *Life* (1920).
[2] *Ibid.* 101.
[3] Schweitzer, I. 161; Spitta, III. 247. Herr Grasnick, of Berlin, died in 1877.
[4] Spitta, III. 238. See also pp. 22, 23 *infra*.
[5] They are the following in the Novello Edition: xviii. 1, 2, 5, 16, 23, 24, 28, 38, 41, 43, 50, 54, 58, 59, 64, 72, 73, 83; xix. 14, 16, 21, 22, 28, 32.
[6] Schweitzer, I. 215; Spitta, II. 712.

Sebastian Bach," among which are many spurious movements. In 1846 it was in the possession of Herr Gleichauf[1]. It was made by *Johann Nepomuk Schelble* (1789-1837), founder of the Frankfort Caecilienverein and one of the earliest Bach conductors[2].

The Leipzig Stadtbibliothek contains the Bequest of *Carl Ferdinand Becker* (1804-77), editor of the *Choralgesänge* and Professor of the Organ in the Leipzig Conservatorium.

In the Königsberg Universitätsbibliothek is a collection of Organ Chorals made by *Johann Gottfried Walther* (1684-1748), Bach's contemporary at Weimar[3]; and also the *Gotthold Bequest*.

Of private collections the most important is that of Herr Kämmersinger Joseph Hauser, of Carlsruhe. It was largely used by Griepenkerl in 1846, when it was in the possession of the singer Franz Hauser (1794-1870), a friend of Mendelssohn and an avid Bach collector[4]. Included in the collection is a volume of "50 variirte und fugirte Choräle" in the handwriting of *Johann Christoph Oley*, organist at Aschersleben (d. 1789), and a MS. "Der anfahende Organist" in the handwriting of *Herr Dröbs*, a pupil of J. C. Kittel, which contains Organ movements by Bach.

[1] Peters, v. Pref.
[2] Schweitzer, I. 245.
[3] Spitta, I. 381.
[4] Schweitzer, I. 251.

THE TEXTS 17

Philipp Spitta, Bach's biographer, possessed a large collection of Bach MSS. which he placed at the disposal of the Bachgesellschaft in 1893. It contained the collection of *Friedrich Wilhelm Rust*, of Dresden (1739–96), grandfather of the prolific editor of the Bachgesellschaft's volumes[1]; a collection of Organ movements made by *Johann Gottfried Walther* of Weimar, at one time in the possession of Herr Frankenberger, Director of Music at Sondershausen; a MS. "Verschiedene variirte Choräle von den besten Meistern älterer Zeit" made by *Michael Gotthardt Fischer* and dated 1793; a collection of Organ Chorals made by Bach's uncle *Johann Christoph Bach*, organist at Eisenach; and a collection of J. S. Bach's "variirten und fugirten Chorälen vor 1 und 2 Claviere und Pedal," made by *Johann Gottfried Schicht* (1753–1823), Cantor of St Thomas', Leipzig (1810–23), through whose influence the Motetts were published by Breitkopf and Haertel in 1803[2]. Other collections drawn upon in 1846 and 1893 were those of the publishers *Breitkopf and Haertel*; *S. W. Dehn* (1799–1858), sometime Keeper of the Department of Music in the Königliche Bibliothek[3]; and *Christian Friedrich Schwenke* (1767–1822),

---
[1] Schweitzer, I. 253.
[2] *Ibid.* I. 252 n.; II. 295.
[3] *Ibid.* I. 252.

successor to Philipp Emmanuel Bach at Hamburg and an industrious Bach collector[1].

Finally must be mentioned an important MS. once in the possession of Bach's first cousin, *Andreas Bach* (b. 1713), which contains fourteen of Sebastian's Organ Preludes, including the Choral "Gottes Sohn ist kommen" (N. xviii. 42)[2].

In the following pages the derivation of the miscellaneous Preludes from the MS. sources named in this section is indicated.

The "*Orgelbüchlein*"

The Autograph of the *Orgelbüchlein* is in the Royal Library, Berlin. It is a small quarto of ninety-two sheets bound in paper boards, with leather back and corners, and bears the following title:

"Orgel-Büchlein Worinne einem anfahenden Organisten Anleitung gegeben wird, auff allerhand Arth einen Choral durchzuführen, anbey auch sich im Pedal studio zu habilitiren, indem in solchen darinne befindlichen Choralen das Pedal gantz obligat tractiret wird.

  Dem Höchsten Gott allein zu Ehren,
  Dem Nechsten, draus sich zu belehren.

Autore Joanne Sebast. Bach p.t. Capellae Magistro S.P.R. Anhaltini-Cotheniensis."

"A Little Organ Book, wherein the beginner may learn to perform Chorals of every kind and also acquire skill in the

---

[1] Schweitzer, i. 252 n.   [2] Spitta, i. 629.

THE "ORGELBÜCHLEIN" 19

use of the Pedal, which is treated uniformly obbligato throughout.
To God alone the praise be given
For what's herein to man's use written.
Composed by Johann Sebast. Bach, pro tempore Capellmeister to His Serene Highness the Prince of Anhalt-Cöthen."

According to the title-page, the Autograph was written at a time when Bach could describe himself as "pro tempore" in the service of Prince Leopold of Anhalt-Cöthen. His appointment to Cöthen was dated August 1, 1717[1], though he did not enter upon his duties until Christmas 1717[2]. To that date he held the positions of Concertmeister and Court Organist at Weimar, where the death of the Capellmeister, Johann Samuel Drese, in 1716, had opened the prospect of obtaining that vacant post. When it was given to Drese's son, Bach resolved to push his fortunes elsewhere, and, still bound to Weimar, accepted the Cöthen post in the summer of 1717. A petition for release from his Weimar duties was rejected. On November 6, 1717, he was placed under arrest "for obstinately insisting that his resignation should be accepted at once," and remained in confinement for a month. He was not released until December 2, 1717, when he was permitted at length to resign his Weimar appointments[3].

[1] Spitta, II. 5.   [2] Schweitzer, I. 106.
[3] *Ibid.* I. 106 n.

"As may be seen by the title-page," writes Spitta[1], the *Orgelbüchlein* was "written at Cöthen." The conclusion has been adopted by later writers and is accepted in the Novello Edition. It does not survive examination, however. Bach describes himself on the title-page as "pro tempore" in the service of Cöthen. Spitta explains the phrase as Bach's manner of stating the fact, that though the Autograph was written at Cöthen, its contents had been composed at Weimar. But, surely, if that was Bach's intention, it would have been more natural to state on the title-page (which, after all, was not written for publication) the earlier position he had since vacated. In other words, writing at Cöthen, as Spitta supposes, we should expect Bach to call himself "sometime Concertmeister to the Duke of Saxe-Weimar."

If Spitta's conclusion is discarded and the Autograph's construction at Weimar is assumed, the puzzling phrase "pro tempore" falls in smoothly with the facts known to us. Between August 1 and December 2, 1717, Bach was by appointment Capellmeister to His Highness of Anhalt-Cöthen. But as his Weimar master refused to release him from service and even put him in prison for begging his resignation, Bach might reasonably describe as "pro tempore" an appointment which seemed little

[1] Vol. 1. 647.

likely to become permanent. The conclusion may be stated with confidence, that the Autograph of the *Orgelbüchlein* was written at Weimar between August 1 and December 2, 1717.

It is possible to be more precise. As will be shown, the scheme of the *Orgelbüchlein* can have been in Bach's mind since the autumn of 1715, but can hardly have been formed earlier. As to three-quarters of its programme the *Orgelbüchlein* is incomplete, and most of it was of little practical use to a Church organist. The scheme of the work, and Bach's complete neglect of it in after years, support the conclusion that it was undertaken in a period of leisure and under an immediate impulse of enthusiasm. We are drawn, therefore, to search for a period of exceptional leisure in which Bach was free to sketch and partly write a lengthy work which in after years he never attempted to complete. Such a period presented itself during his incarceration at Weimar in November 1717, and during those weeks, it may be concluded, the Autograph was written.

But the date of the Autograph does not consequently determine the year in which all its forty-six completed movements were composed. Rust's conclusion, in the B.G. Edition of the *Orgelbüchlein*[1], that they cannot have been composed earlier than

[1] B.G. xxv. (2) vii.

the Cöthen period (1718–23) is already disproved. Spitta[1] gives convincing grounds for the conclusion that they were not composed at Cöthen, where Bach had neither an adequate instrument nor duties as an organist, but at Weimar (1708–17), where both incentives existed. For he demonstrates clearly that the Autograph is not the earliest text of the movements it contains. Felix Mendelssohn possessed a MS. in Bach's hand which contained twenty-six, and probably thirty-eight, of its forty-six completed movements. Indeed, Spitta makes out a strong case for the belief that the Mendelssohn MS. itself is a transcript of a still earlier text. It must therefore be concluded that the completed movements of the *Orgelbüchlein* were composed during Bach's residence at Weimar, 1708–17, between his twenty-third and thirty-third years, and assumed their final shape in the Autograph written in November 1717.

Other than the Autograph, no complete copy of the *Orgelbüchlein* exists. But of its separate movements so large a number of MSS. is found as to testify to their vogue among Bach's pupils and contemporaries.

The fullest collection of them, after the Autograph, is in Kirnberger's hand; in 1878 it was in the possession of Professor Wagener of Marburg, whose

[1] Vol. I. 647.

collection is in the Royal Library, Berlin. The collection contains all the completed (forty-six) movements except the first "Liebster Jesu, wir sind hier[1]" and "Komm, Gott, Schöpfer, heiliger Geist." A smaller collection, revised by Bach himself, which contains " Gottes Sohn ist kommen," "Christ lag in Todesbanden," "Vater unser im Himmelreich," "Ich ruf' zu dir, Herr Jesu Christ," "Wenn wir in höchsten Nöthen sein," and "Ach wie nichtig, ach wie flüchtig," was in 1878 in the possession of Wilhelm Rust, who acquired it from his grandfather, F. W. Rust.

Copies of six movements, "Herr Christ, der ein'ge Gottes-Sohn,"'"O Mensch, bewein' dein' Sünde gross," "Durch Adams Fall ist ganz verderbt," "Es ist das Heil uns kommen her," " Ich ruf' zu dir, Herr Jesu Christ," and " Wer nur den lieben Gott lässt walten," originally belonging to Bach's pupil Krebs, were in the possession of Court Organist Reichardt in 1846 and of Herr Ferdinand Roitzsch of Leipzig in 1878.

The Royal Library, Berlin, possesses copies of eight of the movements in the handwriting of Johann Gottfried Walther, Organist of the Town Church at Weimar during Bach's residence there : "Lob sei dem allmächtigen Gott," "Gelobet seist du, Jesu Christ," "Vom Himmel hoch da komm ich her," " Jesu, meine Freude," " Das alte Jahr vergangen

---
[1] It is omitted in the Novello Edition.

ist," " Mit Fried' und Freud' ich fahr' dahin," " Herr Gott, nun schleuss den Himmel auf," and "Heut' triumphiret Gottes Sohn."

MSS. of "Herr Christ, der ein'ge Gottes-Sohn," and "Es ist das Heil uns kommen her" are in a collection of Choral arrangements made by Walther of Weimar, in the possession (1878) of Herr Frankenberger, Director of Music at Sondershausen. Twenty-eight of the Preludes, in the handwriting of Johann Christoph Oley, organist at Aschersleben (d. 1789), are in the Hauser Collection: "Nun komm, der Heiden Heiland," "Gottes Sohn ist kommen," "Herr Christ, der ein'ge Gottes-Sohn," " Lob sei dem allmächtigen Gott," "Puer natus in Bethlehem," "Gelobet seist du, Jesu Christ," "Der Tag, der ist so freudenreich," "Vom Himmel hoch da komm ich her," " In dulci jubilo," "Lobt Gott, ihr Christen, alle gleich," "Jesu, meine Freude," "Christum wir sollen loben schon," "Wir Christenleut'," "In dir ist Freude," " Mit Fried' und Freud' ich fahr' dahin," "Christe, du Lamm Gottes," "Christus, der uns selig macht," " O Mensch, bewein' dein' Sünde gross," " Wir danken dir, Herr Jesu Christ," " Hilf Gott, dass mir's gelinge," "Christ ist erstanden," "Erstanden ist der heil'ge Christ," "Komm, Gott, Schöpfer, heiliger Geist," " Herr Jesu Christ, dich zu uns wend'," " In dich hab' ich gehoffet, Herr," " Wenn wir in höchsten Nöthen sein," "Alle Menschen müssen sterben," and "Ach wie nichtig, ach wie flüchtig."

An old MS. of twelve of the Preludes is in the University Library, Königsberg: "Herr Christ, der ein'ge Gottes-Sohn," "Lob sei dem allmächtigen Gott," "Gelobet seist du, Jesu Christ," "Lobt Gott, ihr Christen, alle gleich," "Jesu, meine Freude," "Wir Christenleut'," "Christe, du Lamm Gottes," "Erschienen ist der herrliche Tag," "Liebster Jesu, wir sind hier" (*distinctius*), "Ich ruf' zu dir, Herr Jesu Christ," "In dich hab' ich gehoffet, Herr," and "Alle Menschen müssen sterben."

Griepenkerl mentions (1846) other copies by Dröbs, Oley, and Schelble.

Hence, apart from the Mendelssohn Autograph and Kirnberger's MS., the only Preludes in the *Orgelbüchlein* not found in closely contemporary texts are "Da Jesus an dem Kreuze stund," "Dies sind die heil'gen zehn Gebot'," "Helft mir Gott's Güte preisen," "Jesus Christus, unser Heiland" (both), "O Lamm Gottes unschuldig," and "Vom Himmel kam der Engel Schaar."

Mendelssohn's MS. contained twenty-six of the Preludes: "Das alte Jahr vergangen ist," "In dir ist Freude," "Mit Fried' und Freud' ich fahr' dahin," "Christe, du Lamm Gottes," "O Lamm Gottes unschuldig," "Da Jesus an dem Kreuze stund," "O Mensch, bewein' dein' Sünde gross," "Christus, der uns selig macht," "Wir danken dir, Herr Jesu Christ," "Hilf Gott, dass mir's gelinge," "Herr Gott, nun schleuss den Himmel auf," "Christ lag in Todesbanden," "Jesus Christus, unser Heiland," "Christ ist erstanden," "Erstanden ist der heil'ge Christ," "Heut' triumphiret Gottes Sohn," "Erschienen ist der herrliche Tag," "Es ist das Heil uns kommen her," "Ich ruf' zu dir, Herr Jesu Christ," "In dich hab' ich gehoffet, Herr" (*alio modo*), "Liebster Jesu, wir sind hier" (*distinctius*), "Dies sind die heil'gen zehn Gebot'," "Vater unser im Himmelreich," "Durch Adams Fall ist ganz verderbt," "Komm, Gott, Schöpfer, heiliger Geist," and "Herr Jesu Christ, dich zu uns wend'." The last six movements Mendelssohn detached (three leaves) from the MS. and gave to his wife and Madame Clara Schumann. In 1880 the first two of the three leaves were in the possession of the wife of Professor Wach, Leipzig. The last was in that year in Madame Schumann's keeping[1].

The ninety-two sheets of the Autograph were planned by Bach to contain 164 movements upon the melodies of 161 hymns; three hymns (Nos. 50–1, 97–8, 130–1) being represented by two movements in each case. Of the 164 projected movements only forty-six were written, two of them (Nos. 50–1) to the same melody ("Liebster Jesu, wir sind hier").

[1] Spitta, I. 648.

A fragment (two bars) of a forty-seventh movement, upon Johann Rist's hymn, "O Traurigkeit, O Herzeleid," was inserted:

The pages of the Autograph, other than those which contain the completed movements, are merely inscribed with the names of the hymns whose melodies Bach proposed to place upon them. Hence, the *Orgelbüchlein* contains forty-six Preludes and the titles of 118 unwritten ones. Why did Bach fail to complete a work conceived, as the title-page bears witness, in so lofty a spirit? Schweitzer suggests[1] that the unused tunes lack the opportunities for poetic and pictorial expression that Bach required. If so, it is strange that 116 of the 161 hymns selected by Bach himself should be of that character. In fact, as Mr Newman points out in the Preface to the Novello Edition, Schweitzer's hypothesis is not sound. Many of the unused tunes in the *Orgelbüchlein* are as capable of poetic

[1] Vol. I. 287.

and pictorial treatment as those Bach actually used there. Moreover elsewhere he has given some of them precisely the expression of which Schweitzer assumes them to be incapable.

The true reason for Bach's failure to complete the *Orgelbüchlein* is found in the character of that work. Whatever may have been the circumstances that moved him to plan it and partially to write it, no practical incentive to its completion can be discovered. If, as has been asserted, Bach designed it as an exercise for his youthful son Friedemann, its forty-six completed movements were at least adequate as an Organ "tutor." As a Church organist, the completed portion of it alone was of practical use to Bach himself. To establish the statement it is necessary to examine the contents of the Autograph.

When Griepenkerl edited the *Orgelbüchlein* in 1846 he suppressed all reference to the movements Bach projected but did not write, and—a more serious fault—printed the completed movements in alphabetical order, alleging, with consummate audacity, that "Bach himself attached no value to the order of succession"! On the contrary, Bach wrote the hymns into the Autograph in accordance with a carefully thought-out programme, which, however, he left concealed. The order in which the hymns appear in the Autograph is the only clue to it. In 1878 Rust pointed out, in the Preface to the Bachgesellschaft's Edition, that "the Chorals of the *Orgelbüchlein* are in the order of the Church's year." But Rust's analysis probed no deeper than the early movements and is inaccurate for the rest.

In the *Musical Times* of January 1917 the present writer exposed for the first time the complete scheme Bach had in mind in the *Orgelbüchlein*. He was able later to point out[1] that Bach modelled it upon a Hymn-book issued in November 1715 for the neighbouring duchy of Saxe-Gotha-Altenburg, edited by Christian Friedrich Witt (d. 1716), Capellmeister at Gotha. It bears the title:

"Psalmodia sacra, Oder: Andächtige und schöne Gesänge, So wohl des Sel. Lutheri, als anderer Geistreichen Männer, Auf Hochfl. gnädigste Verordnung, In dem Fürstenthum Gotha und Altenburg, auf nachfolgende Art zu singen und zu spielen. Nebst einer Vorrede und Nachricht. Gotha, Verlegts Christoph Reyher, 1715."

A copy of the book in the British Museum has another title (*Neues Cantional*: Gotha and Leipzig, 1715), but its contents are identical with the Gotha publication.

A collation of the Autograph and Witt's Hymnbook shows that the latter provided Bach with 159 of the 161 hymns the *Orgelbüchlein* names. Nos. 6

[1] See the *Musical Times* for February—March 1917.

and 83 of the *Orgelbüchlein* are not in Witt. Whence Bach took them cannot be stated and is immaterial; both were accessible in other collections. The *Orgelbüchlein*, in fact, is a condensed Hymnary and, for convenience, may be divided into two Parts. The first, and shorter, Part follows the seasons and festivals of the Church's year, with one apparent omission. The second Part, almost wholly incomplete, contains hymns arranged in groups that conform to the divisions customary in Hymn-books of Bach's period. Part I was planned to contain sixty Preludes, of which thirty-six were composed. Part II was designed to include one hundred and four Preludes, of which only ten were written. Five of its eleven groups contain not a single completed movement; one contains three; two contain two apiece; three contain one apiece.

The complete scheme of the *Orgelbüchlein* is set out hereunder, with notes upon the hymns and melodies Bach proposed to use. The hymns are named in the order in which Bach wrote them into the Autograph, and are grouped under the seasons or headings he intended them to illustrate but neglected to indicate. In order to show the close correspondence between the *Orgelbüchlein* and Witt's Hymn-book, the latter's group-headings are printed alongside those supplied to Bach's scheme, the figures in brackets stating the numbers of the hymns in Witt's corresponding group and revealing the extent to which Bach drew upon them. Similarly the numerical order of the hymns in the *Orgelbüchlein* is annotated by an indication of their position in Witt's book. Titles in capitals indicate the forty-six completed movements of the *Orgelbüchlein*. Unless the contrary is stated, Witt's and Bach's tunes are identical[1].

PART I.

CHURCH SEASONS AND FESTIVALS.

* Bach uses the melody elsewhere in his concerted Church music or Organ works.

† A four-part setting of the melody is among the *Choralgesänge*.

Advent *Advents-Lieder* (3–17).

*1 (4) NUN KOMM, DER HEIDEN HEILAND.
*†2 (5) GOTTES SOHN IST KOMMEN, or, GOTT, DURCH DEINE GÜTE. (In Canone all' Ottava, a 2 Clav. e Pedale.)
*3 (17) HERR CHRIST, DER EIN'GE GOTTES-SOHN, or, HERR GOTT NUN SEI GEPREISET.
*4 (15) LOB SEI DEM ALLMÄCHTIGEN GOTT.
In Witt the hymn is set to the tune of No. 9 *infra*.

The Advent section calls for no comment. Bach selects from Witt four of his fifteen hymns on the season, altering the order of one, No. 4 (15), in order to end upon a note of joy in the approaching

[1] In Nos. 50–1, 97–8, 130–1 Bach duplicates the hymn. In the first case he does so for reasons stated *infra*. In the other cases, his melody not being Witt's, he proposes a second movement *alio modo*, i.e. on his own preferred melody.

Incarnation. The other hymns invoke the coming Saviour.

        Christmas   *Auf Weynachten* (18–53).
* 5 (35) PUER NATUS IN BETHLEHEM.
  6   Lob sei Gott in des Himmels Thron.
      The hymn is not in Witt. It is by Michael Sachse (1542–1618) and was sung to the tune "Gelobet seist du, Jesu Christ." As Bach treats that tune in No. 7 *infra*, it is to be inferred that he had in mind here the melody proper to the hymn, by J. Michael Altenburg, first printed in 1623 (Zahn, No. 1748).
*† 7 (19) GELOBET SEIST DU, JESU CHRIST (a 2 Clav. e Pedale).
*† 8 (20) DER TAG, DER IST SO FREUDENREICH (a 2 Clav. e Pedale).
* 9 (21) VOM HIMMEL HOCH DA KOMM ICH HER.
*10 (22) VOM HIMMEL KAM DER ENGEL SCHAAR (a 2 Clav. e Pedale).
*† 11 (36) IN DULCI JUBILO (Canone doppio all' Ottava a 2 Clav. e Pedale).
*† 12 (32) LOBT GOTT, IHR CHRISTEN, ALLZUGLEICH.
*† 13 (337) JESU, MEINE FREUDE.
* 14 (34) CHRISTUM WIR SOLLEN LOBEN SCHON (Corale in Alto).
* 15 (33) WIR CHRISTENLEUT'.

Bach arranges the Christmas hymns in an order different from Witt's. The result is to transform a haphazard series of tunes into a Christmas Mystery. No. 5 announces the Incarnation and describes the homage of the Wise Men. Nos. 6 and 7 are acts of praise and thanksgiving for the Nativity. In No. 8 the Angels give the glad tidings to the shepherds. Nos. 9 and 10 picture the Manger at Bethlehem. In No. 11 we listen to the Angels' carol there. The next three hymns are songs of thanksgiving; the second of them (No. 13), transferred from another section of Witt's Hymn-book, being an act of intimate personal homage, very characteristic of Bach. The inversion of Witt's order for the last two hymns is intentional. "Wir Christenleut'" summarizes the lesson of the Christmas season—he who stands steadfast on the fact of the Incarnation shall never be confounded. On that note Bach prefers to end.

New Year   *Auf das Neue Jahr* (54–72).
* 16 (56) HELFT MIR GOTT'S GÜTE PREISEN.
† 17 (57) DAS ALTE JAHR VERGANGEN IST (a 2 Clav. e Pedale).
18 (62) IN DIR IST FREUDE.

The three hymns follow Witt's order. The first two look back upon the old year. The third is instinct with the hope and promise of the new one.

Purification of the B.V.M.   *Auf Lichtmess* (78–83).
*† 19 (80) MIT FRIED' UND FREUD' ICH FAHR' DAHIN.
20 (81) HERR GOTT, NUN SCHLEUSS DEN HIMMEL AUF (a 2 Clav. e Pedale).

Bach omits, or appears to omit, the Epiphany (Witt, Nos. 73–77), which falls between the New Year and the Feast of the Purification. No. 19, however, is in modern use as an Epiphany hymn, and No. 20, which recalls the Song of Simeon, is not less appropriate. Probably Bach intended the two hymns to do duty for both contiguous festivals.

  Passiontide *Vom Leiden Christi* (90-138).
*† 21 (104) O LAMM GOTTES UNSCHULDIG (Canone alla Quinta).
* 22 (103) CHRISTE, DU LAMM GOTTES (in Canone alla Duodecima a 2 Clav. e Pedale).
*† 23 (95) CHRISTUS, DER UNS SELIG MACHT (in Canone all' Ottava).
 24 (113) DA JESUS AN DEM KREUZE STUND.
*† 25 (96) O MENSCH, BEWEIN' DEIN' SÜNDE GROSS (a 2 Clav. e Pedale).
 26 (135) WIR DANKEN DIR, HERR JESU CHRIST, DASS DU - FÜR UNS GESTORBEN BIST.
† 27 (94) HILF GOTT, DASS MIR'S GELINGE (Canone alla Quinta a 2 Clav. e Pedale).
 28 (124) O Jesu, wie ist dein' Gestalt.

  The hymn is attributed to Melchior Franck. It is in ten stanzas, addressed to the Feet (st. ii), Knees (st. iii), Hands (st. iv, v), Side (st. vi), Breast (st. vii), Heart (st. viii), and Face (st. ix) of Jesus. Witt sets it to the tune "Wie schön leuchtet der Morgenstern." As Bach introduces that melody in No. 120 *infra*, it is probable that he intended to use the proper melody of Franck's (?) hymn here. It was published, with the hymn, in 1627 and is by Franck himself (Zahn, No. 8360). Both hymn and melody are found in the Gotha *Cantional* of 1646, and therefore have a strong Saxon tradition.

† 29 (127) O Traurigkeit, O Herzeleid.

  The hymn, by Johann Rist, written for special use on Good Friday, is described as a "Klägliches Grab-Lied über die trawrige Begräbnisse unseres Heylandes Jesu

THE "ORGELBÜCHLEIN" 35

Christi." In Witt the hymn is set to its own melody, published, with the hymn, in 1641. Bach intended to use it here, as the sketch of the opening bars in the Autograph shows[1]. There is a four-part setting of it among the *Choralgesänge*, No. 288.

30 (290) Allein nach dir, Herr Jesu Christ, verlanget mich.

The hymn is by Nikolaus Selnecker. In Witt it is set to a melody probably by Witt himself (Zahn, No. 8544). Perhaps Bach intended to use it, but there are earlier tunes (Zahn, Nos. 8541–2).

† 31 (129) O [Ach] wir armen Sünder.

The hymn, a Litany, is by Hermann Bonn (*c.* 1504–48). The melody to which it is set in Witt dates at least from the end of the fourteenth century, when it was sung to the hymn "Eya der grossen Liebe." It is found in association with Bonn's hymn in 1561 (Zahn, No. 8187*c*). There is a four-part setting of it among Bach's *Choralgesänge*, No. 301.

* 32 (108) Herzliebster Jesu, was hast du verbrochen.

The hymn is by Johann Heermann and occurs in the *St Matthew Passion* and *St John Passion*. It is set in Witt to Johann Crüger's melody (1640), which Bach uses in the *Passions*, but not elsewhere.

33 (126) Nun giebt mein Jesus gute Nacht.

This long (21 stanzas) Good Friday hymn by Johann Rist does not appear to have a melody proper to itself. In Witt it is set to the melody of "Herr Jesu Christ, wahr Mensch und Gott" (Zahn, No. 340*c*), a tune which Bach has not used elsewhere. See No. 128 *infra*.

In the Passiontide section Bach entirely discards Witt's order and follows the stages of the great tragedy in their sequence. The first three hymns call

[1] See *supra*, p. 27.

us to Calvary. No. 24 stations us before the Cross. No. 25 challenges mankind to own its guilt in Christ's martyrdom. No. 26, in another mood, gives thanks for the approaching Atonement. In No. 27, a long ballad of the Passion, the death and sufferings of the Saviour are consummated. No. 28 is a passionate invocation of the pierced Hands, Feet, and Side. No. 29 is sung at the Saviour's burial. Christ being dead, Bach hastens to utter (No. 30) a fervent song of faith, followed by two hymns of remorse and self-accusation. No. 33 leaves the Saviour sleeping in the Tomb. The section is a miniature of the greater *Passion* written twelve years later.

Easter   Von der Auferstehung Jesu Christi (139-157).
*† 34 (140) CHRIST LAG IN TODESBANDEN.
† 35 (144) JESUS CHRISTUS, UNSER HEILAND, DER DEN.
*† 36 (141) CHRIST IST ERSTANDEN.
† 37 (143) ERSTANDEN IST DER HEIL'GE CHRIST.
* 38 (146) ERSCHIENEN IST DER HERRLICHE TAG (a 2 Clav.
          e Pedale in Canone).
† 39 (145) HEUT' TRIUMPHIRET GOTTES SOHN.

The Easter section closely follows Witt's order. Bach begins it with introductory hymns (Nos. 34–36) which summon us to the festival. The last two hymns are songs of triumph, "Heut' triumphiret" being placed out of Witt's order so as to end on the thought of Death conquered. The centre of the section is held by "Erstanden ist der heil'ge

Christ," a dialogue between the Virgin Mary and the Angel at the Tomb, which states the circumstances of the Resurrection, the central thought of the festival.

Ascension Day   *Von der Himmelfahrt Jesu Christi*
(158–167).

40 (160) Gen Himmel aufgefahren ist.

The hymn is a translation of the Latin " Coelos ascendit hodie." It is set in Witt to a melody by Melchior Franck (1627) which is in very general use (Zahn, No. 189). There can be little doubt that Bach intended to introduce it here. The hymn is also sung to an older melody (Zahn, No. 187a), which dates from the middle of the sixteenth century.

† 41 (165) Nun freut euch, Gottes Kinder, all.

The hymn is by Erasmus Alberus (d. 1553). It is set in Witt to a melody of which there is a four-part setting among the *Choralgesänge*, No. 260.

Whit Sunday   *Auf das heiliges Pfingst-Fest* (168–184).

42 (169) Komm, heiliger Geist, erfüll' die Herzen deiner Gläubigen.

Luther's version of the antiphon "Veni Sancte Spiritus reple tuorum." It is set in Witt to the old Latin melody (Zahn, No. 8594) which Bach, no doubt, intended to introduce here.

* 43 (170) Komm, heiliger Geist, Herre Gott.

Another version, by Luther, of the antiphon "Veni Sancte Spiritus reple tuorum." It is set in Witt to the old melody which Bach uses elsewhere in Cantatas 59, 172, 175, and a Motett; also in the *Eighteen Chorals*.

*† 44 (171) KOMM, GOTT, SCHÖPFER, HEILIGER GEIST.

*† 45 (173) Nun bitten wir den heil'gen Geist.

One of the few vernacular pre-Reformation hymns, with stanzas added by Luther. The tune occurs in

Cantatas 169 and 197, and there is another harmonization of it in the *Choralgesänge*, No. 254.

† 46 (172) Spiritus Sancti gratia, *or*, Des heil'gen Geistes reiche Gnad.

The hymn is a German version of the Latin "Spiritus Sancti gratia Apostolorum pectora implevit sua gratia, donans linguarum genera." It is set in Witt to a melody by Melchior Vulpius (Zahn, No. 2601) published in 1609 and repeated in the Gotha *Cantional* of 1646. On the other hand, there exists a sixteenth century melody to the hymn (Zahn, No. 370a) which Johann H. Schein modernized in 1627 and of which a four-part setting is among Bach's *Choralgesänge*, No. 63. Schein was one of Bach's predecessors at Leipzig and the four-part setting may be presumed to have been written for one of the lost Leipzig Cantatas.

47 (174) O heil'ger Geist, du göttlich's Feu'r.

An anonymous hymn, set in Witt to a melody by Melchior Vulpius (Zahn, No. 2027) published in 1609 and repeated in the Gotha *Cantional* of 1646.

48 (176) O heiliger Geist, O heiliger Gott.

The hymn, probably by Johann Niedling (1602–1668), is set in Witt to a melody (Zahn, No. 2016a) which dates from 1650. Witt may have taken it from Freylinghausen (1704), where it also occurs.

The Whitsuntide section closely follows Witt's order and needs no exegesis.

Trinity (Before the Sermon)   *Vor der Predigt* (240–241).

*† 49 (240) HERR JESU CHRIST, DICH ZU UNS WEND'.

*† 50 (241) LIEBSTER JESU, WIR SIND HIER (in Canone alla Quinta a 2 Clav. e Pedale).

*† 51 (241) LIEBSTER JESU, WIR SIND HIER (distinctius).

Trinity   *Auf Trinitatis* (185–200).

† 52 (185) Gott, der Vater, wohn' uns bei.

The hymn is by Luther. It is set in Witt to the original

melody, of which Bach has a four-part setting in the *Choralgesänge*, No. 113.

*† 53 (188) Allein Gott in der Höh' sei Ehr'. Nikolaus Decius' version of the "Gloria in excelsis Deo." Its melody occurs in Cantatas 85, 104, 112, and 128. There is a four-part setting of it among the *Choralgesänge*, No. 12.

† 54 (189) Der du bist Drei in Einigkeit. The hymn is by Luther. It is set in Witt to the melody "O lux beata trinitas," of which there is a four-part setting in the *Choralgesänge*, No. 61, where Bach follows Schein's reconstruction of the melody.

The Trinity section contains six numbers, of which only the last three hymns are found in Witt's Trinity group. Nos. 49 and 50 are taken by Bach from Witt's "Vor der Predigt" (Before the Sermon) section. That Bach intended them for Trinity use is to be inferred from the irrelevance of a general "Before the Sermon" group of hymns between the Whitsuntide and Trinity sections. In regard to No. 49 it is not improbable that local use at Weimar attached it to Trinity, to whose season it is generally relevant. The hymn is attributed to a former Duke of Saxe-Weimar. Its fourth stanza is appropriate to the season:

> To God the Father, God the Son,
> And God the Spirit Three in One,
> Be honour, praise, and glory given
> By all on earth, and Saints in Heaven.

No. 50 acquires a Trinity significance through its second stanza:

> All our knowledge, sense, and sight
> Lie in deepest darkness shrouded,
> Till Thy Spirit breaks our night
> With the beams of truth unclouded.

The strongest reason for believing that Bach intended both hymns to be attached to the Trinity group is in the fact that he copied into the Autograph two movements upon the second hymn, "Liebster Jesu, wir sind hier," which differ so little textually that it is impossible to suppose his reason for duplicating the tune to have been a musical one. Witt, in fact, only offered two hymns, whereas Bach's attention to symbolism moved him to pay separate homage to the three Persons of the Trinity. The regular Trinity hymns (Nos. 52–54) also are three in number.

St John the Baptist   Am Tage Johannis des Täufers (201–4).
55 (201) Gelobet sei der Herr, der Gott Israel.
    This version of the *Benedictus* is by Erasmus Alberus, and in Witt's book is directed to be sung to the plainsong of the *Magnificat*. As Bach introduces that melody in the next movement it may be concluded that he did not propose to use it here also. The melody proper to the hymn is dated 1564 (Zahn, No. 5854).

Visitation of the B.V.M.   Auf Mariä Heimsuchung
(205–207).
*† 56 (205) Meine Seel' erhebt den Herren.
    The *Magnificat*. Bach uses its melody (Tonus Peregrinus) in Cantata 10. There are two Organ movements upon it and two four-part settings in the *Choralgesänge*, Nos. 120, 121.

THE "ORGELBÜCHLEIN" 41

Bach omits the Annunciation. Six hymns for that festival are in Witt (Nos. 84-89).

St Michael the Archangel   Auf Michaelis Tag (208-215).

*† 57 (209) Herr Gott, dich loben alle wir.

The hymn is by Paul Eber. The melody was composed by Louis Bourgeois and was set originally to Psalm 134 ("Or sus, serviteurs du Seigneur") in 1551. The hymn and melody occur in Cantata 130, and there are three four-part settings of the tune in the *Choralgesänge*, Nos. 129, 130 (? J. S. B.), 132. It is familiar as the "Old Hundredth."

† 58 (208) Es steh'n vor Gottes Throne.

The hymn is by Ludwig Helmbold. It is set in Witt to a tune by Joachim von Burck (1541?-1610), published in 1594. There is a four-part setting of it among the *Choralgesänge*, No. 93.

Feasts of the Apostles   Auf der Apostel Tage (216-218).

*† 59 (216) Herr Gott, dich loben wir.

Luther's version of the *Te Deum* and its melody are in Cantatas 16, 119, 120, 190. There is an Organ movement upon it and a four-part setting in the *Choralgesänge*, No. 133.

* 60 (217) O Herre Gott, dein göttlich Wort.

Anark of Wildenfels' (?) hymn is set in Witt to its original melody. Bach uses it in Cantata 184.

PART II.

THE CHRISTIAN LIFE.

The Ten Commandments   Von den zehen Geboten (221-225).

*† 61 (222) DIES SIND DIE HEIL'GEN ZEHN GEBOT'.

62 (221) Mensch, willst du leben seliglich.

The hymn is by Luther. In Witt it is directed to be sung to the melody "Dies sind die heil'gen zehn Gebot'."

As Bach uses the latter in No. 61 *supra*, presumably he had in mind the proper (1524) melody of the hymn (Zahn, No. 1956) for use here.

63 (219) Herr Gott, erhalt' uns für und für.
    Ludwig Helmbold's hymn is set in Witt to its proper melody, by Joachim von Burck (Zahn, No. 443), published in 1594. The hymn appears to have no other melody.

The Creed   Vom Glauben (226–229).

* 64 (228) Wir glauben all' an einen Gott, Vater.
    The hymn is by Tobias Clausnitzer. It is set in Witt to the melody which Bach uses in N. xix. 30.

Prayer   Vom Gebeth (230–239).

*† 65 (232) VATER UNSER IM HIMMELREICH.

Holy Baptism   Von der Tauffe (243–245).

*† 66 (243) Christ, unser Herr, zum Jordan kam.
    The melody of Luther's hymn occurs in Cantatas 7, 176, and the Organ works. There is also a four-part setting of it among the *Choralgesänge*, No. 43.

Nos. 61 to 66 form a group of Catechism hymns. Bach and Witt (Nos. 219–45), whom he follows, treat the heads of the Catechism in the customary order. Bach interchanges Nos. 61 and 62, using the former, as being more definitive, to introduce the Ten Commandments group.

Penitence and amendment   Buss-Lieder (246–270).

*67 (261) Aus tiefer Noth schrei ich zu dir.
    The hymn is by Luther. Its familiar melody also is probably by him. Bach uses it in Cantata 38 as well as in the *Clavierübung*. Witt uses another (1525) tune (Zahn, No. 4438*a*).

THE "ORGELBÜCHLEIN" 43

*†68 (258) Erbarm' dich mein, O Herre Gott.
The hymn is by Erhart Hegenwalt. The melody, probably by Johann Walther, was published with the hymn in 1524. Bach uses it in the miscellaneous Preludes. There is a four-part setting of it among the *Choralgesänge*, No. 78.

*†69 (286) Jesu, der du meine Seele.
Johann Rist's hymn is set in Witt to a melody published in 1662 to Harsdörffer's "Wachet doch, erwacht, ihr Schläfer." Bach uses it in Cantatas 78 and 105, and there are three four-part settings of it among the *Choralgesänge*, Nos. 185-187.

*†70 (280) Allein zu dir, Herr Jesu Christ.
The hymn is by Johannes Schneesing. The melody also is attributed to him. It occurs in Cantata 33. There is a four-part setting of it among the *Choralgesänge*, No. 15.

*†71 (265) Ach Gott und Herr.
The authorship of the hymn is disputed. The melody is used by Bach in Cantata 48 and among the miscellaneous Preludes. A four-part setting of it is among the *Choralgesänge*, No. 3.

*†72 (283) Herr Jesu Christ, du höchstes Gut.
The hymn is by Bartholomäus Ringwaldt. The melody occurs in a variety of forms, Witt's being the Tenor of a four-part setting of the tune "Wenn mein Stündlein" (Zahn, Nos. 4484, 4486). Bach uses it in Cantatas 48, 113, 166, 168, and there is a four-part setting of it among the *Choralgesänge*, No. 141.

*†73 (253) Ach Herr, mich armen Sünder.
The hymn is by Cyriacus Schneegass. Its tune is also known as "Herzlich thut mich verlangen." Bach employs it in Cantatas 25, 135, 153, 159, 161 and the miscellaneous Preludes. There are two four-part settings of it among the *Choralgesänge*, Nos. 157, 158.

INTRODUCTION

*74 (282) Wo soll ich fliehen hin.
> The hymn is by Johann Heermann. The melody Witt uses is perhaps by Caspar Stieler. Bach uses it in two Cantatas of the Weimar period, Nos. 163 and 199. The melody "Wo soll ich fliehen hin," which he uses elsewhere, is more correctly styled "Auf meinen lieben Gott" (see No. 136 *infra*).

75 (267) Wir haben schwerlich.
> The melody of this anonymous hymn is taken by Witt from a five-part setting in the Gotha *Cantional* of 1648 (Zahn, 2099). Bach has not made use of it elsewhere.

*76 (291) DURCH ADAMS FALL IST GANZ VERDERBT.
*77 (292) ES IST DAS HEIL UNS KOMMEN HER.

In the Penitential group Bach draws upon Witt's corresponding section and his "Faith" and "Justification by Faith" hymns. He begins (Nos. 67, 68) with a cry of despair:

> Out of the depths I cry to Thee,
> Lord, hear me, I implore Thee;

and

> Behold, I was all born in sin,
> My mother conceived me therein.

He adds words of comfort; Johann Rist's (No. 69)

> Jesu, Who, in sorrow dying,
> Didst deliverance bring to me;

and Schneesing's (No. 70)

> Lord Jesus Christ, in Thee alone
> My only hope on earth I place.

But the mood of despair returns (No. 71):

> Alas! my God! my sins are great,
> My conscience doth upbraid me,
> And now I find in my sore strait
> No man hath power to aid me;

and again (No. 72):
> Jesus, Thou Source of every good,
> Pure Fountain of Salvation,
> Behold me bowed beneath the load
> Of guilt and condemnation;

and again (No. 73):
> A sinner, Lord, I pray Thee,
> Recall Thy dread decree;
> Thy fearful wrath, O spare me,
> From judgment set me free.

There falls (No. 74) a ray of hope:
> My heavy load of sin
> To Thee, O Lord, I bring;
> ....
> From out Thy Side love floweth,
> And saving grace bestoweth.

After a final (No. 75) act of contrition, the section ends with heartening comfort: Lazarus Spengler's (No. 76)
> He that hopeth in God steadfastly
> Shall never be confounded;

and Paul Speratus' (No. 77)
> Salvation hath come down to us
> Of freest grace and love.

It is characteristic of Bach's temperament that the last two hymns, with their message of comfort, are the only completed movements in the section.

Holy Communion   Vom Abendmahl des Herrn (308–333).
*†78 (320) Jesus Christus, unser Heiland, Der von uns.
> The hymn is by Luther. The tune also is attributed to him. It occurs in four Organ Preludes, and there is a four-part setting of it among the *Choralgesänge*, No. 206.

†79 (324) Gott sei gelobet und gebenedeiet.
  The hymn is by Luther, and the melody is based on pre-Reformation material. There is a four-part setting of it among the *Choralgesänge*, No. 119.
80 (633) Der Herr ist mein getreuer Hirt.
  The hymn is by Wolfgang Meusel. It is set in Witt to a melody (Zahn, No. 4432*a*) not used by Bach elsewhere. In the Cantatas he invariably sets the hymn to Decius' "Allein Gott in der Höh' sei Ehr'" (see No. 53 *supra*).
81 (319) Jetzt komm ich als ein armer Gast.
  The hymn, whose first line also reads, "Ich komm jetzt als ein armer Gast," is by Justus Sieber (1628-95). In Witt it is directed to be sung to the melody "Herr Jesu Christ, du höchstes Gut" (see No. 72 *supra*). Bach has not used the hymn's proper melody (Zahn, No. 4646) elsewhere.
82 (322) O Jesu, du edle Gabe.
  The hymn is by Johann Böttiger (1613-72). It is set in Witt to a melody (Zahn, No. 3892*b*) which Bach has not used elsewhere.
83   Wir danken dir, Herr Jesu Christ, Dass du das Lämmlein.
  The hymn is by Nikolaus Selnecker. It is not in Witt. Bach has not used its melody (Zahn, No. 479 or 480) elsewhere.
*84 (317) Ich weiss ein Blümlein hübsch und fein.
  The anonymous hymn is set in Witt to a melody used by Bach in Cantata 106, and also known as "Ich hab' mein Sach' Gott heimgestellt."
*†85 (293) Nun freut euch, lieben Christen, g'mein.
  Luther's hymn has two melodies. Of the older (1524) there is a four-part setting among the *Choralgesänge*, No. 261. The second (1529 or 1535) occurs in the *Christmas Oratorio*, Cantata 70, the miscellaneous Preludes, and in a four-part setting among the *Choralgesänge*,

No. 262. The second tune has been attributed to Luther, and for that reason perhaps Bach preferred it. Witt also uses it.

*†86 (384) Nun lob', mein' Seel', den Herren.
 The hymn is by Johann Graumann. The melody, probably composed by Johann Kugelmann, is used by Bach in Cantatas 17, 28, 29, 51, 167, Motett 1. There are four-part settings of it among the *Choralgesänge*, No. 269, 270.

Of the nine hymns in the Holy Communion group only five (Nos. 78, 79, 81, 82, 84) are found in Witt's corresponding section. The rest are drawn from other parts of Witt's book or (No. 83) are introduced from outside it. Bach is working out a "programme" of his own. The section begins with Luther's "Jesus Christus, unser Heiland," which Bach used many years later for the Eucharistic hymn in the *Clavierübung*. It is an invitation to the Holy Table:

> Christ Jesus, our Redeemer born,
> Who from us did God's anger turn,
> That we never should forget it,
> Gave He us His flesh to eat it.
> Who will draw near to that table
> Must take heed, all he is able.
> Who unworthy thither goes,
> Thence death, instead of life, he knows.

No. 79, Luther's "Gott sei gelobet," is a prayer that the communicant may worthily receive Christ's Flesh and Blood.

No. 80, transferred from another section of Witt's book, brings the communicant to the Holy Table:

> The Lord He is my Shepherd true,
> My steps He safely guideth;
> With all good things in order due
> His bounty me provideth.

No. 81 is an act of devotion before receiving the Sacramental Food:

> Thy poor unworthy guest, O Lord,
> I place me at Thy Table.

No. 82 is an act of thanksgiving after communicating:

> From my sins Thy Blood hath cleansed me,
> From Hell's flames Thy love hath snatched me.

No. 83 is a grateful invocation of the atoning Lamb of God.

In No. 84 the worshipper apostrophizes the rich gift vouchsafed to him.

The last two hymns (Nos. 85, 86), drawn from other parts of Witt's book, end upon a note of thanksgiving.

The common weal　　*Von denen drey Haupt-Ständen*
(471-473).

87 (473) Wohl dem, der in Gottes Furcht steht.
　　The hymn is by Martin Luther. In Witt it is directed to be sung to the tune " Wo Gott zum Haus nicht giebt sein' Gunst." As that melody occurs in No. 88 *infra* Bach had in mind to introduce here, perhaps, an older tune (Zahn, No. 298) associated with Luther's hymn. He has not used it elsewhere.

†88 (472) Wo Gott zum Haus nicht giebt sein' Gunst.
The hymn is attributed to Johann Kolross. The melody, which dates from 1535, belongs also to Luther's "Wohl dem, der in Gottes Furcht steht." A four-part setting of it is among the *Choralgesänge*, No. 389.

The section does not need comment. Bach includes in it two of the three hymns allotted by Witt to "The Three Estates."

Christian life and experience   *Vom Christlichen Leben und Wandel* (514-597).

*89 (694) Was mein Gott will, das g'scheh' allzeit.
Albrecht Margrave of Brandenburg-Culmbach's hymn and the French melody associated with it occur in Cantatas 65, 72, 92, 103, 111, 144, and in the *St Matthew Passion*.

*90 (514) Kommt her zu mir, spricht Gottes Sohn.
The hymn is by Georg Grüenwald. Bach uses the melody in Cantatas 74, 86, 108.

*91 (299) ICH RUF' ZU DIR, HERR JESU CHRIST.

†92 (531) Weltlich Ehr' und zeitlich Gut.
The hymn is by Michael Weisse. It is set in Witt to a melody (Zahn, No. 4977) which Bach has not used elsewhere. There is a four-part setting of the original melody of the hymn in the *Choralgesänge*, No. 351.

*†93 (542) Von Gott will ich nicht lassen.
The melody of Ludwig Helmbold's hymn occurs in Cantatas 11, 73, 107, and in the Organ Preludes. There are three four-part settings of it among the *Choralgesänge*, Nos. 324-326.

†94 (525) Wer Gott vertraut.
The first stanza of the hymn is by Joachim Magdeburg. It is set in Witt to a version of the original (1572) melody found in Calvisius in 1597. There is a four-part setting of it among the *Choralgesänge*, No. 366.

95 (526) Wie's Gott gefällt, so gefällt mir's auch.
The hymn is by Ambrosius Blaurer (1492-1564). It is set in Witt to "Was mein Gott will, das g'scheh' allzeit" (No. 89 *supra*). Its proper melody (Zahn, No. 7574) bears a likeness to the latter. Bach has not used it elsewhere.

*† 96 (527) O Gott du frommer Gott.
The hymn is by Johann Heermann. It is set in Witt to an anonymous melody which Bach uses in Cantatas 24, 71, 164. There is a four-part setting of it among the *Choralgesänge*, No. 282. Elsewhere in the Cantatas Bach uses a second melody, and for the Partite a third.

Excepting Nos. 89 and 91, the hymns in the "Christian Life" section are taken from Witt's corresponding group. Bach varies Witt's order, but his own does not indicate a "programme."

In time of trouble   Vom Creutz und Verfolgung (598-658).

*97 (606) In dich hab' ich gehoffet, Herr.
The hymn is by Adam Reissner. It is set in Witt to Calvisius' melody, which Bach uses in Cantatas 52 and 106, the *St Matthew Passion*, the *Christmas Oratorio*, and the Organ Preludes.

98 (606) IN DICH HAB' ICH GEHOFFET, HERR (Alio modo).
Witt's tune is that indicated in No. 97 *supra*.

99 (630) Mag ich Unglück nicht widerstahn.
The melody (Zahn, No. 8113) of this anonymous hymn does not occur elsewhere in Bach.

*† 100 (656) WENN WIR IN HÖCHSTEN NÖTHEN SEIN.

*† 101 (601) An Wasserflüssen Babylon.
The hymn and the melody are by Wolfgang Dachstein. Bach uses the melody elsewhere in the Organ Preludes, and there is a four-part setting of it among the *Choralgesänge*, No. 23.

*† 102 (638) Warum betrübst du dich, mein Herz.
The hymn is attributed to Hans Sachs. It is set in

Witt to the ancient tune which Bach uses in Cantatas 47 and 138 and of which there are four-part settings in the *Choralgesänge*, Nos. 331, 332.

103 (639) Frisch auf, mein' Seel', verzage nicht.

The hymn is by Caspar Schmucker. Witt directs it to be sung to the tune "Was mein Gott will" (see No. 89 *supra*). Its proper melody is found in the Gotha *Cantional* of 1648 (Zahn, No. 7578). Bach has not used it elsewhere.

* 104 (604) Ach Gott, wie manches Herzeleid.

The hymn is attributed to Martin Moller. Witt directs it to be sung to the tune "Vater unser im Himmelreich" (see No. 65 *supra*). In Cantatas 3, 44, 58, 118, 153 Bach uses another melody for the hymn (see No. 139 *infra*).

† 105 (605) Ach Gott, erhör' mein Seufzen und Wehklagen.

The hymn is by Jakob Peter Schechs (1607–59). It is set in Witt to a melody of which there is a four-part setting among the *Choralgesänge*, No. 2.

106 (723) So wünsch' ich nun ein' gute Nacht.

The hymn is by Philipp Nicolai. It is set in Witt to a melody (Zahn, No. 2766) which Bach has not used elsewhere.

107 (641) Ach lieben Christen, seid getrost.

The hymn is by Johannes G. Gigas. Witt directs it to be sung to the melody "Wo Gott der Herr nicht bei uns hält." Bach also associates the two. (See No. 119 *infra*.) He has not used elsewhere the melody proper to "Ach lieben Christen."

108 (598) Wenn dich Unglück thut greifen an.

The hymn is anonymous. It is set in Witt to a melody (Zahn, No. 499) which Bach has not used elsewhere.

† 109 (552) Keinen hat Gott verlassen.

The hymn is anonymous. It is set in Witt to a reconstruction of the melody of the "Rolandslied," of which there is a four-part setting among the *Choralgesänge*, No. 217.

110 (632) Gott ist mein Heil, mein' Hülf' und Trost.
  The hymn is anonymous. It is set in Witt to a melody by Bartholomäus Gesius (Zahn, No. 4421) which Bach has not used elsewhere.
111 (599) Was Gott thut, das ist wohlgethan, Kein einig.
  The hymn is by J. Michael Altenburg. Witt directs it to to be sung to the tune "Kommt her zu mir, spricht Gottes Sohn" (see No. 90 *supra*). Its proper melody is in the Gotha *Cantional* of 1648 (Zahn, No. 2524). Bach has not used it elsewhere.
*112 (550) Was Gott thut, das ist wohlgethan, Es bleibt gerecht.
  The hymn is by Samuel Rodigast. Its melody is used by Bach frequently in the Cantatas and in the "Three Wedding Chorals."
*†113 (553) WER NUR DEN LIEBEN GOTT LÄSST WALTEN.

The section "In Time of Trouble" contains seventeen hymns, four of which (Nos. 106, 109, 112, 113) are not in Witt's corresponding group. Bach also disturbs Witt's order. He deliberately selects No. 97, a fervent expression of faith, to begin it. The succeeding eight hymns (Nos. 99–106) indicate moods of distress and despair, culminating in No. 106, with its hopeless cry:

> Farewell, vain, worthless world, farewell!
> Farewell to friends, farewell to life!

Then the mood changes. The last seven hymns breathe courage and assurance, and Bach ends with, perhaps, his favourite consolatory hymn, Georg Neumark's "Wer nur den lieben Gott":

> Think not amid the hour of trial
> That God hath cast thee off unheard.

THE "ORGELBÜCHLEIN" 53

(a) *The Church Militant*   *Von der Christlichen Kirchen und Worte Gottes* (476-497).

*114 (480) Ach Gott, vom Himmel sieh darein.
The hymn is by Martin Luther. It is set in Witt to the original melody. Bach uses it in Cantatas 2, 77, 153.

†115 (481) Es spricht der Unweisen Mund wohl.
The hymn is by Martin Luther. There is a four-part setting of its proper melody (attributed to Luther) among the *Choralgesänge*, No. 92.

*†116 (482) Ein' feste Burg ist unser Gott.
The melody of Luther's hymn occurs in Cantata 80 and the Organ Preludes, and there are two four-part settings of it among the *Choralgesänge*, Nos. 74, 75.

*†117 (483) Es woll' uns Gott genädig sein.
The hymn is by Martin Luther. Its melody occurs in Cantatas 69 and 76, and there are two four-part settings of it among the *Choralgesänge*, Nos. 95, 96.

*118 (485) Wär' Gott nicht mit uns diese Zeit.
The hymn is by Luther. The melody, attributed either to him or to Johann Walther, is used by Bach in Cantata 14.

*†119 (486) Wo Gott der Herr nicht bei uns hält.
The hymn is by Justus Jonas. Bach uses its melody in Cantatas 73, 114, and 178, and there are four-part settings of it among the *Choralgesänge*, Nos. 383, 385, 388.

*†120 (479) Wie schön leuchtet der Morgenstern.
The hymn is by Philipp Nicolai, to whom also the tune is attributed. Bach uses the melody in Cantatas 1, 36, 37, 49, 61, 172, and an Organ Prelude. There is a four-part setting of it among the *Choralgesänge*, No. 375.

(b) *God's Holy Word.*

*121 (610) Wie nach einem Wasserquelle.
The hymn is by Ambrosius Lobwasser (1515-85). Louis Bourgeois' melody, to which it is set in Witt, occurs in

Cantatas 13, 19, 25, 30, 32, 39, 70, 194. "Ainsi qu'on oit le cerf bruire" is its original title. In German hymnody it is known as "Freu' dich sehr, O meine Seele."
*122 (477) Erhalt' uns, Herr, bei deinem Wort.
The hymn is by Luther. Bach uses its melody in Cantatas 6 and 126.
123 (520) Lass' mich dein sein und bleiben.
The hymn is by Nikolaus Selnecker. In Witt it is directed to be sung to "Ich dank' dir, lieber Herre" (see No. 144 *infra*), or "Ich freu' mich in dem Herren" (Zahn, No. 5427). Neither the latter nor the hymn's proper melody is used by Bach elsewhere.

While Witt's corresponding group illustrates promiscuously "The Christian Church" and "God's Word," Bach prefers to treat the two ideas separately. Hence, the section contains two parts: (*a*) "The Church Militant," Nos. 114–120; and (*b*) "God's Holy Word," Nos. 121–123. In the first part, with one important modification, Bach follows Witt's order. He begins (No. 114) with Luther's version of Psalm 12, the fourth stanza of which sets forth the Church's mission:

> Grant her, O Lord, to keep the faith
> Amid a faithless nation,
> And keep us safe from sinful scathe
> At length to reach salvation.
> Though men their part with Satan take,
> No powers of Hell can ever shake
> The Church's sure foundation.

To the taunt (No. 115; Luther's Psalm 14), "The fool hath said in his heart, There is no God," the

THE "ORGELBÜCHLEIN" 55

Church (Luther's Psalm 46) (No. 116) answers confidently:

> A stronghold sure our God is He.

In No. 117 (Luther's Psalm 67) the Church prays for the enlargement of her bounds:

> That Thy way may be known on earth,
> Thy grace among all nations.

Nos. 118 and 119 (two versions of the 124th Psalm) picture the Church militant and victorious:

> Our help on God's own name doth stand,
> Who hath made heaven and earth.

The last hymn (No. 120) is a vision of the risen Church glorious, the Spouse of Christ.

The second part is prefaced appropriately (No. 121) by Psalm 42, wherein the Church declares her longing for the pure waters of God's Word. In No. 122 she prays for grace to remain constant. No. 123 expresses the same thought; but, as is so often the case with Bach, in an intimate and personal manner.

In time of War   Um Friede (498-513).

124 (498) Gieb Fried', O frommer, treuer Gott.

The hymn is by Cyriacus Schneegass. Witt directs it to be sung to the melody "Durch Adams Fall" (see No. 76 *supra*). Its proper melody is in the Gotha *Cantional* of 1648. Bach has not used it elsewhere.

*125 (499) Du Friedefürst, Herr Jesu Christ.

The hymn is by Jakob Ebert. Its melody, by Bartholomäus Gesius, is used by Bach in Cantatas 67, 116, and 143.

*126 (502) O grosser Gott von Macht.
　　The hymn is by Balthasar Schnurr. Its melody, attributed to Melchior Franck, is used by Bach in Cantata 46.

　　In the above group Bach picks out the three best known hymns from Witt's larger selection.

　　Death and the Grave　　*Vom Sterben und Begräbnissen*
　　　　　　　　　　　　　　　　(659-742).

*†127 (678) Wenn mein Stündlein vorhanden ist.
　　The hymn and its melody are by Nikolaus Herman. Bach uses the tune in Cantatas 15, 31, 95, and there are four-part settings of it among the *Choralgesänge*, Nos. 353-355.

†128 (697) Herr Jesu Christ, wahr Mensch und Gott.
　　The hymn is by Paul Eber. Witt sets it to a tune (Zahn, 340c) which Bach has not used elsewhere. In Cantata 127 he uses a melody by Louis Bourgeois. Among the *Choralgesänge*, No. 146, there is a four-part setting of another melody, doubtfully attributed to Eccard, to which also the hymn was sung.

†129 (661) Mitten wir im Leben sind.
　　Luther's version of the antiphon "Media vita in morte sumus." There is a four-part setting of its melody among the *Choralgesänge*, No. 252.

†130 (660) Alle Menschen müssen sterben.
　　The hymn is by Johann Georg Albinus. It is set in Witt to a melody by Jakob Hintze (1622-1702), of which a four-part setting (with variations from Witt's text) is among the *Choralgesänge*, No. 17. In Cantata 162 and No. 131 *infra* Bach uses two other melodies.

131 (660) ALLE MENSCHEN MÜSSEN STERBEN (Alio modo).
　　Bach's melody here is not Witt's.

*†132 (722) Valet will ich dir geben.
　　The hymn is by Valerius Herberger. The melody, by Melchior Teschner, occurs in the *St John Passion*,

THE "ORGELBÜCHLEIN" 57

Cantata 95, and the Organ Preludes. There is a four-part setting of it among the *Choralgesänge*, No. 314.

133 (733) Nun lasst uns den Leib begraben.

The hymn is by Michael Weisse. It is set in Witt to a melody (Zahn, No. 352) which Bach has not used elsewhere.

*†134 (719) Christus, der ist mein Leben.

The melody of this anonymous hymn is used by Bach in Cantata 95, and there are four-part settings of it among the *Choralgesänge*, Nos. 46, 47.

*†135 (698) Herzlich lieb hab' ich dich, O Herr.

The hymn is by Martin Schalling. The melody occurs in Cantatas 149, 174, and the *St John Passion*. There is a four-part setting of it among the *Choralgesänge*, No. 152.

*136 (695) Auf meinen lieben Gott.

The hymn is attributed to Sigismund Weingärtner. Bach uses its melody in Cantatas 5, 89, 136, 148, 188, and two of the Organ Preludes ("Wo soll ich fliehen hin").

137 (680) Herr Jesu Christ, ich weiss gar wohl.

The hymn is by Bartholomäus Ringwaldt. Witt directs it to be sung to the tune "Herr Jesu Christ, du höchstes Gut" (see No. 72 *supra*). Its proper melody (Zahn, No. 4525) is not used by Bach elsewhere.

*†138 (684) Mach's mit mir, Gott, nach deiner Güt'.

The hymn is by Johann Hermann Schein. Witt directs it to be sung to the melody "Wie soll ich doch die Güte dein'." The latter, actually, is Schein's own melody to his hymn, and is used by Bach in Cantatas 139, 156, and the *St John Passion*. There is a four-part setting of it among the *Choralgesänge*, No. 237.

*†139 (703) Herr [O] Jesu Christ, mein's Lebens Licht.

The hymn is by Martin Behm. Its melody is generally associated with the hymn "Ach Gott, wie manches Herzeleid," and is used by Bach for it in Cantatas 3, 44,

58, 118, 153. Among the *Choralgesänge*, No. 145, is a four-part setting of another melody to which also the hymn was sung.

140 (720) Mein' Wallfahrt ich vollendet hab'.
The hymn is by Ludwig von Hörnigk (d. 1667). Witt directs it to be sung to the tune "Was mein Gott will" (see No. 89 *supra*). Bach has not used its proper melody (Zahn, No. 5704a) elsewhere.

†141 (743) Gott hat das Evangelium.
The hymn is by Erasmus Alberus. There is a four-part setting of its melody among the *Choralgesänge*, No. 116.

142 (744) Ach Gott, thu' dich erbarmen.
The hymn is by M. R. Müntzer. Its melody (Zahn, No. 7228a) is not used by Bach elsewhere.

In the above section all but the last two hymns (Nos. 141, 142) are taken from Witt's corresponding group. But they are arranged in Bach's order and with a definite design. Nos. 127–129 are prayers of the soul facing death, calm and confident. Nos. 130, 132, and 133 place us at the graveside. Nos. 134–140 breathe over the dead clay the assurance of a future life. Nos. 141 and 142 proclaim the Last Judgment and the day-dawn of Eternity.

Morning hymns   Morgen-Gesänge (410–429).
*143 (419) Gott des Himmels und der Erden.
The hymn is by Heinrich Albert. Witt directs it to be sung to the melody "Freu' dich sehr, O meine Seele." In the *Christmas Oratorio* Bach sets the hymn to Albert's own tune.

*†144 (411) Ich dank' dir, lieber Herre.
The hymn is by Johann Kolross. The melody, secular in origin, is used by Bach in Cantata 37. There are

THE "ORGELBÜCHLEIN" 59

two four-part settings of it among the *Choralgesänge*, No. 176, 177.

†145 (412) Aus meines Herzens Grunde.
The hymn is attributed, probably inaccurately, to Johannes Mathesius (1504-65). Its melody (properly "Herzlich thut mich erfreuen") is found in a four-part setting among the *Choralgesänge*, No. 30.

†146 (414) Ich dank' dir schon durch deinen Sohn.
The melody of this anonymous hymn is found in a four-part setting among the *Choralgesänge*, No. 179.

† 147 (415) Das walt' mein Gott.
The hymn is attributed to Basilius Förtsch. A four-part setting of the melody is among the *Choralgesänge*, No. 59.

Evening hymns   *Abend-Gesänge* (430-446).

*† 148 (431) Christ, der du bist der helle Tag.
The hymn is by Erasmus Alberus. Bach has used the melody for a set of Variations. There is also a four-part setting of it among the *Choralgesänge*, No. 33.

†149 (430) Christe, der du bist Tag und Licht.
The hymn is by Wolfgang Meusel. There is a four-part setting of the melody among the *Choralgesänge*, No. 34.

*†150 (434) Werde munter, mein Gemüthe.
The hymn is by Johann Rist. Bach uses the melody in the *St Matthew Passion* and Cantatas 55, 146, 147, 154. There are four-part settings of it among the *Choralgesänge*, Nos. 363, 364.

*†151 (435) Nun ruhen alle Wälder.
The hymn is by Paul Gerhardt. Its melody is also known as "O Welt, ich muss dich lassen." Bach uses it in the *St Matthew Passion, St John Passion*, and Cantatas 13, 44, 97. There are four-part settings of it among the *Choralgesänge*, Nos. 289, 290, 291, 298.

INTRODUCTION

Grace at meals   *Tisch-Gesänge* (449-461).

†152 (452) Danket dem Herrn, denn er ist sehr freundlich.
The hymn is by Johann Horn. Its melody belongs to a four-part setting of the words "Vitam quae faciunt beatiorem" (Zahn, No. 12). Both its Descant and Tenor passed into use as hymn tunes. Witt sets the hymn to the Tenor melody, of which there is a setting among the *Choralgesänge*, No. 53.

*153 (455) Nun lasst uns Gott, dem Herren.
The hymn is by Ludwig Helmbold. Its tune, also known as "Wach auf, mein Herz, und singe," is used by Bach in Cantatas 79, 165, 194.

†154 (456) Lobet den Herrn, denn er ist sehr freundlich.
The hymn is anonymous. A four-part setting of its melody is among the *Choralgesänge*, No. 232.

*155 (457) Singen wir aus Herzensgrund.
Bach uses the melody of this anonymous hymn in Cantata 187.

For good weather   *Um gut Wetter* (462-463).

156 (462) Gott Vater, der du deine Sonn.
The hymn and its melody (Zahn, No. 380) are by Nikolaus Herman. Bach has not used the tune elsewhere.

The life eternal   *Von Jüngsten Gericht und ewigen Leben* (743-762).

†157 (336) Jesu, meines Herzens Freud'.
The hymn is by Johann Flittner (1618-1678). The original melody (Zahn, No. 4797) is in a minor mode. There is a four-part setting of it, in a major key, among the *Choralgesänge*, No. 202.

†158 (284) Ach, was soll ich Sünder machen.
The hymn is by Johann Flittner. There is a four-part setting of the melody among the *Choralgesänge*, No. 10.

THE "ORGELBÜCHLEIN" 61

*159 (665) ACH WIE NICHTIG, ACH WIE FLÜCHTIG.
  The hymn is by Michael Franck. Its first line is one of four syllables only, and should read "Ach wie flüchtig." It appears in that form in Witt. Why Bach changed it is not apparent. He uses the melody in Cantata 26.

160 (659) Ach, was ist doch unser Leben.
  The hymn is by Johann Rosenthal (1615-90). The melody (Zahn, No. 1208) is not used by Bach elsewhere.

161 (672) Allenthalben, wo ich gehe.
  The hymn, entitled "Verlangen bey Christo zu seyn," is anonymous. Bach has not used the melody (Zahn, No. 1338*b*) elsewhere.

*162 (607) Hast du denn, Jesu, dein Angesicht.
  The hymn is by Ahashuerus Fritsch. Bach uses its melody in Cantata 57 and also in the Organ Prelude "Kommst du nun, Jesu, vom Himmel herunter."

*†163 (125) Sei gegrüsset, Jesu gütig.
  The hymn is by Christian Keimann. The melody, probably by Gottfried Vopelius, is used by Bach for a set of Organ Variations, and there is a four-part setting of it among the *Choralgesänge*, No. 307.

*164 (308) Schmücke dich, O liebe Seele.
  The hymn is by Johann Franck. Crüger's melody is used by Bach in Cantata 180 and in the *Eighteen Chorals*.

It is remarkable that for his concluding section Bach completely disregards Witt's corresponding group. In no other part of the *Orgelbüchlein* is his concentration upon a plan of his own more apparent. He begins (No. 157) with Flittner's "Jesus-Lied," whose closing lines, undoubtedly, were particularly before him:

> When Death calls me, O sustain me,
> Thou Consoler,
> Jesu, Comforter.

It is followed by another of Flittner's hymns (No. 158), which its author inscribed "Omnia si perdam, Jesum servare studebo" (Though I lose all, yet will I cling to Jesus). Its seven stanzas end with the refrain:

> Jesu, from Thee ne'er I'll part.

Then come two reflective hymns upon the transitoriness of human life (Nos. 159, 160). The mood changes. The last four hymns of the group look across the gulf of death. No. 161 is inscribed by its author "Longing to be with Jesus":

> There's a land that looms before me,
> Where nor death nor sin I'll see,
> Where, 'mid Angels who adore Thee,
> I shall pure and glorious be.

In No. 162, a dialogue between Jesus and the Soul, the Soul bids farewell to earth:

> Vain earth, farewell!
> Lost is thy deadening spell!
> Heavenward my wings are poised.

In the last stanza of the hymn (No. 162) the Soul receives its Master's summons to Paradise:

> Welcome! ah welcome! O child whom the Father's love brings Me!
> Heaven is thine, enter in, never, O never, to weary!
> Here shalt thou be
> Of all earth's troubles heart-free,
> Radiant and happy in glory.

In No. 163 the Soul prays for strength to meet the searching ordeal:

> Jesus, Master, dearest treasure,
> Christ my Saviour, my heart's pleasure,
> Hands and pierced Side O show me,
> Give me strength to see and know Thee.
> Let me all Thy love inherit
> And meet death in Thy sure merit.

So, sustained and strengthened, the Soul wings its flight Heavenward (No. 164):

> Soul, array thyself with gladness;
> Leave the gloomy caves of sadness;
> Come from doubt and dusk terrestrial,
> Gleam with radiant light celestial:
> For the Lord, divine and gracious,
> Full of gifts both rare and precious,
> He of love itself the essence,
> Bids Thee to His sacred presence.

It is impossible to follow the unfolding plan of the *Orgelbüchlein* without discerning in its author a man whose personality exhibits the sure fabric of moral grandeur. It reveals in the young man of thirty the simple, confiding trust in God that was his thirty-five years later, when the call of Death came to him almost as his failing breath dictated the words:

> Before Thy throne, my God, I stand,
> Myself, my all are in Thy hand.

It is of interest to observe Bach's fidelity to the hymns and melodies he included in the *Orgelbüch-*

lein. It has been shown elsewhere[1] that he introduces 154 hymns into the *Passions*, Oratorios, Cantatas, and Motetts. Exactly half (77) are in the *Orgelbüchlein*: Nos. 1, 3, 5, 7, 9, 12, 13, 14, 15, 16, 19, 21, 22, 23, 25, 32, 34, 36, 38, 43, 44, 45, 55, 56, 57, 59, 60, 65, 66, 67, 69, 70, 71, 72, 73, 74, 76, 77, 80, 86, 89, 90, 91, 93, 96, 97, 102, 104, 107, 112, 113, 114, 116, 117, 118, 119, 120, 122, 125, 126, 127, 128, 130, 132, 134, 135, 136, 137, 138, 139, 144, 150, 153, 155, 159, 162, 164.

The relation between the *Orgelbüchlein* and the hymn tunes (132) Bach introduces into his vocal and Organ works is less easy to establish. Since only forty-six of the 164 movements (163 melodies; Nos. 50 and 51 being identical) are written and two bars of another are sketched (No. 29), there remain one hundred and seventeen movements in regard to which we can only conjecture, though with some certainty, the tune Bach had in mind. But assuming that he proposed to use in the *Orgelbüchlein* the tune which he associates with the particular hymn elsewhere, we conclude that only thirty-four of its 163 melodies are not found in his vocal and Organ works or among his *Choralgesänge*: Nos. 6, 28, 30, 33, 40, 42, 47, 48, 55, 62, 63, 75, 80, 81, 82, 83, 87, 95, 99, 103, 106, 107, 108, 110, 111, 123, 124, 133, 137, 140, 142, 156, 160, 161. The *Orgelbüchlein* therefore was

[1] *Bach's Chorals*, Part II. 46.

designed to contain 98 of the 132 hymn melodies that Bach used throughout the whole range of his art.

It follows from what has been written that some, at least, of the completed movements of the *Orgelbüchlein* may have been composed before the publication of Witt's Hymn-book in November 1715. Three of them undoubtedly are based on melodic texts not found in Witt (Nos. 4, 98, 131). In three cases (Nos. 14, 27, 44), while using Witt's tune, Bach clearly follows another text than Witt's. In another instance the same conclusion presents itself, though less positively (No. 36).

On the other hand, there are movements for which it seems certain that Bach must have had Witt's text before him, or another identical with it; in particular, " Das alte Jahr," " Herr Gott, nun schleuss," and "In dir ist Freude." Witt refers in his Preface to an older Hymn-book upon which his own was based, and gives constant page references to it. There can be little doubt that he referred to the Gotha *Cantional* of 1646, or a later edition. Bach's familiarity with the Gotha Hymn-book of 1715 makes it reasonable to suppose that the earlier Gotha compilation was known and used in Weimar. Unfortunately there is no copy of it in this country, and for the moment it is impossible to collate Witt's book with it. Zahn's volumes, however, show that in very many cases Witt's melodic texts reproduce those of the earlier book.

After his removal to Leipzig in 1723 it is shown that Bach took his melodic texts from the Hymnbooks of Leipzig musicians, such as Vetter and Schein. On the other hand, the melodic texts of the four-part settings among the *Choralgesänge* seem very generally to conform to the Hymn-books of the Weimar period. Equally of the Organ movements other than those of the *Orgelbüchlein*, a collation of their melodic texts makes it evident that in them too Bach generally followed the Gotha tradition.

The subject is a large one, rendered difficult by the inaccessibility of the Hymn-books upon which its solution depends. Meanwhile the revelation of Witt's Hymn-book and Gotha tradition as Bach's guides during the early period of his musical career, in which the bulk of his Organ work was composed, offers a stable foundation for further research.

The "*Clavierübung*," Part III

The full title of the work is:

"Dritter Theil der Clavier Übung bestehend in verschiedenen Vorspielen über die Catechismus- und andere Gesænge, vor die Orgel: Denen Liebhabern, und besonders denen Kennern von dergleichen Arbeit, zur Gemüths Ergezung verfertiget von Johann Sebastian Bach Kœnigl. Pohlnischen, und Churfürstl. Sæchs. Hoff-Compositeur,

THE "CLAVIERÜBUNG" 67

Capellmeister, und Directore Chori Musici in Leipzig. In Verlegung des Authoris."

"The Third Part of the Clavier-Exercise, containing various Preludes on the Catechism and other Hymns, for the Organ. Composed for amateurs and lovers of such works, and for their recreation, by Johann Sebastian Bach, Composer to the Royal and Electoral Court of Poland-Saxony, Capellmeister and Director of the Music, Leipzig. Published by the Author."

The work was published in 1739, or at latest at Easter 1740; price, three thalers[1].

The larger part of the book consists of a series of movements which employ Luther's hymns to illustrate the Lutheran Catechism:

The Ten Commandments ("Dies sind die heil'gen zehn Gebot'").
The Creed ("Wir glauben all' an einen Gott, Schöpfer").
Prayer ("Vater unser im Himmelreich").
Baptism ("Christ unser Herr zum Jordan kam").
Penitence ("Aus tiefer Noth schrei ich zu dir").
Holy Communion ("Jesus Christus, unser Heiland, Der von uns").

In a characteristic mood of reverence, Bach prefaces his exposition of Lutheran dogma with an invocation of the Trinity—a Litany to the Three Persons, and "Allein Gott in der Höh' sei Ehr'."

So far the *Clavierübung* is homogeneous in design. Bach, however, added six irrelevant numbers:

(1) He prefaced the volume with a Prelude in E flat major.

[1] Spitta, III. 213 n.

(2) As a closing voluntary he printed a Fugue in E flat major, known as "St Anne's" from the likeness of its opening subject to that tune. The similar tonality of the opening Prelude and closing Fugue emphasizes the homogeneity of the numbers that lie between them.

(3–6) Between the last of the Catechism Chorals and the closing Fugue he inserted four movements marked "Duetto," written for the Cembalo Clavicembalo, or "Flügel," and irrelevant to the rest of the book, though its other movements were also appropriate to the Cembalo.

The Catechism hymns are presented in duplicate, in long and short movements. So also is the introductory "Kyrie," of whose three sections there are two sets. The "Gloria" ("Allein Gott in der Höh' sei Ehr'") is triplicated; each Person of the Trinity being addressed in a separate movement. Schweitzer is of opinion[1] that the long movements were composed for the *Clavierübung* circa 1739, and that the short movements date from an earlier period. He suggests that Bach had in mind Luther's longer and shorter Catechisms and proposed to distinguish them: the first by a series of lengthy movements sublimely symbolic; the second by Preludes of the childish simplicity characteristic of Luther's shorter exegesis.

[1] Vol. I. 290.

THE "CLAVIERÜBUNG" 69

The complete scheme of the *Clavierübung* is as follows, the capitals A and B standing respectively for the long and short movements:

Voluntary.

Praeludium pro Organo pleno.

Invocation of the Trinity.

A. { Kyrie, Gott Vater in Ewigkeit (Canto fermo in Soprano. a 2 Clav. e Pedale).
Christe, aller Welt Trost (Canto fermo in Tenore. a 2 Clav. e Pedale).
Kyrie, Gott heiliger Geist (a 5. Canto fermo in Basso. Con Organo pleno). }

B. { Kyrie, Gott Vater in Ewigkeit (Alio modo. Manualiter).
Christe, aller Welt Trost.
Kyrie, Gott heiliger Geist. }

{ Allein Gott in der Höh' sei Ehr' (a 3. Canto fermo in Alto).
Allein Gott in der Höh' sei Ehr' (a 2 Clav. e Pedale).
Allein Gott in der Höh' sei Ehr' (Fughetta. Manualiter). }

The Ten Commandments.

A. Dies sind die heil'gen zehn Gebot' (Canto fermo in Canone. a 2 Clav. e Pedale).
B. Dies sind die heil'gen zehn Gebot'(Fughetta. Manualiter).

The Creed.

A. Wir glauben all' an einen Gott (In Organo pleno).
B. Wir glauben all' an einen Gott (Fughetta. Manualiter).

Prayer.

A. Vater unser im Himmelreich (Canto fermo in Canone. a 2 Clav. e Pedale).
B. Vater unser im Himmelreich (Alio modo. Manualiter).

Baptism.

A. Christ unser Herr zum Jordan kam (a 2 Clav. e Canto fermo in Pedale).
B. Christ unser Herr zum Jordan kam (Alio modo. Manualiter).

Penitence.

A. Aus tiefer Noth schrei ich zu dir (a 6. In Organo pleno con Pedale doppio).
B. Aus tiefer Noth schrei ich zu dir (a 4. Alio modo. Manualiter).

Holy Communion.

A. Jesus Christus, unser Heiland, Der von uns (a 2 Clav. e Canto fermo in Pedale).
B. Jesus Christus, unser Heiland, Der von uns (Fuga. a 4. Manualiter).

Interludes.

Duetto I [E mi. 3/8].
Duetto II [F ma. 2/4].
Duetto III [G ma. 12/8].
Duetto IV [A mi. ¢].

Voluntary.

Fuga a 5 pro Organo pleno.

Schübler's "*Sechs Choräle*"

The title-page of the original edition is as follows:

"Sechs Chorale von verschiedener Art auf einer Orgel mit 2 Clavieren und Pedal vorzuspielen, verfertiget von Johann Sebastian Bach, Königl. Pohln. und Chur-Saechs. Hoff-Compositeur, Capellm. u. Direct. Chor-Mus. Lips.

In Verlegung Joh. Georg Schüblers zu Zella am Thüringer Walde.

Sind zu haben in Leipzig bey Herrn Capellm. Bachen, bey dessen Herrn Söhnen in Berlin und Halle, u. bey dem Verleger zu Zella."

"Six Chorals in various forms for an Organ with two manuals and Pedal, composed by Johann Sebastian Bach, Composer to the Royal and Electoral Court of Poland-Saxony, Capellmeister and Director of the Music, Leipzig. Published by Johann Georg Schübler at Zella in the Thuringian Forest. To be had in Leipzig from Herr Capellmeister Bach, from his sons in Berlin and Halle, and from the publisher in Zella."

The reference to Bach's sons establishes the date of the publication as in or after 1746. The "son in Halle" was Bach's eldest, Wilhelm Friedemann, who was appointed Organist there in 1746. The "son in Berlin" was Carl Philipp Emmanuel, who had been appointed Clavier accompanist to Frederick the Great of Prussia in 1740.

A copy of the original edition of the *Sechs Choräle* was extant in 1847. Presumably it had been in the possession of Bach himself or of a member of his family; for it was corrected throughout in Bach's hand, with his directions for playing the movements. It was in Forkel's Collection and from him passed to Griepenkerl[1]. On the latter's death it came into the possession of Professor S. W. Dehn, Keeper of the Music in the Royal Library,

---

[1] Peters, vi. Pref.

Berlin, who died in 1858. Writing in 1878, Rust declares its then locality unknown to him. Rust possessed a second and Hauser of Carlsruhe a third copy[1].

After 1744 Bach appears to have abandoned the composition of Church Cantatas, which to that point occupied so much of his time at Leipzig, and devoted himself to his Organ works. During the last five years of his life the Canonic Variations on "Vom Himmel hoch," the *Musikalisches Opfer* (Musical Offering) to Frederick the Great, and the *Sechs Choräle* were published. The *Kunst der Fuge* (Art of Fugue) appeared shortly after Bach's death. Excepting the Canonic Variations, all of these works were engraved by Johann Georg Schübler of Zella[2].

Zella is a small town of 4000 inhabitants, twenty miles south of Gotha in the Thuringian Forest, about one hundred miles from Leipzig. That Bach should publish his music there is curious but explicable. The place is distinguished for the manufacture of arms, and Spitta[3] conjectures Schübler to have been the son of a gunstock maker there. The link between him and Bach appears to have been Johann Schmidt, Organist at Zella until 1746,

---

[1] B.G. xxv. (2) xv.
[2] Spitta, III. 203 n., however, disputes Rust's conclusion that Schübler engraved the *Kunst der Fuge*.
[3] Vol. III. 238 n.

when he resigned in favour of his son. Spitta identifies Johann Schmidt as the Johann Christoph Schmidt who, in 1713, copied out a Clavier Prelude of Bach's for his own use. If the identification is correct, the acquaintance of Bach and Schmidt was of long standing. Schmidt's, or another's, intervention, at any rate, seems to account for Bach's business relations with Zella during the last five years of his life.

The *Sechs Choräle* were published by Schübler at Zella between 1746 and Bach's death in 1750[1]. They are distinguished from the rest of Bach's Organ music by the fact that five of them positively, and the sixth with practical certainty, are arrangements of movements from his recently composed Leipzig Church Cantatas[2]. They are printed in the following order, to which, however, no significance attaches:

1. *Wachet auf, ruft uns die Stimme* (Canto fermo in Tenore).
    An arrangement of the fourth movement of Cantata 140, the Tenor Unison Choral, "Zion hört die Wächter singen[3]." In the Cantata the melody is sung by the Tenor or Tenors in unison. In the Prelude it is assigned to an eight-foot stop on the "sinistra" manual. The Cantata was composed in 1731, or later.

[1] Wilhelm Rust, who edited them for the Bach Society, dates their publication *c.* 1747-49.
[2] See Parry, *J. S. Bach*, pp. 390, 535.
[3] *Bach's Chorals*, Part II. 407.

2. *Wo soll ich fliehen hin*, or *Auf meinen lieben Gott* (a 2 Clav. e Pedale).

The movement, no doubt, is adapted from a lost Cantata.

3. *Wer nur den lieben Gott lässt walten* (a 2 Clav. e Pedale).

An arrangement of the fourth movement of Cantata 93, a Soprano-Alto *Duetto*, "Er kent die rechten Freudenstunden[1]," in which the melody is played by the Violins and Violas in unison. In the Organ movement it is given to a four-foot stop on the Pedals. The Cantata was composed in 1728 (?).

4. *Meine Seele erhebt den Herren* (a 2 Clav. e Pedale).

An arrangement of the fifth movement of Cantata 10, an Alto-Tenor *Duetto*, "Er denket der Barmherzigkeit[2]," in which the melody is played by the Oboes and Tromba in unison. In the Organ movement it is given to the "dextra" manual. The Cantata was composed *c.* 1740.

5. *Ach bleib' bei uns, Herr Jesu Christ* (a 2 Clav. e Pedale).

An arrangement of the third movement of Cantata 6, the Soprano Unison Choral, "Ach bleib' bei uns, Herr Jesu Christ[3]," in which the voice has the melody. In the Organ movement it is given to the "dextra" manual. The Cantata was composed in 1736.

6. *Kommst du nun, Jesu, vom Himmel herunter* (a 2 Clav. e Pedale).

An arrangement of the second movement of Cantata 137, the Alto Unison Choral, "Lobe den Herren, der Alles so herrlich regieret[4]," in which the voice has the melody. In the Organ movement it is given to a four-foot stop on the Pedals. The Cantata was composed in 1732 (?).

---

[1] *Bach's Chorals*, Part II. 321.
[2] *Ibid.* 157.
[3] *Ibid.* 147.
[4] *Ibid.* 399.

THE CANONIC VARIATIONS 75

The Canonic Variations on "Vom Himmel hoch da komm ich her"

The work has the following title-page:

"Einige canonische Veränderungen über das Weihnachtslied: 'Vom Himmel hoch, da komm ich her,' vor die Orgel mit 2 Clavieren und dem Pedal von Johann Sebastian Bach, Königl. Pohl. und Chursächs. Hoff-Compositeur, Capellmeister u. Direct. Chor. Mus. Lips. Nürnberg in Verlegung Balth. Schmids."

"Canonic Variations upon the Christmas Carol 'Vom Himmel hoch da komm ich her' for an Organ with two manuals and Pedal. By Johann Sebastian Bach, Composer to the Royal Polish and Electoral Court of Saxony, Capellmeister and Director of the Music, Leipzig. Nürnberg: Published by Balthasar Schmidt."

The title-page bears no date, but the publication number "28" affords a clue. C. P. E. Bach's Clavier Concerto in D major, also published by Schmidt, bears the number "27" and the date admittedly is 1745. The "Variations" therefore must have been brought out subsequently to Emmanuel's Concerto, i.e. in or after 1745. That they were presented by Bach to Mizler's "Sozietät der musikalischen Wissenschaften," upon becoming a member of it in June 1747, is an admitted fact. According to the "Necrology" Bach gave the work to the Society "vollständig gearbeitet" (completely worked-out) "and it was afterwards engraved on copper." If this statement is accurate, Balthasar Schmidt can have published nothing between Emmanuel's Concerto and the Variations, two years later. The supposition is so improbable, that Bach must be held to have engraved the work before he presented it to the Mizler Society. In other words, its publication is to be assigned to the period in which the *Schübler Chorals* also made their appearance[1]. The Autograph is in the Royal Library, Berlin.

The "Sozietät der musikalischen Wissenschaften" was founded at Leipzig in 1738. Its promoter, Lorenz Christoph Mizler, a student at Leipzig from 1731 to 1734, was in that period Bach's pupil for composition and the Clavier. His Society being somewhat academic in its outlook, Bach was only induced to join it in the summer of 1747—Handel had been elected an honorary member two years before (1745)[2].

The character of the Society to some extent explains the form of the composition Bach presented to it as his diploma work. His purpose, Schweitzer remarks[3], was "to pack into a single Choral the whole art of canon." The work consists of five Variations:

I (In Canone all' Ottava).

A Trio. The canon is between the two manuals; the Pedal having the unembellished melody.

---

[1] See Spitta, III. 294. In B.G. xlvi, p. xxi n. Kretzschmar dates the work "1723" but offers no proof.
[2] See Spitta, III. 22–25.   [3] Vol. I. 283.

THE CANONIC VARIATIONS 77

II (Alio modo in Canone alla Quinta).

Like the first Variation, the movement is a Trio, the *cantus* being on the Pedal, and the canon between the two manuals. The canonic subject has a close affinity to the Choral melody; or, more correctly, suggests either by anticipation (bars 1 and 16) or by repetition (bar 10) the lines of the *cantus*, in the Pachelbel manner.

III (In Canone alla Settima).

In four parts. The canon is between the Pedal and the second manual. The melody is on the first manual over a free part *cantabile*.

IV (In Canone all' Ottava per augmentationem).

In four parts. The canon is between the first manual and the Bass of the second. The melody is on the Pedal. The middle part on the second manual has a free subject.

V (L' altra sorte del Canone al rovescio: (1) alla Sesta, (2) alla Terza, (3) alla Seconda, e (4) alla Nona).

The movement is a *tour-de-force*. For the first thirteen bars the melody is in the Treble and below it a canon by inversion at the sixth. From bars 14 to 26 the melody is in the Bass of the second manual in canon with the first by inversion at the third. For bars 27 to 39 the melody is in the Pedal and above it is the canon by inversion at the second. In bars 40 to 51 the melody is again in the Treble in canon with the Pedal by inversion at the ninth. In every one of the foregoing divisions the part not engaged in canon has a free subject; the Pedal in the first two sections, the first manual in the third, the second manual in the fourth. The last five bars are in five parts. Bach introduces into them actually all four lines of the melody, embellished with a profusion of little canons in diminution, "which seem to be tumbling over one another in their eagerness to get into the scheme before the inexorable limits of formal proportion shut the door with the final cadence[1]."

Bach turned again to this work in the last weeks of his life. A corrected fair copy of the printed edition is in the Autograph containing the *Eighteen Chorals* in the Royal Library, Berlin.

The "Achtzehn Choräle"

The Autograph of the *Eighteen Chorals* or *Great Chorals* is in the Berlin Royal Library. It once belonged to Philipp Emmanuel Bach. The manuscript bears the following title:

"Achtzehn Choräle von verschiedener Art auf einer Orgel mit 2 Clavieren und Pedal vorzuspielen, verfertiget von Johann Sebastian Bach, Königl. Poln. und Churf. Sächs. Hof-Compositeur, Capellm. und Direct. Chor. Mus. Lips."

[1] Parry, p. 541.

THE "ACHTZEHN CHORÄLE" 79

" Eighteen Chorals in various forms for an Organ with two manuals and Pedal, composed by Johann Sebastian Bach, Composer to the Royal and Electoral Court of Poland-Saxony, Capellmeister and Director of the Music, Leipzig."

Bach worked upon the manuscript during the illness that terminated fatally on July 28, 1750. The first fifteen Chorals are Bach's holograph. Nos. 16 and 17 are in his son-in-law Altnikol's handwriting. Of the last movement, No. 18, "Vor deinen Thron tret' ich hiemit," only the first twenty-five and a half bars are written in the MS. The remaining nineteen and a half bars have been supplied from the *Art of Fugue*, in which the movement also is found. The conclusion hardly can be evaded that Bach, tardily obsessed by desire to publish in the last five years of his life, was preparing the *Eighteen Chorals* for the engraver when death called him.

In addition to the Autograph and original edition of the *Art of Fugue*, early and authoritative MSS. of several of the *Eighteen Chorals* are extant. The Kirnberger Collection in the Amalienbibliothek of the Joachimsthal Gymnasium contains copies of thirteen of them: Nos. 1, 2, 3, 4, 5, 6, 7, 8, 9, 11, 12, 13, and 17. Among the MSS. of Krebs, another of Bach's pupils, are copies of Nos. 7 and 12. In the handwriting of Oley (Hauser Collection) are copies of seven: Nos. 1, 2, 3, 4, 7, 8, and 9.

The University Library of Königsberg possesses early copies of Nos. 7 and 12. Besides these there are earlier versions of twelve: Nos. 1, 2, 3, 5 (three readings), 6, 8, 9, 10 (two readings), 11, 13, 14, 15. They are found in the Krebs, Kirnberger, and Walther Collections. Bach's Autograph of one of these earlier versions (No. 10) is in the Berlin Royal Library. The Autograph of the early version of No. 14 is also there[1].

Wilhelm Rust's conclusion that the *Eighteen Chorals* were composed during the Leipzig period is contested by Spitta and Schweitzer[2] and is generally held to be inaccurate. For the most part their composition dates from the Weimar period, when Bach was still influenced by Buxtehude, Pachelbel, and Böhm. The large number of early texts of them supports the conclusion.

The *Eighteen Chorals* appear in the Autograph in the following order, to which no significance attaches. Every movement except No. 18 is headed "di J. S. Bach":

1. *Komm, heiliger Geist, Herre Gott* (Fantasia. Canto fermo in Pedale).
2. *Komm, heiliger Geist, Herre Gott* (Alio modo. a 2 Clav. e Pedale).
3. *An Wasserflüssen Babylon* (a 2 Clav. e Pedale).
4. *Schmücke dich, O liebe Seele* (a 2 Clav. e Pedale).

[1] B.G. xxv. (2) xx.   [2] Vol. 1. 290.

THE "ACHTZEHN CHORÄLE" 81

5. *Herr Jesu Christ, dich zu uns wend'* (Trio. a 2 Clav. e Pedale).
6. *O Lamm Gottes unschuldig* (3 Versus).
7. *Nun danket alle Gott* (a 2 Clav. e Pedale. Canto fermo in Soprano).
   Parry remarks[1] on the fidelity with which the movement follows the scheme of the so-called "Pachelbel Choralvorspiel," in the anticipation of each phrase of the melody by the accompanying parts in shorter notes than the *cantus*.
8. *Von Gott will ich nicht lassen* (Canto fermo in Pedale).
9. *Nun komm, der Heiden Heiland* (a 2 Clav. e Pedale).
10. *Nun komm, der Heiden Heiland* (Trio. a due Bassi e Canto fermo).
11. *Nun komm, der Heiden Heiland* (In Organo pleno. Canto fermo in Pedale).
12. *Allein Gott in der Höh' sei Ehr'* (a 2 Clav. e Pedale. Canto fermo in Soprano).
    "To many people," Schweitzer remarks[2], the movement "seems very youthful." He finds it "purely in the style of Böhm."
13. *Allein Gott in der Höh' sei Ehr'* (a 2 Clav. e Pedale. Canto fermo in Tenore).
14. *Allein Gott in der Höh' sei Ehr'* (Trio. a 2 Clav. e Pedale).
    Even in this miscellaneous Collection Bach inserts the Trinity Hymn three times.
15. *Jesus Christus, unser Heiland, Der von uns* (Sub Communione. Pedaliter).
16. *Jesus Christus, unser Heiland, Der von uns* (Alio modo).
17. *Komm, Gott, Schöpfer, heiliger Geist* (In Organo pleno con Pedale obligato).
    The first seven and part of the eighth bars are textually an almost exact copy of the *Orgelbüchlein* movement on the melody.

[1] *Op. cit.* 538.   [2] Vol. 1. 292.

18. *Vor deinen Thron tret' ich*, or *Wenn wir in höchsten Nöthen sein*.

The foundation of the movement is the earlier Prelude in the *Orgelbüchlein*. In the present movement, however, the four lines of the *cantus* are separated and the elaborate embroidery of the *canto fermo* is discarded. The new material is in the interludes.

MELODIES

ACH BLEIB' BEI UNS, HERR JESU CHRIST.

Melody: "Danket dem Herrn, heut' und allzeit"

Seth Calvisius 1594

i. Ah Jesu Christ, with us abide,
For now, behold, 'tis eventide :
And bring, to cheer us through the night,
Thy Word, our true and only light.

ii. In times of trial and distress
Preserve our truth and steadfastness,
And pure unto the end, O Lord,
Vouchsafe Thy Sacraments and Word.

iii. O Jesu Christ, Thy Church sustain ;
Our hearts are wavering, cold, and vain :
Then let Thy Word be strong and clear
To silence doubt and banish fear.

iv. O guard us all from Satan's wiles,
From worldly threats and worldly smiles,
And let Thy saints in unity
Know Thee in God and God in Thee.

v. The days are evil : all around
Strife, errors, blasphemies abound,
And secret slander's withering eye,
And soft-tongued, sleek hypocrisy.

* * *

ix. From these and all of God abhorred,
O Christ, protect us by Thy Word ;
Increase our faith and hope and love,
And bring us to Thy fold above.

Nikolaus Selnecker (1532-92)   Tr. *Benjamin Hall Kennedy*[1].

Nikolaus Selnecker's "Ach bleib' bei uns, Herr Jesu Christ," was first published in his *Geistliche Psalmen* (Nürnberg, 1611). Actually only stanzas iii–ix are by him, being an addendum to Melanchthon's "Vespera jam venit, nobiscum Christe maneto"

[1] *Hymnologia Christiana* (Lond. 1863), No. 41. The original hymn has nine stanzas.

ACH BLEIB' BEI UNS, HERR JESU CHRIST 85

(St Luke, xxiv. 29). The Alto melody (*supra*), which also bears the name of Selnecker's hymn, is found in a four-part setting of the hymn "Danket dem Herrn, heut' und allzeit," by Seth Calvisius, in 1594. As a separate melody, however, its Alto part is at least as old as 1589. Bach uses it in the movement *infra*, in Cantata 6 (1736), and *Choralgesänge*, Nos. 1, 313. His text is invariable. Its variations of the original are not traced in Zahn. In Witt (No. 476) the hymn is set to another melody, as in the Gotha *Cantional* (Zahn, No. 613).

[1]

N. xvi. 10[1]. The movement is No. 5 of the *Schübler Chorals*, an arrangement of the Soprano Unison Choral in Cantata 6, where the *obbligato* is played by the Violoncello piccolo[2]. The movement paints the placid evening scene upon the road to Emmaus.

[1] The reference is to the Novello Edition. To identify the movement in the other Editions, refer to the Table on pp. 2–11 *supra*.
[2] See *Bach's Chorals*, Part II. 146.

Ach Gott und Herr.

Melody: "*Ach Gott und Herr*"
Johann Crüger's version 1640

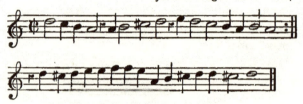

i. Alas! my God! my sins are great,
   My conscience doth upbraid me;
   And now I find that at my strait
   No man hath power to aid me.

ii. And fled I hence, in my despair,
    In some lone spot to hide me,
    My griefs would still be with me there,
    Thy hand still hold and guide me.

iii. Nay, Thee I seek;—I merit nought,
     Yet pity and restore me;
     Be not Thy wrath, just God, my lot;
     Thy Son hath suffered for me.

iv. If pain and woe must follow sin,
    Then be my path still rougher.
    Here spare me not; if heaven I win,
    On earth I gladly suffer.

v. But curb my heart, forgive my guilt,
   Make Thou my patience firmer,
   For they must miss the good Thou wilt,
   Who at Thy teachings murmur.

vi. Then deal with me as seems Thee best,
Thy grace will help me bear it,
If but at last I see Thy rest,
And with my Saviour share it.

Johann Major (1564-1654) or Martin Rutilius (1550-1618)
Tr. *Catherine Winkworth*[1].

The Lenten hymn, "Ach Gott und Herr," is attributed to Johann Major of Jena or Martin Rutilius of Weimar. It was published as a broadsheet in 1613, and with the melody in 1625. The composer of the tune is unknown. Johann Crüger reconstructed it (*supra*) in his *Newes vollkömliches Gesangbuch* (Berlin, 1640). A major version of his reconstruction appeared fifteen years later (1655). Bach employs it in Cantata 48 (*c.* 1740), *Choralgesänge*, No. 3, and the first two Organ movements *infra*, where his text differs from Witt's (No. 265), which very closely follows the original (1625) version[2].

There are three Organ movements on the melody:

[2]

N. xviii. 1. Six MSS. of the movement exist, one of them Kirnberger's and another in the Krebs "Sammelbuch." A third attributes the movement

---

[1] *Chorale Book for England* (London, 1865), No. 107. The original hymn has six stanzas of six lines, 1 and 2, 4 and 5, 3 and 6 rhyming.

[2] See *Bach's Chorals*, Part II. 237, where the 1625 and 1655 texts of the tune are printed.

to Johann Gottfried Walther of Weimar, no doubt incorrectly. A variant text of it is in B.G. xl. 152, of which there are three MSS., one of which (Hauser) is inscribed "Vers. 4" and another (Schelble-Gleichauf) "Vers. 3." The latter MS. contains seven movements on the *cantus* by Bach and Walther. That Bach communicated to Walther his own treatments of the melody is an obvious inference.

[3]

N. xviii. 2. In one of the eleven MSS. of the movement (Schelble-Gleichauf) the composition, like No. 2 above, is attributed to Walther and is marked "Vers. 4." Bach's authorship does not appear to be in doubt. Ernst Naumann (B.G. xl. Introd. xvii) suggests that Bach communicated it to Walther when they were neighbours in Weimar.

[4]

N. xviii. 3. Unlike Nos. 2 and 3 the movement is in a minor key (B mi.) and follows closely the original (1625) and Witt's versions of the tune. A copy of it in the Krebs MSS. is marked "J. S. B." Another copy is in the Königsberg University Library, among the Walther MSS. The facts therefore point to Bach's composition of all three movements in the Weimar years. In the same period, it is to be observed, Bach

ACH GOTT UND HERR   89

included the melody among the Penitential hymns of the *Orgelbüchlein* (No. 71).

In none of the three movements is there apparent an intention to distinguish the stanzas of the hymn by musical treatment.

ACH WIE FLÜCHTIG.

Melody: "*Ach wie flüchtig*" Michael Franck 1652

i. O how cheating,
O how fleeting,
Is our earthly being!
'Tis a mist in wintry weather,
Gathered in an hour together,
And as soon dispersed in ether.

ii. O how cheating,
O how fleeting,
Are our days departing!
Like a deep and headlong river
Flowing onward, flowing ever,
Tarrying not and stopping never.

* * *

iv. O how cheating,
O how fleeting,
Is all earthly beauty!
Like a summer floweret flowing,
Scattered by the breezes, blowing
O'er the bed on which 'twas growing.

* * *

vi. O how cheating,
O how fleeting,
Is all earthly pleasure!
'Tis an air-suspended bubble,
Blown about in tears and trouble,
Broken soon by flying stubble.

vii. O how cheating,
O how fleeting,
Is all earthly honour!
He who wields a monarch's thunder,
Tearing right and law asunder,
Is to-morrow trodden under.

* * *

xiii. O how cheating,
O how fleeting,
All—yes! all that's earthly!
Every thing is fading, flying,
Man is mortal, earth is dying,
Christian! live on Heaven relying.
Michael Franck (1609-67)   Tr. *Sir John Bowring*[1].

The melody, "Ach wie flüchtig," was written by Michael Franck for his hymn. Words and melody were published together in 1652. In Cantata 26 (*c.* 1740), where the Choral is introduced twice, and in the *Orgelbüchlein* Bach's text of the *cantus* is uniform with Witt's (No. 665) and is based upon a reconstruction of the melody, perhaps by Johann Crüger, published in 1661[2]. The closing cadence is a combination of the original (1652) and Crüger's texts. It dates from 1679. The title of the hymn is correctly stated in the Cantata. Bach heads the *Orgelbüchlein* movement "Ach wie nichtig, ach wie flüchtig." Actually, "Ach wie flüchtig" is the first

---

[1] *Hymns* (London, 1825), No. 35. In Franck's setting each half of every stanza is sung twice. The original has thirteen stanzas.

[2] It is printed in *Bach's Chorals*, Part II. 193.

line of the first and succeeding odd stanzas, and "Ach wie nichtig" the first line of the even stanzas.

There is a single Organ movement on the melody:

[5]

N. xv. 121. The hymn occurs in the section on "The Life Eternal" in the *Orgelbüchlein*. In treating the melody Bach was moved by the word "Nebel" (mist) in the fourth line of the first stanza, and the image of man's life as

> a mist in wintry weather,
> Gathered in an hour together,
> And as soon dispersed in ether.

He therefore accompanies the melody with restless, gliding semiquavers that flicker across the movement like shadowy ghosts, or clouds driven across the sky, while the three-note phrases on the Pedals echo the words "wie nichtig." Towards the end of his life, about a quarter of a century after the *Orgelbüchlein* was sketched, Bach again used the melody, in Cantata 26. So constant and invariable is his musical language that, in the opening movement of the Cantata, a Choral Fantasia, Franck's hymn drew from him a similar treatment of the melody.

Alle Menschen müssen sterben.

Melody: "Alle Menschen müssen sterben" Anon. 1687

i. Hark! a voice saith, All are mortal,
   Yea, all flesh must fade as grass,
   Only through Death's gloomy portal
   To a better life ye pass,
   And this body, formed of clay,
   Here must languish and decay,
   Ere it rise in glorious might,
   Fit to dwell with saints in light.

ii. Therefore, since my God doth choose it,
    Willingly I yield my life,
    Nor I grieve that I should lose it,
    For with sorrows it was rife;
    And my Saviour suffered here
    That I might not faint nor fear,
    Since for me He bore my load
    And hath trod the same dark road.

iii. For my sake He went before me,
     And His death is now my gain;
     Peace and hope He conquered for me;
     So without regret or pain
     To His lovely home I go,
     From this land of toil and woe,
     Glad to reach that blest abode
     Where I shall behold my God.

   iv. There is joy beyond our telling
       Where so many saints are gone;
       Thousand thousands there are dwelling,
       Worshipping before the throne;
       There the Seraphim on high
       Brightly shine, and ever cry
       "Holy, Holy, Holy, Lord!
       Three in One for aye adored!"

           *   *   *

   vi. O Jerusalem, how clearly
       Dost thou shine, thou city fair!
       Lo! I hear the tones more nearly
       Ever sweetly sounding there!
       Oh what peace and joy hast thou!
       Lo the sun is rising now,
       And the breaking day I see
       That shall never end for me!

   vii. Yea, I see what here was told me,
       See that wondrous glory shine,
       Feel the spotless robes enfold me,
       Know a golden crown is mine;
       So before the throne I stand,
       One amid that glorious band,
       Gazing on that joy for aye
       That shall never pass away!

Johann Georg Albinus (1624–79) Tr. *Catherine Winkworth*[1].

Johann Georg Albinus' hymn, "Alle Menschen müssen sterben," written in 1652 for the funeral of Paul von Henssberg, a Leipzig merchant, was published in that year as a broadsheet, with a five-part setting by Johann Rosenmüller. The written movement (*alio modo*) in the *Orgelbüchlein* treats a tune

---

[1] *Chorale Book for England*, No. 196. The original hymn has eight stanzas. Stanzas v and viii are omitted in the translation.

ALLE MENSCHEN MÜSSEN STERBEN 95

(*supra*) first published, with the hymn, in *Das grosse Cantional: oder Kirchen-Gesangbuch* (Darmstadt, 1687). Its author is not identified. Bach's variation of its second line is found in 1692, of the sixth in 1710, and of the last line in 1711. Witt (No. 660) uses another melody for the hymn (*Choralgesänge*, No. 17), and Bach a third in Cantata 162 (1715)[1]. There is a single Organ movement on the melody.

[6]

N. xv. 119. The 1687 melody is treated in the "Death and the Grave" section of the *Orgelbüchlein*. The rhythm ♪ ♫♫ ♫ ♪ ♫♫ ♫ is used by Bach invariably to suggest blissful joy, here as in the Preludes "Herr Christ, der ein'ge Gottes-Sohn" (N. xv. 9), "O Gott, du frommer Gott" (N. xix. 52; Partita 9), "Gelobet seist du" (N. xv. 15), "Vater unser im Himmelreich" (N. xv. 105), "Jesu, meine Freude" (N. xv. 31), and "Lob sei dem allmächtigen Gott" (N. xv. 11). That Bach should introduce the rhythm into a hymn on Death is due to his disregard of the sinister message of the first stanza. He concentrates upon stanza iv's "joy beyond our telling" and the vision of "wondrous glory" unfolded in stanza vii. The movement is a song of triumph over death, not a dirge for the dead and dying, nor merely instinct with the "tender melancholy" Spitta finds in it.

[1] It is printed in *Bach's Chorals*, Part II. 434.

MELODIES

ALLEIN GOTT IN DER HÖH' SEI EHR'.

Plainsong: "*Gloria in excelsis Deo*" 1545

i. To God on high all glory be,
And thanks, that He's so gracious,
That hence to all eternity
No evil shall oppress us:
His word declares good-will to men,
On earth is peace restored again
Through Jesus Christ our Saviour.

ALLEIN GOTT IN DER HÖH' SEI EHR'

ii. We humbly Thee adore, and praise,
And laud for Thy great glory:
Father, Thy kingdom lasts always,
Not frail, nor transitory:
Thy power is endless as Thy praise,
Thou speak'st, the universe obeys:
In such a Lord we're happy.

iii. O Jesus Christ, enthroned on high,
The Father's Son beloved,
By Whom lost sinners are brought nigh,
And guilt and curse removed;
Thou Lamb once slain, our God and Lord,
To needy prayers Thine ear afford,
And on us all have mercy.

iv. O Comforter, God Holy Ghost,
Thou source of consolation,
From Satan's power Thou wilt, we trust,
Protect Christ's congregation,
His everlasting truth assert,
All evil graciously avert,
Lead us to life eternal.

Nikolaus Decius (d. 1541)   Tr. *Moravian Hymn-book*[1].

The melody, "Allein Gott in der Höh' sei Ehr'," was adapted by Nikolaus Decius for his translation of the "Gloria in excelsis," and was published with it in 1539[2]. The melody is a shortened version of the plainsong Easter "Gloria in excelsis" (the first eleven lines or phrases of which are printed *supra*), being made up of phrases 3-4, 7-8, 11. Bach uses the melody in the Organ movements *infra*; Cantatas

[1] Ed. 1877, No. 199. The original hymn has four stanzas.
[2] It is printed in *Bach's Chorals*, Part II. 305. Phrases 3-4 (*supra*) are repeated.

85, 104, 112, 128 (*c.* 1725-35); *Choralgesänge*, No. 12. His text is practically invariable, and closely conforms to Witt's (No. 188).

Among the Organ works there are ten movements upon the melody; three in the *Clavierübung*; three among the *Eighteen Chorals*; and four miscellaneous Preludes. There exists also a set of seventeen Variations (B.G. xl. 195), whose genuineness is doubtful. Almost invariably Bach uses the melody to express the adoration of the Angelic hosts, and in scale passages pictures the throng of them ascending and descending between earth and heaven.

[7] [8] [9]

N. xvi. 39, 40*, 41. The three movements are in the *Clavierübung*, and offer separate acts of homage to each Person of the Trinity. There is further symbolic significance in the fact that every movement is in the form of a Trio.

B.G. xl. 208 (P. vi. 96) prints from the Schelble-Gleichauf MSS. a movement that apparently is the original of No. 8, than which it is shorter and more concentrated. It is a Trio, the *cantus* being given to the Treble. In No. 9 the final ascending cadence represents the withdrawal of the heavenly host.

[10] [11] [12]

N. xvii. 56, 60, 66. The three movements are among the *Eighteen Chorals*. The first (No. 10)

ALLEIN GOTT IN DER HÖH' SEI EHR'

Schweitzer regards as a youthful work[1]. The last thirty-one bars of No. 12 (*Adagio*) seem to be inspired by the first stanza of the hymn:

> On earth is peace restored again
> Through Jesus Christ our Saviour.

The ascending cadence again represents the departing host of angels.

An older text of No. 11 is in B.G. xxv. (2) 180 (P. vi. 100). Two copies of it are among the Krebs MSS. Of No. 12 an older version exists (B.G. xxv. (2) 183; P. vi. 97) in Bach's Autograph.

[13]

N. xviii. 4. The composition reveals Bach's method of accompanying hymns and probably was written for the instruction or use of a pupil. Indeed, the MS. is in Kellner's Collection. It is inscribed "di Johann Seb. Bach."

[14]

N. xviii. 5. The movement, of which copies are in the Schicht and Schelble MSS., differs from the others on the melody in that it omits to picture the thronging angels. Spitta[2] doubts whether the movement is by Bach, and observes that his nephew Bernhard Bach wrote somewhat in this style. Parry[3] finds "a quaint waywardness in the accompaniment which is fascinating." He makes the suggestion

---

[1] Vol. I. 292.   [2] Vol. I. 656.   [3] *Op. cit.* 504.

that, as in the case of No. 5 of the *Schübler Chorals*, the movement originally was designed for a voice with Violoncello piccolo accompaniment[1].

[15]

N. xviii. 7 (Fuga). The movement comes to us through three MSS. in the Royal Library, Berlin, one of them by Oley. It is in the Pachelbel form, a Fugue in three parts upon the first two lines of the melody, which is introduced at the close as a *cantus firmus* on the pedal. A similar scheme occurs in the setting of the *Magnificat* (N. xviii. 75).

In No. 15 the ascending cadence paints the Angelic host's withdrawal to heaven.

[16]

N. xviii. 11. The attribution of the movement to Bach rests upon a Krebs MS. in the Berlin Library marked "J. S. B.": a "ganz correcte Handschrift," Naumann calls it. The movement is in three parts, as, significantly, are six of the ten movements on the melody.

[1] See p. 85 *supra*.

An Wasserflüssen Babylon.

Melody: "An Wasserflüssen Babylon"
Wolfgang Dachstein 1525

i. At the ryvers of Babilon,
   There sat we downe ryght hevely;
   Even whan we thought upon Sion,
   We wepte together sorofully.
   For we were in soch hevynes,
   That we forgat al our merynes,
   And lefte of all oure sporte and playe:
   On the willye trees that were thereby
   We hanged up oure harpes truly,
   And morned sore both nyght and daye.

ii. They that toke us so cruelly,
    And led us bounde into pryson,
    Requyred of us some melody,
    With wordes full of derision.
    When we had hanged oure harpes alwaye,
    This cruell folke to us coulde saye:
    Now let us heare some mery songe,
    Synge us a songe of some swete toyne,
    As ye were wont to synge at Sion,
    Where ye have lerned to synge so longe.

iii. To whome we answered soberly:
Beholde now are we in youre honde:
How shulde we under captivite
Synge to the Lorde in a straunge londe?
Hierusalem, I say to the,
Yf I remember the not truly,
My honde playe on the harpe no more:
Yf I thynke not on the alwaye,
Let my tonge cleve to my mouth for aye,
And let me loose my speache therfore.

iv. Yee, above all myrth and pastaunce,
Hierusalem, I preferre the.
Lorde, call to thy remembraunce
The sonnes of Edom ryght strately,
In the daye of the destruction,
Which at Hierusalem was done;
For they sayd in theyr cruelnes,
Downe with it, downe with it, destroye it all;
Downe with it soone, that it may fall,
Laye it to the grounde all that there is.

v. O thou cite of Babilon,
Thou thy selfe shalt be destroyed.
Truly blessed shall be that man
Which, even as thou hast deserved,
Shall rewarde the with soch kyndnesse
As thou hast shewed to us gyltlesse,
Which never had offended the.
Blessed shall he be that for the nones[1]
Shall throwe thy chyldren agaynst the stones,
To brynge the out of memorie.

Wolfgang Dachstein (d. c. 1561) Tr. *Bishop Myles Coverdale*[2].

[1] For the nonce, for the purpose.
[2] *Remains* (Parker Society, 1846), p. 571. The original hymn has five stanzas.

The hymn and melody appeared together in the third part of the *Teutsch Kirchēamt mit lobgsengen* (Strasbourg, 1525). The words are by Wolfgang Dachstein, to whom the melody also is assigned. He was Organist of Strasbourg Cathedral, and later, having become a Protestant, of St Thomas' Church there. He died *circa* 1561.

There are two movements upon the melody in the Organ works—in the *Eighteen Chorals* and among the miscellaneous movements (Fünfstimmig). Griepenkerl states that Krebs' copies of the two are marked respectively "Vers 2" and "Vers 1." They display a close relation in tonality, atmosphere, and construction. Both are in G major. Both are inspired by the word "Wasserflüssen" (waves). In quavers, against the crotchets of the *cantus*, the accompaniment ripples on pellucidly in a figure which, in No. 18 especially, is reminiscent of Schubert's familiar "Barcarolle." Though No. 17 is six bars longer than No. 18, the two movements are otherwise similar. Practically they are built upon the same Bass, and their contrapuntal accompaniment to the *cantus* is constructed out of the opening two lines of the melody. In No. 17 the close is prolonged upon a final (tenth) statement of the opening phrase of the *cantus*. The melody also occurs in *Choralgesänge*, No. 23. In the penultimate bar (*supra*) E flat for E natural as the sixth note was general after 1653. Witt (No. 601) has it and also Bach's B natural as the penultimate note of bar 4 *supra*. Of Bach's B natural as the third note of bars 2 and 4 Zahn (No. 7663) affords no earlier example.

[17]

N. xvii. 18. The movement is No. 3 of the *Eighteen Chorals*. Schweitzer[1] finds in it the evident influence of Georg Böhm, Organist of St John's Church, Lüneburg, from 1698 to his death in 1734 (?). Spitta[2], on the other hand, detects in it the example of Dietrich Buxtehude (1637–1707), Organist of St Mary's Church, Lübeck, but concurs with Schweitzer in regarding the movement as an early essay of Bach's. He dates its composition *circa* 1712, during the Weimar period.

No. 17 is not the oldest form of the movement. B.G. xxv. (2) 157 (P. vi. 103) prints an older version of it which may be distinguished as No. 17*a*. In the year 1720, as will be shown, Bach revised No. 17*a* and produced No. 18. No. 17 seems to have been the final text, prepared for the collection upon which Bach was at work at the time of his death. With what art he creates (cf. No. 18 where the impression is less evident) an atmosphere of languor congruous to stanza i of the hymn!

[18]

N. xviii. 13 was the result of a revision of No. 17*a*,

[1] Vol. I. 292.   [2] Vol. I. 616.

whose occasion Spitta suggests with plausibility. In the autumn of 1720 Bach visited Hamburg, where the post of Organist in the Church of St James was vacant. Johann Reinken, the veteran Organist of St Catherine's Church there, came to hear Bach play, and complimented him upon an improvisation, in the broad Böhm-Buxtehude manner, upon the melody "An Wasserflüssen Babylon," a theme which Reinken himself had treated in a Prelude[1]. Spitta suggests[2] that Bach revised the Hamburg improvisation (No. 17a) and sent Reinken No. 18. Having regard to Reinken's age and traditions it was natural that Bach should offer him a composition in the manner of Böhm (Reinken's pupil) and Buxtehude rather than in the new forms Bach was originating. While preserving the framework of No. 17a, Bach added a second Pedal part, an addition which entailed removing the *cantus* from the Tenor, where it lies in Nos. 17a and 17, to the Treble[3].

The single MS. of No. 18 is in the Royal Library, Berlin, inscribed " J. S. B." by Krebs.

[1] For Bach's visit to Hamburg, see Forkel (trans. Terry), p. 20.
[2] Vol. I. 617.
[3] Spitta points out (I. 608) that the characteristics of the Buxtehude form were melodic ornamentation, richness of harmony and tone, the constant employment of two manuals, one having the *cantus*, and the frequent use of the double Pedal (*pedale doppio*).

Aus tiefer Noth schrei ich zu dir.

Melody: "*Aus tiefer Noth schrei ich zu dir*"
?Martin Luther 1524

i. Out of the depths I cry to Thee,
   Lord, hear me, I implore Thee!
   Bend down Thy gracious ear to me,
   Let my prayer come before Thee!
   If Thou rememberest each misdeed,
   If each should have its rightful meed,
   Who may abide Thy presence?

ii. Our pardon is Thy gift. Thy love
    And grace alone avail us;
    Our works could ne'er our guilt remove,
    The strictest life must fail us,
    That none may boast himself of aught,
    But own in fear Thy grace hath wrought
    What in him seemeth righteous.

iii. And thus my hope is in the Lord,
     And not in mine own merit;
     I rest upon His faithful word
     To them of contrite spirit;
     That He is merciful and just—
     Here is my comfort and my trust,
     His help I wait with patience.

AUS TIEFER NOTH SCHREI ICH ZU DIR

iv. And though it tarry till the night,
And round till morning waken,
My heart shall ne'er mistrust His might,
Nor count itself forsaken.
Do thus, O ye of Israel's seed,
Ye of the Spirit born indeed,
Wait for our God's appearing.

v. Though great our sins and sore our woes,
His grace much more aboundeth;
His helping love no limit knows,
Our utmost need it soundeth;
Our kind and faithful Shepherd, He
Who shall at last set Israel free
From all their sin and sorrow.

Martin Luther (1483–1546)   Tr. *Catherine Winkworth*[1].

Written in 1523, Luther's free translation of Psalm 130 was first published in 1524, along with the melody. The tune is known as "Luther's 130th" and with some probability may be regarded as his composition. Bach makes little use of it. It occurs only in the movements *infra* and Cantata 38 (*c.* 1740). It is among the unwritten movements of the *Orgelbüchlein*. Bach's melodic text is invariable. Witt (No. 261) uses another (1525) melody for the hymn.

There are two movements upon the melody in the *Clavierübung*. They are the only ones in that collection, as Sir Hubert Parry points out[2], which completely reproduce the Pachelbel type.

---

[1] *Chorale Book for England*, No. 40. The original hymn has five stanzas.
[2] *Op. cit.* p. 472.

[19]

N. xvi. 68. The movement is in six parts and is the glory of the *Clavierübung*. Not even the giants among Bach's predecessors introduce a double pedal throughout[1]. A piece of pure music of unsurpassable grandeur, the Prelude seems to derive its inspiration from the mood expressed in stanza iii of the hymn:

> And thus my hope is in the Lord,
> I rest upon His faithful word,
> Here is my comfort and my trust.

At the thirteenth bar from the end Bach introduces a rhythm of joy that rolls on with increasing fervour to its climax of fruition and content. The addition of Trombones to the Pedal *cantus* enhances its impressiveness.

[20]

N. xvi. 72. The movement becomes, like No. 19, a song of triumph at the close.

---

[1] See Spitta, III. 217.

CHRIST, DER DU BIST DER HELLE TAG.

Melody: "Christ, der du bist der helle Tag"   Anon. 1568

i. Lord Christ, Thou art the heavenly Light
Who dost disperse the shades of night.
All radiant, Thou, the Father's Son,
Dost spread the brightness of His throne.

ii. O dearest Lord, e'er guard our sleep,
From foes' assault our slumbers keep,
And let us find in Thee our rest,
Nor be by Satan's wiles opprest.

iii. E'en though our weary eye-lids fall,
O keep our hearts true to Thy call.
Above us stretch Thy sheltering hand,
Lest Sin or Shame our dreams should brand.

iv. We pray Thee, Jesus, Christ and Lord,
'Gainst Satan's cunning help afford;
May he whose fell hosts camp around
Ne'er drag us with him to the ground.

v. Sure, 'tis Thy heart's most precious Blood
Has won our souls Thy brotherhood;
And so indeed the Father meant
Ere to our world Thyself He sent.

 vi. O set Thine angels round our bed,
   And may our thoughts to Thee be led;
   That guarded so, north, east, south, west,
   From Satan's lures we find sure rest.
 vii. Safe in Thy care so shall we sleep,
   While wakeful angels watch do keep.
   O God Eternal, Three in One,
   For ever may Thy praises run.

Erasmus Alberus (*c.* 1500-53)   Tr. *C. S. T.*[1]

The evening hymn "Christ, der du bist der helle Tag," or, as was its original title, "Christe, du bist der helle Tag," is a translation of the Ambrosian Lenten hymn "Christe, qui lux es et dies," written by Erasmus Alberus, the son of a pastor, born at Sprendlingen *circa* 1500. After studying at Wittenberg under Luther and Melanchthon, Alberus worked as a schoolmaster until, in 1528, he was appointed pastor at Sprendlingen and Götzenhain. Later he settled at Magdeburg, and was present during the long siege of the city in 1550-51. In 1552 he was appointed preacher at St Mary's Church, Neu Brandenburg, and died in 1553. His hymns were written specially for children and have been ranked after Luther's in the literature of the Reformation.

"Christe, du bist der helle Tag" was published in *Die Morgengeseng für die Kinder* (Nürnberg *c.* 1556). In 1565 the hymn was published in the

---

[1] The original hymn has seven stanzas.

CHRIST, DER DU BIST DER HELLE TAG 111

Hamburg *Enchiridion Geistliker Leder und Psalmen* along with another melody than that which Bach uses. The latter was published, with the hymn, in Cyriacus Spangenberg's *Christlichs Gesangbüchlein, Von den Fürnembsten Festen, durchs gantze Jhar* (Eisleben, 1568). There is no indication of the composer's identity. The tune has a pre-Reformation tone, and not improbably is a form of the old melody of "Christe, qui lux es et dies." Bach uses it in the Variations *infra* and *Choralgesänge*, No. 33. In the former his text exactly follows Witt (No. 431). The other setting shows Bach to have followed another text than Witt's. It will be observed that the second line of the *cantus* in the Variations differs from the original (1568) version. Bach's variant is found as early as 1597. In the *Choralgesänge* he adopts a statement of the first line of the melody which dates from at least 1581.

[21]

N. xix. 36. These "Choralvariationen," it is generally agreed, are a youthful work written while Bach was under the influence of Böhm. Spitta assigns their composition to *circa* 1701-2, when Bach was in his sixteenth or seventeenth year, resident at Lüneburg, and therefore in contact with Böhm, who was organist there[1]. Schweitzer[2] points out that the number of Variations corresponds to

[1] Vol. I. 213.   [2] Vol. I. 282.

the number of stanzas in the hymn. But the inference that each Variation pictures the corresponding stanza does not survive examination. It is difficult to imagine Bach tempted to distinguish in seven pictures moods so placid and invariable as the hymn maintains. He is not even moved, as in maturer years he might have been, by references to Satan and the angels; though the convolutions of the accompanying figure in Variations II, IV, VI may have been prompted by the image of the Serpent. On the other hand, it need not follow that the numerical correspondence between the hymn stanzas and the Variations is fortuitous. The opening broad and simple treatment of the melody looks like a statement of the *cantus* as a preliminary to singing the first stanza. The remaining movements may have been designed as improvisations between the stanzas. They are not in the ordinary sense Variations at all, but movements in Fantasia form written for the two-manualed "Pedalflügel." The Pedal is introduced only in the last (seventh) Variation and is marked "con Pedale se piace" (i.e. *ad libitum*).

The text of the Variations in Peters' edition was printed from a MS. once the possession of Forkel. Copies also exist in the Hauser Collection. Naumann records (1893) that the Autograph was "formerly" in the possession of Capellmeister Guhr.

CHRIST IST ERSTANDEN.

Melody: "Christ ist erstanden"   Anon. 1535

i. Christe is now rysen agayne
   From His death and all His payne:
   Therfore wyll we mery be,
   And rejoyse with Him gladly.
         Kirieleyson.

ii. Had He not rysen agayne,
    We had ben lost, this is playne:
    But sen He is rysen in dede,
    Let us love Hym all with spede.
         Kirieleyson.

iii. Now is tyme of gladnesse,
     To synge of the Lorde's goodnesse:
     Therfore glad now wyll we be,
     And rejoyse in Hym onely.
         Kirieleyson.

Traditional   Tr. *Bishop Myles Coverdale*[2].

[1] The melody of stanza ii is identical with that of stanza i.
[2] *Remains*, p. 563. The original hymn has three stanzas.

The ancient Easter Carol, "Christ ist erstanden," dates back at least to the thirteenth century. The melody is found in print in 1513. With the words it occurs in a text of 1535 [1529]. Bach uses it in Cantata 66 (1731); *Choralgesänge*, No. 36; and the movements *infra*. Zahn does not reveal the source of his variations: nor does Bach follow Witt (No. 141). Probably they are his own.

[22]

N. xv. 83. The movement is among the Easter tunes of the *Orgelbüchlein* and is the only one there in which Bach sets all the verses of the hymn. His melodic text closely fits the words of each stanza:

> Christ ist erstanden
> Von der Marter alle;
> Des soll'n wir alle froh sein;
> Christ soll unser Trost sein.
>   Kyrieleis.
> Wär er nicht erstanden,
> Die Welt die wär vergangen;
> Seit dass er erstanden ist,
> So loben wir den Vater Jesu Christ.
>   Kyrieleis.
> Hallelujah!
> Hallelujah! Hallelujah!
> Des soll'n wir alle froh sein.
> Christ soll unser Trost sein.
>   Kyrieleis.

Through all three verses, Spitta comments[1], there flows "a fresh vitality as of the rising sun."

[1] Vol. I. 600.

CHRIST IST ERSTANDEN 115

A four-part setting of the melody is in B.G. xl.
173. Copies of it are in the Forkel and Hauser
MSS. In one copy it is inscribed "Versio IV."

CHRIST LAG IN TODESBANDEN.

Melody: "Christ lag in Todesbanden"   Anon. 1524

i. Christ lay in Death's dark prison,
  It was our sin that bound Him;
  This day hath He arisen,
  And sheds new life around Him.
  Therefore let us joyful be
  And praise our God right heartily.
  So sing we Hallelujah!
    Hallelujah!

ii. O'er Death no man could prevail,
  If mortal e'er came near him;
  Through guilt all our strength would fail,
  Our sinful hearts did fear him.

8—2

  Therefore Death did gain the day,
  And lead in triumph us away,
  Henceforth to dwell emprisoned.
   Hallelujah!
iii. Now Jesus Christ, the Son of God,
  For our defence hath risen,
  Our grievous guilt He hath removed,
  And Death hath bound in prison.
  All his might Death must forego,
  For now he's nought but idle show,
  His sting is lost for ever.
   Hallelujah!
iv. How fierce and dreadful was the strife
  When Life with Death contended;
  For Death was swallowed up by Life
  And all his power was ended.
  God of old, the Scriptures show,
  Did promise that it should be so.
  O Death, where's now thy victory?
   Hallelujah!
v. The Paschal Victim here we see,
  Whereof God's Word hath spoken;
  He hangs upon the cruel tree,
  Of saving love the token.
  His blood ransoms us from sin,
  And Death no more can enter in,
  Now Satan cannot harm us.
   Hallelujah!
vi. So keep we all this holy feast,
  Where every joy invites us;
  Our Sun is rising in the East,
  It is our Lord Who lights us.
  Through the glory of His grace
  Our darkness will to-day give place.
  The night of sin is over.
   Hallelujah!

vii. With grateful hearts we all are met
To eat the bread of gladness.
The ancient leaven now forget,
And every thought of sadness.
Christ Himself the feast hath spread,
By Him the hungry soul is fed,
And He alone can feed us.
Hallelujah!

Martin Luther (1483-1546)   Tr. *Paul England*[1].

Luther's Easter hymn, "Christ lag in Todesbanden," was first published in 1524, and is described as the Easter Carol "Christ ist erstanden" "improved." The melody, to a greater extent than the words, is drawn from the ancient hymn. It was published with Luther's hymn in 1524 in two forms[2], and is a reconstruction of the original melody of which, no doubt, Johann Walther was the author. In the Organ works, Cantatas 4 and 158 (1708-24), and *Choralgesänge*, Nos. 38, 39, Bach uses the form printed *supra*. The B natural which he almost invariably substitutes for A as the first note of the fifth phrase of the tune is in Witt (No. 140), as also is C sharp for C natural as the third note of the fourth phrase. For G sharp as the second note of the first phrase Zahn reveals no earlier authority.

The melody occurs in three movements among the Organ works:

[1] Cantata 4, Novello's edition. The original hymn has seven stanzas.
[2] See the second in *Bach's Chorals*, Part II. 138.

118   MELODIES

[23]

N. xv. 79. The short movement is instinct with the triumph of Easter. The Pedal, its jubilant rhythm notwithstanding, interprets the sinister word "Todesbanden" (Death's dark prison). The semiquaver Pedal phrases may symbolize the rolling away of the sepulchral stone.

[24]

N. xviii. 16. (Fantasia). The movement is a Trio, formal and probably written for the "Pedalflügel." Early copies (six) of it exist in the Kirnberger and other collections. In three of them the movement concludes with the following simple setting. It is omitted in the Novello Edition.

A variant text of the movement (without the concluding Choral) is in B.G. xl. 153 (P. vi. 104). A single MS. of it exists (Schelble-Gleichauf). It differs from No. 24 in that the *cantus* is on the Pedal instead of in the Alto.

[25]

N. xviii. 19. There are three MSS. of the movement, none of them authoritative; one, however, bears the inscription "di Gio. Bast. Bach." The conversation between the Great and Choir manuals in the Novello Edition is distinguished in the Bach Society's Edition by a series of "forte" and "piano" passages[1]. The fact, along with the final crotchet E, shows that Bach wrote the movement for the two-

---

[1] They are identically reproduced in the Peters edition.

120   MELODIES

manualed "Pedalflügel[1]." Hence Spitta infers that it was composed at Lüneburg, where Bach had no Organ at his absolute disposal. In general character it resembles the first movement of Cantata 38 (*c.* 1740) on the first stanza of the hymn.

Besides the above movements, B.G. xl. 174 prints another (P. ix. 56), in which the *cantus* is on the Pedal. The MS. of it exists among forty-six "Choralvorspiele," doubtfully attributed to Bach, in the Royal Library, Berlin. A copy of it is also among the Schelble-Gleichauf MSS.

CHRIST UNSER HERR ZUM JORDAN KAM.

Melody: "*Christ unser Herr zum Jordan kam*"
? Johann Walther 1524

[1] See Spitta, I. 214. On the Organ there would be no need to strike the E. On the Flügel, on the other hand, the E sustained in the preceding chord already would have ceased to be heard.

CHRIST UNSER HERR ZUM JORDAN KAM

i. To Jordan when our Lord had gone,
His Father's pleasure willing,
He took His baptism of St.John,
His work and task fulfilling ;
Therein He would appoint a bath
To wash us from defilement,
And also drown that cruel Death
In His blood of assoilment :
'Twas no less than a new life.

ii. Let all then hear and right receive
The baptism of the Father,
And what a Christian shall believe
To shun where heretics gather.
Water indeed, not water mere
In it can do His pleasure,
His holy Word is also there
With Spirit rich, unmeasured :
He is the one baptizer.

iii. This clearly He to us by word
Hath shown, nor less by vision ;
The Father's voice men plainly heard
At Jordan tell His mission.
He said, This is My own dear Son,
In Whom I am well contented :
To you I send Him, every one—
That you may hear, I have sent Him,
And follow what He teaches.

iv. Also God's Son Himself here stands
In His humanity tender ;
The Holy Ghost on Him descends,
In dove's appearance hidden,
That not a doubt should ever rise
That, when we are baptizéd,
All the three Persons do baptize ;
And so, here recognizéd,
Themselves give to dwell with us.

v. Christ to His scholars says : Go forth,
Give to all men acquaintance
That lost in sin lies the whole earth,
And must turn to repentance.
Who trusts, and is baptized, each one
Is thereby blest for ever,
Is from that hour a new-born man,
And, thenceforth dying never,
The kingdom shall inherit.

vi. But in this grace who puts no faith
Abides in his trespasses,
And is condemned to endless death,
Deep down in hell's abysses.
Nothing avails his righteousness,
And lost are all his merits ;
The old sin than nothing makes them less—
The sin which he inherits ;
And help himself he cannot.

vii. The eye but water doth behold,
As from man's hand it floweth ;
But inward faith the power untold
Of Jesus Christ's blood knoweth.
Faith sees therein a red flood roll,
With Christ's blood dyed and blended,
Which hurts of all kinds maketh whole,
From Adam here descended,
And by ourselves brought on us.

Martin Luther (1483-1546)   Tr. *George Macdonald*[1].

Martin Luther's Baptismal hymn, "Christ unser Herr zum Jordan kam," was written, probably, in 1541. Johann Walther's (?) melody, set to another of Luther's hymns, had been published seventeen

[1] *Exotics* (London, 1876), p. 98. The original hymn has seven stanzas.

years earlier (1524). In 1543 it was attached to "Christ unser Herr" and since has remained its distinctive melody. It occurs in the Organ movements *infra*; Cantatas 7, 176 (*c.* 1735); *Choralgesänge*, No. 43. Bach's text is invariable. Zahn does not reveal early authority for his variations of the orginal text (G for A as the first note of the second phrase *supra*; B for A as the first note of the fifth phrase). Both details are found in Witt (No. 243).

[26]

N. xvi. 62. As in the Choral Fantasia on the first stanza that opens Cantata 7, Bach lets the word "Jordan" guide his treatment of the melody. Here, as there, the quick flowing stream is the background of his picture. While the Cantata movement is a setting of the first stanza of the hymn, the conclusion may be hazarded that in No. 26 Bach had the seventh stanza in his mind. Had the first been before him it is difficult to believe that he would have omitted to emphasize lines 7 and 8 in his customary chromatic idiom:

> And also drown that cruel Death
> In His blood of assoilment.

Bach seeks rather to emphasize the contrast suggested in the first four lines of the seventh stanza:

> The eye but water doth behold,
> As from man's hand it floweth;
> But inward faith the power untold
> Of Jesus Christ's blood knoweth.

Thus interpreted, the strong, reliant melody over which Jordan ripples acquires a new significance.

[27]

N. xvi. 67. The word "Jordan" also inspires this movement, which is constructed upon the first phrase of the melody, presented in four forms in the first eight bars: (1) the first phrase of the melody in the Treble line of bars 1-4; (2) its inversion in the Bass of bars 4-8; (3) an accelerated form of it in the Bass of bars 2-4; (4) the inversion of the accelerated form in the Treble of bars 6-8. The four motives, Schweitzer points out[1], "are worked into an extremely realistic picture of great and small waves rising and falling and overwhelming each other." It is a picture, he adds, for the eye rather than the ear.

Christe, du Lamm Gottes.

Melody: "*Christe, du Lamm Gottes*"   Anon. 1557

gieb uns dei-nen Frie-den. A . . . . men .

[1] Vol. II. 59.

i. Christ, Thou Lamb of God,
   Thou that bear'st the sins of men,
   Have mercy on us!

ii. Christ, Thou Lamb of God,
    Thou that bear'st the sins of men,
    Have mercy on us!

iii. Christ, Thou Lamb of God,
     Thou that bear'st the sins of men,
     Grant to us Thy peace!

"Agnus Dei"   Tr. *C. S. T.*

The melody, "Christe, du Lamm Gottes," is among those which the reformed Church took over from its predecessor. The hymn is a translation of the "Agnus Dei." With the melody it appears in a text of 1557. Bach uses it in the *Orgelbüchlein*; Cantatas 23, 127 (1724–*c.* 1740); and in the "Kyrie" of the Mass in F. His text follows Witt (No. 103).

[28]

N. xv. 61. The "Agnus Dei" is a petition to Christ for forgiveness and pity. Bach also sees the Cross, thrice pictured in the three clauses of the hymn, and weaves round it poignant harmonies indicative of Christ's suffering.

[1] The original has three clauses.

CHRISTUM WIR SOLLEN LOBEN SCHON.

Melody: "A solis ortus cardine"   Anon. 1537

i. Christ, Whom the Virgin Mary bore,
We now with humble hearts adore;
O might all nations, tribes, and tongues,
To our Immanuel raise their songs.

ii. God, Who to all things being gave,
The fallen human race to save,
Assumed our feeble flesh and blood,
And for our debt as surety stood.

*   *   *

vi. He Who the wants of all supplies
Now in a manger helpless lies;
He Who the whole creation feeds
An earthly mother's nursing needs.

vii. The angels at His birth rejoice,
And sing His praise with cheerful voice;
The shepherds, hearing Christ is born,
To Jesus, our chief Shepherd, turn.

CHRISTUM WIR SOLLEN LOBEN SCHON 127

viii. Thanks to the Father now be given,
 Who sent His Son to us from heaven;
 Thanks to the Son Who saves the lost;
 Thanks to our Guide, the Holy Ghost.
Martin Luther (1483-1546) Tr. *C. Kinchen*[1].

WAS FÜRCHT'ST DU, FEIND HERODES, SEHR.

i. Herod, why dreadest thou a foe,
 Because the Christ comes born below?
 He seeks no mortal kingdom thus,
 Who brings His kingdom down to us.

ii. After the star the wise men go.
 That light the true Light them did show;
 They signify, with presents three,
 This child, God, Man, and King to be.

iii. In Jordan baptism He did take,
 This Lamb of God, for our poor sake;
 Thus He Who never did a sin
 Hath washed us clean both out and in.

iv. A miracle straightway befell:
 Six pots of stone they saw, who tell,
 Of water full, which changed its sort,
 And turned to red wine at His word.

v. Praise, honour, thanks to Thee be said,
 Jesus, born of the holy maid;
 With the Father and the Holy Ghost,
 Now, and henceforward, ending not.
Martin Luther (1483-1546) Tr. *George Macdonald*[2].

[1] *Moravian Hymn-book*, ed. 1877, No. 46. The original hymn has eight stanzas, of which iii-v are omitted in the translation.

[2] *Exotics*, p. 50. The original hymn has five stanzas.

Both words and melody of Luther's "Christum wir sollen loben schon" are adapted from Coelius Sedulius' Christmas hymn, "A solis ortus cardine," whose melody is printed *supra* from a text of 1537. The adaptation of the tune to Luther's stanzas was probably undertaken by Johann Walther, in whose Hymn-book, printed at Wittenberg in 1524, it first appeared[1]. Bach uses the tune, in its original form, in Cantata 121 (*c.* 1740) and in two Organ Preludes. Witt (No. 34) prints the tune in another form.

[29]

N. xv. 33. The movement is in the Christmas section of the *Orgelbüchlein*. Schweitzer[2] points out that Bach's habit was not to employ an actual motive to express ecstatic and spiritual joy, but to give it utterance in an "exuberant musical arabesque," *e.g.* the Violin *obbligato* in the "Laudamus te" of the B minor Mass. It is not rash to select stanza i of Luther's hymn as the one Bach illustrates in this movement:

> O might all nations, tribes, and tongues,
> To our Immanuel raise their songs.

The arabesque enfolding the *cantus* (in the Alto) "embraces a whole world of unutterable joy."

---

[1] It is printed in *Bach's Chorals*, Part II. 368.
[2] Vol. ii. 66.

CHRISTUM WIR SOLLEN LOBEN SCHON

[30]

N. xviii. 23. The movement is among the miscellaneous Preludes, and receives the alternative title of Luther's hymn, " Was fürcht'st du, Feind Herodes, sehr." The definition has no musical significance; the movement being merely a short "Choralvorspiel" in Fughetta form upon the first line of the melody. The hymn is a translation of the second part (*Hostis Herodes impie*) of Sedulius' text and was in use at Epiphany (Witt, No. 73).

The movement is in the Kirnberger MS. and there are eight other texts of it in the Voss, Forkel, and Kittel Collections. In two of them the Prelude is specifically attributed to Bach.

CHRISTUS, DER UNS SELIG MACHT.

Melody: "Patris Sapientia"   1531

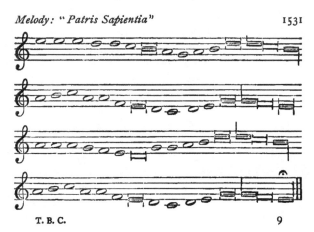

i. Christ, by Whose all-saving Light
   Mankind benefited,
   Was for Sinners in the Night
   As a Thief committed.
   Dragged before a wicked Court
   Of the Jewish Clergy;
   Where they tried their worst Effort
   'Gainst the Lord of Mercy.

ii. Sentenced early by this Crew,
   As the worst of Sinners,
   Came to Pilate, who foreknew
   This Tumult's Beginners:
   Though he judged Him innocent
   Of their Accusation,
   Yet to Herod He was sent
   For his Arbitration.

iii. Then His holy Flesh was torn
   With inhuman Lashes,
   And His blessed Head in Scorn
   Crowned of sinful Ashes:
   Cloathed in a Purple Dress,
   Mocked, and beat, and bruised;
   Thus the Source of Holiness
   Was by Sin misused.

iv. Then at Noon the Son of God
   To the Cross was nailed,
   Where His fervent Prayer and Blood
   For our Sins prevailed:
   The Spectators shook their Head,
   Had Him in derision,
   Till the Sun-light mourning fled
   From so sad a Vision.

v. When at Three they heard Him call:
   Why am I forsaken?
   Strait was Vinegar mixed with Gall
   Offered, but not taken:

CHRISTUS, DER UNS SELIG MACHT.

  Then to God His Spirit went,
  Shaking the Earth with Wonder,
  Gave the Vail a thorough Rent,
  Cleft the Rocks asunder.

vi. At the approaching Evening Tide,
  Criminals Bones were broken;
  But the Spear pierced Jesus' Side,
  For a lasting Token:
  Which poured forth a double Flood
  Of a cleansing Nature.
  Both the Water and the Blood
  Wash the guilty Creature.

vii. Joseph, when the Eve was come,
  Took his dearest Master,
  Laid Him in his Stately Tomb,
  Hewn in Alabaster;
  Nicodem, now void of Fear,
  Brought the richest Spices:
  Thus these holy Men paid here
  Their last Sacrifices.

viii. Grant, O Jesu, blessed Lord,
  By Thy Cross and Passion,
  Thy blest Love may be adored
  By the whole Creation:
  Hating Sin, the woful Cause
  Of Thy Death and Suffering,
  Give our Heart to obey Thy Laws
  As the best Thanks-offering.

Michael Weisse (1480?-1534)   Tr. *John Christian Jacobi*[1].

---

[1] *Psalmodia Germanica* (London, 1765), p. 24. The original hymn has eight stanzas.

Both words and melody of the hymn, "Christus der uns selig macht," are adapted from the Latin "Patris Sapientia, veritas divina." The words are by Michael Weisse and were first published, with the tune, in 1531. The melody occurs also in the *St John Passion* (1723), Nos. 12, 35; *Choralgesänge*, No. 48; and the *Orgelbüchlein*.

Bach is not consistent in his statement of the melody. In the *Choralgesänge* and *Orgelbüchlein* he adopts the early 1531 text. In the *St John Passion* he uses a Leipzig reconstruction of the tune which dates from 1598[1]. Witt (No. 95) uses the older form.

[31]

N. xv. 64. The movement is one of the Passiontide Preludes in the *Orgelbüchlein*. Its fierce intensity is inspired by the first stanza of the hymn, and particularly by the words

> Where they tried their worst effort.
> 'Gainst the Lord of Mercy.

An older text of the movement—that of the Mendelssohn Autograph[2]—is in B.G. xxv. (2) 149 (P. v. 108).

---
[1] It is printed in *Bach's Chorals*, Part II. 491.
[2] See Spitta, I. 649.

DA JESUS AN DEM KREUZE STUND.

Melody: "*Da Jesus an dem Kreuze stund*" Anon. 1545

i. When Jesus on the Cross was found,
His Body pierced with many a Wound,
With Torture very bitter ;
The dying Words, which He then spake,
With a still Heart consider.

ii. First He does to His Father speak
In Heaven's Kingdom, sweetly meek ;
"What they to Me are doing,
Father! forgive, they know it not":
Here He's Love's Pattern shewing.

iii. Weigh next the Mercy and Relief
Which God bestows upon the Thief;
He the poor Heart addresses,
"Verily thou shalt in Paradise
To-day feel My Caresses."

iv. Thirdly observe the tender Care
Which He still for His House did bear;
"Woman, lo! there is thy Son :
John! see thy Mother there"; and this
Was the first Cross's Union.

v. The fourth Word on the Cross accurst
By our Prince spoken was, " I thirst."
With such keen Thirst He's pained
After our Righteousness : but now,
Dear Heart, His Cordial's gained.

vi. Weigh too the Scorn He underwent
As He to God the fifth Word sent,
A Scorn which knew no Measure ;
" My God, my God! why leavest Thou Me?
Am I no more Thy Pleasure?"

vii. The sixth's a very powerful Word,
Which many a Sinner poor has heard,
Out of His Mouth proceeding ;
" It's finished": what? our Happiness :
Through what? His Wounds so bleeding.

viii. " Father!" when all was at an End,
Immanuel says, " I recommend
My Spirit separated
Into Thy Hands." His Body dies,
His Soul's in Life instated.

ix. He who God's Pains in Honour has,
To whom our Saviour gives the Grace
To be in Heart possessing
And weigh these seven Gospel Words,
Enjoys a noble Blessing.

Johann Böschenstein (1472–1539?)

Tr. *Moravian Hymn-book*[1].

The Passiontide hymn, " Da Jesus an dem Kreuze stund," was written by Johann Böschenstein, and is found in an undated broadsheet *circa* 1515. Whether

---

[1] Ed. 1746, Part II. p. 714. The original hymn has nine stanzas.

it is a translation of Peter Bolandus' "Stabat ad lignum crucis" cannot be stated positively.

Böschenstein was born at Esslingen, in Würtemberg, in 1472. In 1514 he published a Hebrew grammar at Augsburg and in 1518 settled at Wittenberg (where Melanchthon was his pupil) as a teacher of Greek and Hebrew. Later he taught Zwingli Hebrew at Zürich. He died in 1539 or 1540 at Nördlingen.

The melody (*supra*) traditionally associated with the hymn appears first in Valentin Babst's *Geystliche Lieder* (Leipzig, 1545), and is there set to the hymn " In dich hab' ich gehoffet, Herr." The large number of texts of the tune found in the latter half of the sixteenth century proves it to be of earlier date than 1545. The first half of it is practically identical with the melody of Luther's " Es woll' uns Gott genädig sein," which is found in use at Strasbourg in 1525[1]. The latter tune was reconstructed by Johann Walther from pre-Reformation material, and, with "Da Jesus an dem Kreuze stund," probably traces to a common, perhaps secular, source.

The tune occurs only in the *Orgelbüchlein*. Bach's form of the *cantus* differs in lines 2, 3, and 4 from the 1545 text. He closely follows Witt (No. 113), whose version is sanctioned generally by sixteenth century usage.

[1] See the melody in *Bach's Chorals*, Part II. 271.

[32]

N. xv. 67. The movement is the centre of the Passiontide section of the *Orgelbüchlein*. The recurring Pedal rhythm, heavy, syncopated, pictures the weary exhaustion of the hanging and suffering Jesus. In two other *Orgelbüchlein* movements Bach conveys an impression of lassitude by the same means. In "Herr Gott, nun schleuss den Himmel auf" (N. xv. 53) he seizes the lines of the first stanza

> My course is run, enough I've striven,
> Enough I've suffered here;
> Weary and sad
> My heart is glad
> That she may lay her down to rest

to represent in the Pedal the stumbling steps of the dying man groping towards his goal. In "Hilf Gott, dass mir's gelinge" (N. xv. 76) Bach fastens on the stanza of the hymn which recalls that Christ

> For our trespas on Croce He hang

and represents the heavy agony of the tortured Saviour in a Pedal rhythm which supports the narrative *cantus* above it.

Were not Bach so naïve in his literalness, it would be extravagant to interpret the seven octave leaps upward[1] that end each statement of the Pedal motive (bars 3, 4, 5, 6, 7, 9, 10) in " Da Jesus an dem Kreuze stund" as expressing the physical effort of the dying Saviour to speak the last seven Words.

[1] In fact the interval in bar 4 is a seventh.

DAS ALTE JAHR VERGANGEN IST.

Melody: "Gott Vater, der du deine Sonn"

Johannes Steurlein 1588

i. The old year now hath passed away,
We thank Thee, O our God, to-day
That Thou hast kept us through the year,
When danger and distress were near.

ii. We pray Thee, O Eternal Son,
Who with the Father reign'st as One,
To guard and rule Thy Christendom
Through all the ages yet to come.

iii. Take not Thy saving Word away,
Our souls' true comfort and their stay;
Abide with us, and keep us free
From errors, following only Thee.

iv. O help us to forsake all sin,
A new and holier course begin,
Mark not what once was done amiss;
A happier, better year be this,

v. Wherein as Christians we may live,
Or die in peace that Thou canst give,
To rise again when Thou shalt come,
And enter Thine eternal home.

vi. There shall we thank Thee, and adore,
With all the angels evermore ;
Lord Jesus Christ, increase our faith
To praise Thy name through life and death.
? Johannes Steurlein (1546-1613)
or Jakob Tapp (d. 1630)   Tr. *Catherine Winkworth*[1].

The New Year hymn, " Das alte Jahr vergangen ist," is first found, as a single stanza of eight lines (stanzas i and ii of the translation), in Clement Stephani's *Schöner ausserlessner deutscher Psalm, und anderer künstlicher Moteten und Geistlichen lieder XX* (Nürnberg, 1568). Twenty years later Johannes Steurlein included the hymn, in six stanzas of four lines, in his *Sieben und Zwantzigk Newe Geistliche Gesenge, Mit vier Stimmen Componiret und in druck der lieben Jugend zu gut verordnet* (Erfurt, 1588). Three of the twenty-seven hymns in the collection are marked as Steurlein's. "Das alte Jahr" is not among them, a fact which makes his alleged authorship doubtful. As early as 1609 the whole hymn was attributed to Jakob Tapp (d. 1630).

On the other hand, the melody (*supra*), which has borne the name of the hymn since 1608, is generally attributed to Johannes Steurlein, son of the first Lutheran pastor at Schmalkalden, where he was born in 1546. About 1580 he became Town-clerk

[1] *Chorale Book for England*, No. 171. The original hymn has six stanzas.

DAS ALTE JAHR VERGANGEN IST 139

of Wasungen, whence he passed in 1589 to Meiningen, of which he became Mayor. He died there in 1613. He was an excellent musician and published various melodies and four-part settings by himself. In 1588 his melody was set to Nikolaus Herman's "Gott Vater, der du deine Sonn," though the latter has a four-line stanza. In 1608 Erhart Bodenschatz attached the tune to "Das alte Jahr vergangen ist" in his *Harmoniae angelicae Cantionum Ecclesiasticarum* (Leipzig, 1608), and thenceforward the hymn and melody have been associated invariably. A four-lined reconstruction of the tune is set to the hymn in the Darmstadt *Cantional* of 1687, and a six-lined version of it, which Bach follows literally in the *Orgelbüchlein* and *Choralgesänge*, Nos. 55, 56, is found in Witt (No. 57), but not earlier in print.

[33]

N. xv. 43. Though the hymn is a prayer for help and comfort during the coming New Year (the old year being referred to incidentally merely in the first stanza), Bach, influenced, perhaps, by the character of the melody, writes a threnody on the year that is gone, and wraps the tune in chromatic counterpoint expressing, in his idiom, poignant grief and regret. A chromatic grief motive is employed for the same purpose in the opening choruses of the B minor Mass and the *St Matthew Passion*. It occurs also in the eighth Partita on "O Gott, du frommer Gott" (N. xix. 51), depicting the torture of the souls awaiting the Judgment summons, of which the corresponding stanza of the hymn speaks. In the *Orgelbüchlein* movement, "Christus, der uns selig macht," Bach introduces it to picture the bitter anguish of Christ, of which the hymn tells (N. xv. 64). The same thought moves him to introduce it "adagissimo" in the final bar of "O Mensch, bewein' dein' Sünde gross" (N. xv. 69).

Schweitzer remarks[1] that the striking major cadence is occasioned by "the consolatory conclusion of the first verse and of the poem in general." In fact the major cadence is as old as the tune.

Das Jesulein soll doch mein Trost.

Melody: "Das Jesulein soll doch mein Trost"
Bartholomäus Helder 1646

[1] Vol. II. 68.

DAS JESULEIN SOLL DOCH MEIN TROST

i. In Jesus is my only joy,
My soul He doth deliver;
He loveth me without alloy,
From Him nought me shall sever.
With deepest love
I gaze above
And yield myself unto Him.
In joy or woe
His path I go,
In living or in dying.

ii. With Thee, sweet Jesus, at my side
Nought can on earth distress me;
E'en though I wade through troubles' tide,
Thy love will hold and bless me.
The Devil's wiles,
Earth's flattering smiles,
Shall not prevail against me;
In Jesus I
My bourne descry:
On Him I soon shall rest me.

iii. The day will dawn, O Jesus mine,
When my dread God will face me,
When freed I'll be from foes malign,
And Thou wilt stoop to embrace me.
Then I shall be
Ever with Thee,
And with Thee throned in glory,
O Saviour dear,
Who far and near
Art hymned in deathless story.

Bartholomäus Helder (d. 1635)   Tr. *C. S. T.*[1]

[1] The original hymn has three stanzas.

Bartholomäus Helder's New Year hymn, "Das Jesulein soll doch mein Trost," was published, with the melody (*supra*), in the *Cantionale Sacrum, Das ist, Geistliche Lieder* (Gotha, 1646). The author-composer, son of the Superintendent in Gotha, was in 1616 pastor at Remstädt, near Gotha, where he died in 1635. Bach uses the melody only in the Organ movement *infra*. His text shows the same variations of the original as Witt's (No. 63).

[34]

N. xviii. 24. The movement is in the form of a Fughetta, and develops to the jubilant climax pictured in the last stanza of the hymn:

> O then I'll be
> Ever with Thee,
> And with Thee throned in glory.

Bach uses only the first and second lines of the tune.

There are five copies of the movement in the Kirnberger, Voss, Forkel, and other Collections.

DER TAG, DER IST SO FREUDENREICH.

Melody: "Der Tag, der ist so freudenreich" Anon. 1535

i. O hail this brightest day of days,
   All good Christian people!
   For Christ hath come upon our ways,
   Ring it from the steeple!
   Of maiden pure is He the Son;
   For ever shall thy praise be sung,
   Christ's fair mother Mary!
   Ever was there news so great?
   God's own Son from heaven's high state
   Is born the Son of Mary!

ii. This day the wondrous Child is born,
    Lent to earth from heaven.
    He comes to cheer a world forlorn,
    Its heavy sin to leaven.
    So, sing ye all the glorious birth
    Which doth redeem our fallen earth,

      And works our salvation.
      Laud to Thee, Child Jesu Christ!
      With mankind Thou'st kept the tryst
      Thou Star of every nation.

iii. As from above the sun his rays
      Poureth down upon us,
      And with his glow renews our days,
      Health and life doth give us ;
      E'en so the Christ Child was He sent
      A maiden's Babe, for our content,
      And for our sweet comfort.
      In a manger was He laid,
      Sinless, and yet undismayed
      To dwell on earth among us.

iv. The shepherds in amaze did stand,
      As from heaven came streaming
      Bright angels in a flaming band,
      Christ the King's birth hymning.
      O Christ the King of Kings where's He?
      False Herod, raging mightily,
      Everywhere doth seek Him
      Whom His mother Jesus dight,
      And doth slay, O wicked wight,
      The children for to catch Him.

Anon.   Tr. *C. S. T.*

The Christmas Carol, "Dies est laetitiae, In ortu regali," dates probably from the fourteenth century. "Der Tag, der ist so freudenreich," an early fifteenth century translation of it, is found in many versions with a varying number of stanzas. The form translated here is in four stanzas, in Joseph Klug's Wittenberg Hymn-book, 1535 [1529], along with the melody.

DER TAG, DER IST SO FREUDENREICH

The tune, whose opening phrase is reminiscent of the Carol "Puer natus in Bethlehem," is that of the Latin "Dies est laetitiae." Bach uses it in the two Organ movements *infra* and *Choralgesänge*, No. 62. His text closely follows Witt's (No. 20).

[35]

N. xv. 18. A Christmas movement in the *Orgelbüchlein*, instinct with the spirit of the opening lines of the hymn:

> O hail this brightest day of days,
> All good Christian people!
> For Christ hath come upon our ways,
> Ring it from the steeple!

The ♪♫ ♪♫ rhythm which pervades the movement uninterruptedly is one of two that Bach employs to express joy and exhilaration. .It is found in "Erschienen ist der herrliche Tag" (N. xv. 91), "In dich hab' ich gehoffet, Herr" (N. xv. 113), "Wir danken dir" (N. xv. 73), and "Von Gott will ich nicht lassen" (N. xvii. 43). "A joyful soaring rhythm," Spitta calls it[1].

[36]

N. xviii. 26. A movement upon the first half of the melody, *i.e.* stanza i, lines 1–4. Its source is a collection of Organ Chorals made by Johann Christoph Bach, of Eisenach, Sebastian's uncle. It is the only one by Bach in the collection.

[1] Vol. I. 600,

Dies sind die heil'gen zehn Gebot'.

Ky - rio - leis

i. These are the holy ten commands,
Which came to us from God's own hands,
By Moses, who obeyed His will,
On the top of Sinai's hill.
                        Kyrioleis.

ii. I am the Lord thy God alone ;
Of Gods besides thou shalt have none ;
Thou shalt thyself trust all to Me,
And love Me right heartily.
                        Kyrioleis.

iii. Thou shalt not speak like idle word
The name of God Who is thy Lord ;
As right or good thou shalt not praise
Except what God does or says.
                        Kyrioleis.

iv. Thou shalt keep holy the seventh day,
That rest thou and thy household may ;
From thine own work thou must be free,
That God have His work in thee.
                        Kyrioleis.

DIES SIND DIE HEIL'GEN ZEHN GEBOT'

v. Honour thou shalt and shalt obey
Thy father and thy mother alway ;
To serve them ready be thy hand,
That thou live long in the land.
    Kyrioleis.

vi. In wrathfulness thou shalt not kill,
Nor hate, nor take revenge for ill,
But patience keep and gentle mood,
And ev'n to thy foe do good.
    Kyrioleis.

vii. Thy marriage-bond thou shalt keep clean,
That even thy heart no other mean ;
Thy life thou must keep pure and free,
Temperate, with fine chastity.
    Kyrioleis.

viii. Money or goods steal not, nor yet
Grow rich by others' blood and sweat ;
Open thou wide thy kindly hand
To the poor man in thy land.
    Kyrioleis.

ix. Thou shalt not lying stories bear,
Nor 'gainst thy neighbour falsely swear ;
His innocence thou shalt rescue,
And hide his shame from man's view.
    Kyrioleis.

x. Thy neighbour's wife or house to win
Thou shalt not seek, or ought within ;
But wish all good to him may be,
As thy own heart doth to thee.
    Kyrioleis.

xi. To us come these commands, that so
Thou, son of man, thy sins mayst know,
And with this lesson thy heart fill,
That man must live for God's will.
    Kyrioleis.

xii. May Christ our Lord help us in this,
For He our mediator is ;
Our own work is a hopeless thing,
Wrath alone all it can bring.
              Kyrioleis.
Martin Luther (1483-1546)   Tr. *George Macdonald*[1].

Luther's versification of the Ten Commandments was published first in 1524, with the tune (*supra*). The latter is an adaptation, probably by Johann Walther, of the melody of the pilgrim song " In Gottes Namen fahren wir[2]." Besides the three Organ movements in which it occurs, Bach uses the melody elsewhere in the accompaniment to the first Chorus of Cantata 77 (*c.* 1725) and *Choralgesänge*, No. 66. Bach's text of the tune is invariable. It is noticeable that he writes G for F as the first note of the fourth line of the stanza (the ninth note of the second line *supra*). Therein he follows Witt (No. 222).

There are three Organ movements on the melody:

[37]

N. xv. 103. The movement is the first of the Catechism hymns in the *Orgelbüchlein*. It is one of three there—the others being N. xv. 39, 115—in which Bach evolves the figures of the counterpoint out of the first line of the tune[3]. In the present instance the device assists his love of literalness.

[1] *Exotics*, p. 84. The original hymn has twelve stanzas.
[2] See *Bach's Chorals*, Part II. 287, for the tune.
[3] Spitta, I. 600.

In the two inner parts that accompany the *cantus* and on the Pedal he introduces the first melodic period of the tune with constant iteration to suggest the rigidity of rule and dogma[1].

[38]

N. xvi. 42. This and the following movement belong to the *Clavierübung*, a work in which Bach tended to indulge in symbolism somewhat extravagantly. His purpose here is to illustrate and enforce the idea of law and of man's bondage to it as a necessity of his moral being. To quote Schweitzer's penetrating analysis[2]: "In a lengthy fantasia each of the separate parts goes its own way, without rhythm, without plan, without theme, without regard for the others. This musical disorder depicts the moral state of the world before the law. Then the law is revealed. It is represented by a majestic canon upon the melody of the Choral, running through the whole movement." Bach had the same idea before him when he introduced the melody into the opening Chorus of the Cantata, "Du sollst Gott, deinen Herren, lieben" (*c.* 1725)[3].

---

[1] I accept this interpretation from Mr Harvey Grace's illuminating article on the *Orgelbüchlein* in the *Musical Times* for October 1, 1920. Schweitzer (II. 59) speaks of the phrase being repeated ten times "in the Pedal," once for each Commandment. This is inaccurate.

[2] Vol. II. 59.

[3] See *Bach's Chorals*, Part II. 288.

MELODIES

[39]

N. xvi. 47. The movement belongs to the shorter set of *Clavierübung* Preludes. It is a Fughetta, in which a counterpoint upon the first line of the melody is carefully stated ten times.

Durch Adams Fall ist ganz verderbt.

Melody: "*Durch Adams Fall ist ganz verderbt*"
Anon. 1535

i. When Adam fell, the frame entire
Of nature was infected;
The source, whence came the poison dire,
Was not to be corrected:
The lust accursed, indulged at first,
Brought death as its production;
But God's free grace
Hath saved our race
From misery and destruction.
* * *
iii. By one man's guilt we were enslaved
To sin, death, and the devil;
But by another's grace are saved
Through faith from all this evil:

And as we all by Adam's fall
. Were sentenced to perdition,
So for us hath
Christ by His death
Regained true life's fruition.

iv. Since God bestowed His only Son
On His rebellious creature,
To save our souls which were undone,
And free our sinful nature
From shame and guilt, by His blood spilt,
His death and resurrection,—
Do not delay,
Make sure this day
Thy calling and election.

* * *

viii. I send my cries unto the Lord,
My heart implores this favour,
To grant me of His living word
A never-failing savour;
That sin and shame may lose their claim
To hinder my salvation:
In Christ, the scope
Of all my hope,
I fear no condemnation.

ix. His word's a lamp unto my feet,
My soul's best information;
My surest guide and path to meet
Eternal consolation:
This light, where'er it doth appear,
Revealeth Christ our Saviour
To all the lost,
Who firmly trust
In Him alone for ever.

Lazarus Spengler (1479–1534)   Tr. *John Christian Jacobi*[1].

[1] *Moravian Hymn-book*, ed. 1877, No. 18. The original hymn has nine stanzas, of which ii, v–vii are omitted in the translation.

Lazarus Spengler's penitential hymn, "Durch Adams Fall ist ganz verderbt," was first published in the Hymn-book which Johann Walther, in collaboration with Luther, issued in 1524. The melody (*supra*) which bears its name did not appear in association with it until the publication of Joseph Klug's Hymn-book at Wittenberg in 1535 [1529]. The tune, the "Pavier Tone," is said to have been sung at the Battle of Pavia in 1525. Bach employs it elsewhere in Cantatas 18 and 109 (1713 : *c.* 1731). In the Organ movements he gives the sixth and last lines eight feet. In Witt (No. 291) and the Cantatas, as in the original, they have seven. Otherwise Bach's text is invariable.

There are two Organ movements on the melody:

[40]

N. xv. 107. One of the movements in the "Penitence and Amendment" section of the *Orgelbüchlein*. Bach interprets the opening line :

<blockquote>When Adam fell.</blockquote>

The *basso ostinato* consists of a series of almost irremediable stumbles or falls. Notice also the pathetic significance of the little phrase accompanying the first note of every line of the melody. But the close in A major enforces the lines :

<blockquote>But God's free grace
Hath saved our race.</blockquote>

DURCH ADAMS FALL IST GANZ VERDERBT 153

[41]

N. xviii. 28. The Fugue is among the miscellaneous movements and its form declares it an early work. The text of it is among Kirnberger's MSS. Five other copies are in the Berlin Royal Library and Hauser MSS. It bears no relation to a particular stanza.

EIN' FESTE BURG IST UNSER GOTT.

Melody: "*Ein' feste Burg ist unser Gott*"

Martin Luther 1535

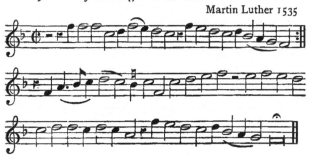

i. A sure stronghold our God is He,
A trusty shield and weapon;
Our help He'll be and set us free
From every ill can happen.
That old malicious foe
Means us deadly woe;
Armed with might from hell
And deepest craft as well,
On earth is not his fellow.

ii. Through our own force we nothing can,
   Straight were we lost for ever;
   But for us fights the proper Man,
   By God sent to deliver.
   Ask ye Who this may be?
   Jesus Christ is He,
   Of Sabaoth Lord,
   Sole God to be adored—
   'Tis He must win the battle.

iii. And were the world with devils filled,
   All eager to devour us,
   Our souls to fear should little yield,
   They cannot overpower us.
   Their dreaded Prince no more
   Harms us as of yore;
   Look grim as he may,
   Doomed is his ancient sway,
   A word can overthrow him.

iv. Still shall they leave that Word His might,
   And yet no thanks shall merit;
   Still is He with us in the fight,
   By His good gifts and Spirit.
   E'en should they take our life,
   Wealth, name, child, or wife—
   Though all these be gone,
   Yet nothing have they won,
   God's kingdom ours abideth.

Martin Luther (1483-1546)   Tr. *Catherine Winkworth*[1].

Luther's hymn is a free translation of Psalm 46 and probably was written for the Diet of Speyer in 1529. The tune was adapted by Luther, certainly

---

[1] *Chorale Book for England*, No. 124. The original hymn has four stanzas.

from the Roman Gradual. Words and melody were published together in 1531 and again in Klug's Wittenberg Hymn-book in 1535. Bach uses the tune in Cantata 80 (1730); *Choralgesänge*, Nos. 74-5; and the movement *infra*. Only in the Organ movement does he exactly follow the 1535 text in the fifth line of the melody (line 2 *supra*). Witt's (No. 482) text shows the same fidelity to the original.

[42]

N. xviii. 30. Observe how triumphantly Bach brings out on the Pedal (p. 32, bars 2-9) two lines of stanza ii:

| Er heist Jesu Christ, | Jesus Christ is He, |
| Der Herr Sabaoth. | Of Sabaoth Lord. |

Copies of the movement are among the Kirnberger, Krebs, and Walther MSS.

ERBARM' DICH MEIN, O HERRE GOTT.

Melody: "*Erbarm' dich mein, O Herre Gott*"
? Johann Walther 1524

i. O God, be mercyfull to me,
　Accordynge to Thy great pitie;
　Washe of, make clene my iniquite:
　I knowlege my synne, and it greveth me
　Agaynst The, agaynst The only
　Have I synned, which is before myne eye:
　Though Thou be judged in man's syght,
　Yet are Thy wordes founde true and ryght.

ii. Beholde, I was all borne in synne,
　My mother conceaved me therin:
　But Thou lovest treuth, and haste shewed me
　Thy wysdome hyd so secretly.
　With fayre ysope, Lorde, sprenkle Thou me;
　Washe Thou me clean; so shall I be
　Whyter than snowe: cause me reioyse,
　Make my bones mery, whom Thou madest lowse.

iii. Lorde, turne Thy face from my wickednesse;
　Clense me from all unryghteousnesse:
　A pure harte, Lorde, make Thou in me,
　Renewe a ryght spirite in my body:
　Cast me not out away from The,
　Nor take Thy Holy Goost from me;
　Make me reioyse in Thy savynge health,
　Thy myghty Spirite strength me for my wealth.

iv. Thy waye shall I shewe to men full of vyce,
　And enstructe them well in Thy service;
　That wicked men and ungodly
　May be converted unto The.
　O God, O God, my Savioure,
　Delyver me from the synne of murther:
　My tonge shall reioyse in Thy mercye;
　Open my lippes, and my mouth shal prayse The.

v. Thou wylt have no bodely offrynge;
　I thought them els to The to brynge.
　God's sacrifice is a troubled spirite;
　Thou wylt not dispise a harte contrite.

ERBARM' DICH MEIN, O HERRE GOTT 157

With Sion, O God, deale gently,
That Hierusalem walles may buylded be:
Then shalt Thou delyte in the ryght offrynge,
Which men shall with theyr calves brynge.

Erhart Hegenwalt (1524) Tr. *Bishop Myles Coverdale*[1].

The hymn, "Erbarm' dich mein, O Herre Gott," a translation of Psalm 51, was published in the *Enchiridion Oder eyn Handbuchlein* (Erfurt, 1524) and in Johann Walther's Wittenberg Hymn-book in the same year, in the latter with the melody *supra*. The author of the hymn, Erhart Hegenwalt, appears to have been a student and graduate of Wittenberg and a contemporary of Luther and Walther there. The melody is reminiscent of "Es woll' uns Gott[2]" and is with great probability Walther's composition. Bach uses it in the Organ movement *infra* and *Choralgesänge*, No. 78. His text, like Witt's (No. 258), closely follows the original.

[43]

N. xviii. 35. The *cantus* is set to an accompaniment unique in Bach's Organ music. Spitta[3] finds a counterpart to it in an arrangement of "Vater unser im Himmelreich," by Böhm, and concludes that Bach's movement was composed at Lüneburg under Böhm's immediate influence, at the period in

---

[1] *Remains*, p. 576. The original hymn has five stanzas.
[2] More generally known as "Christ unser Herr zum Jordan kam." See p. 120 *supra*.
[3] Vol. I. 216.

158 MELODIES

which the Variations upon "Christ, der du bist der helle Tag" were written, i.e. *circa* 1701–2, when Bach was sixteen or seventeen years old. On the other hand, Johann Kuhnau (d. 1722), Bach's predecessor at Leipzig, issued in 1700 six Clavier Sonatas illustrating certain Bible stories. Into the first of them, depicting the fight between David and Goliath, he introduces the melody "Aus tiefer Noth" in the right hand against repeated quaver chords in the left. As a young man Bach probably knew this work. His wistful accompaniment's congruity to the mood of Hegenwalt's hymn is apparent.

The MS. of the movement is in Johann Ludwig Krebs' *Sammelbuch*, marked "J. S. B."

ERSCHIENEN IST DER HERRLICHE TAG.

Melody: "*Erschienen ist der herrliche Tag*"
Nikolaus Herman 1560

ERSCHIENEN IST DER HERRLICHE TAG

i. The day hath dawned—the day of days
Transcending all our joy and praise:
This day our Lord triumphant rose;
This day He captive led our foes.
    Hallelujah!

ii. The Serpent's craft, sin, death, and hell,
This day before the Conqueror fell:
All suffering, sorrow, ill, the name
Of Jesus risen this day o'ercame.
    Hallelujah!

* * *

xiii. The Sun, the Earth, all things adore,
As at His death they mourned before:
All own with joy upon this day
The foe's dominion passed away.
    Hallelujah!

xiv. Then, as is meet, we now will sing
Glad Hallelujahs to our King:
To Thee, Lord, doth our praise pertain,
Who for our joy art risen again.
    Hallelujah!

Nikolaus Herman (*c.* 1485–1561)   Tr. *Arthur T. Russell*[1].

Both words and melody of the Easter hymn, "Erschienen ist der herrliche Tag," are by Nikolaus Herman, and were published together by him in 1560. Bach uses the melody in the *Orgelbüchlein* and Cantatas 67 and 145 (*c.* 1725–30). Always he substitutes E for D as the sixth note of the third line of the stanza (line 2, note 7 *supra*). The in-

---

[1] *Psalms and Hymns* (Cambridge, 1851), No. 113. The original hymn has fourteen stanzas, of which iii–xii are omitted in the translation.

novation dates from a text of 1605 and is found in Witt (No. 146).

[44]

N. xv. 91. The movement is one of the Easter Preludes in the *Orgelbüchlein*. It is pervaded by the rhythm of ecstatic joy which, in the Christmas Prelude, "Der Tag, der ist sehr freudenreich," has already been remarked. The same rhythm is found in the B minor Mass at the words "et expecto resurrectionem mortuorum[1]," and the upward soaring of the final close has the significance here which it bears in the Mass.

ERSTANDEN IST DER HEIL'GE CHRIST.

Melody: "*Erstanden ist der heil'ge Christ*"   Anon. 1607

---

[1] Novello's edition, 1908, p. 153.

ERSTANDEN IST DER HEIL'GE CHRIST

Melody: "Surrexit Christus hodie" Anon. 1531

i. Christ our Lord is Risen to-day,
    Halle-Hallelujah,
Christ, our Life, our Light, our Way,
    Halle-Hallelujah,
The Object of our Love and Faith,
    Halle-Hallelujah,
Who but died to conquer Death,
    Halle-Hallelujah.

ii. The Holy Matrons early come,
  Halle-Hallelujah,
To Bedew their Saviour's Tomb,
  Halle-Hallelujah,
Jesus seek among the Dead,
  Halle-Hallelujah,
Far from those Dark Regions fled,
  Halle-Hallelujah.

iii. Two bright Angels, that appear,
  Halle-Hallelujah,
Thus Salute them: "He's not here,
  Halle-Hallelujah.
"Banish Sorrow, Shout and Sing,
  Halle-Hallelujah,
Welcome to your Risen King,
  Halle-Hallelujah."

Mary   iv. "Beauteous Angels, say what Place,
  Halle-Hallelujah,
Does His charming Presence Grace?
  Halle-Hallelujah.
Bless my Eyes; then bid Rejoyce,
  Halle-Hallelujah.
Then to Praise I'll tune my Voice,
  Halle-Hallelujah."

The Angel   v. "First the Sacred Place behold,
  Halle-Hallelujah,
Did your Breathless Lord infold,
  Halle-Hallelujah.
See the Cloath which bound His Head,
  Halle-Hallelujah,
Proves He's Risen from the Dead,
  Halle-Hallelujah."

Mary	vi.	"True, 'tis so; the empty Urn,
		Halle-Hallelujah,
		Shall my Grief to Transports turn,
		Halle-Hallelujah.
		He's not here: O tell me where,
		Halle-Hallelujah,
		His blest Residence declare,
		Halle-Hallelujah."
The Angel	vii.	"Haste in Faith, prepare to see,
		Halle-Hallelujah,
		Your loved Lord in Galilee,
		Halle-Hallelujah.
		Blest let His Disciples be,
		Halle-Hallelujah,
		With your Sacred Embassy,
		Halle-Hallelujah."
Mary	viii.	"Heralds of our Joy, to you,
		Halle-Hallelujah,
		Grateful Thanks and Love is due,
		Halle-Hallelujah,
		While our God in Praises high,
		Halle-Hallelujah,
		We together Magnify,
		Halle-Hallelujah."
	ix.	The Cross is past, the Crown is won,
		Halle-Hallelujah,
		The Ransom paid, and Death's Sting gone,
		Halle-Hallelujah.
		Let us Feast and Sing and Say,
		Halle-Hallelujah,
		Christ and We have Life to-day,
		Halle-Hallelujah.

Traditional   *Anonymous*[1].

[1] *Lyra Davidica* (London, 1708), p. 12. The original hymn has nineteen stanzas of two lines.

164 MELODIES

The Easter Carol, "Surrexit Christus hodie," of which "Erstanden ist der heil'ge Christ" is a translation, dates at least from the fourteenth century and exists in several forms. The German hymn also is found in many versions, the one here translated being from a broadsheet printed at Nürnberg in 1544. The melody (*supra*) proper to the Latin Carol is found in Michael Weisse's *Ein New Gesengbuchlen* (Jung Bunzlau, 1531), and is the descant melody of a four-part setting (*supra*) in Michael Praetorius' *Musae Sioniae* (Part V, 1607).

The *Choralgesänge*, No. 85, gives a four-part setting of another melody to which the hymn also was sung, whose evolution from the original (1531) tune is revealed in the following three-part setting in Valentin Triller's *Ein Schlesich singebüchlein aus Göttlicher schrifft* (Breslau, 1555), where it appears as the descant to the original melody in the Tenor:

"*Erstanden ist der Herre Christ*"

"*Surrexit Christus hodie*"

ERSTANDEN IST DER HEIL'GE CHRIST 165

In the single Organ movement in which he treats the melody Bach uses the original (1531) tune with the 1607 cadence. His text exactly follows Witt (No. 143).

[45]

N. xv. 89. The movement, one of the Easter Preludes in the *Orgelbüchlein,* expresses the spirit and teaching of the festival. The Pedal, in bold intervals, sounds the message of resurrection, emphasized by the upward rush of the parts in the opening bars, while the animated quaver figure expresses joy. Bach employs a similar association of motives in the Christmas Prelude, "Puer natus in Bethlehem" (N. xv. 13), in which the Pedal performs the obeisances of the Wise Men from the East, while quaver passages exhibit their reverent ecstasy.

ES IST DAS HEIL UNS KOMMEN HER.

Melody: "Es ist das Heil uns kommen her" Anon. 1524

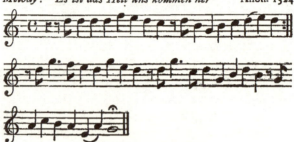

i. Our whole salvation doth depend
  On God's free grace and Spirit;
  Our fairest works can ne'er defend
  A boast in our own merit:
  Derived is all our righteousness
  From Christ and His atoning grace;
  He is our Mediator.

* * *

v. The law cried, Justice must be done,
  And man doomed to damnation;
  But mercy sent the Eternal Son,
  Who purchased our salvation,
  Endured the Cross, despised the shame,
  And answered every legal claim,
  To spare the sons of Adam.

vi. Christ, having all the law fulfilled,
  Thro' His blest Cross and Passion,
  Is now the rock whereon we build
  Our faith and whole salvation:
  He is the Lord our righteousness,
  Whose death hath purchased life and grace,
  And ransomed us for ever.

* * *

ix. The law revealed sin's sinfulness,
Enhanced the accusation;
The gospel brings us saving grace,
Hope, joy, and consolation;
Bids all lay hold on Jesus' Cross:
The law could ne'er retrieve our loss,
Ev'n with our best performance.

x. True faith, by Jesus in us wrought,
By works is manifested;
That faith is empty which is not
By works of love attested:
Yet faith alone us justifies;
Love to our neighbour but implies
We are sincere believers.

*   *   *

Paul Speratus (1484-1551)   Tr. *John Christian Jacobi*[1].

The words and melody of Paul Speratus' (Offer or Hoffer) hymn were published in 1524 in the first Lutheran Hymn-book. Bach uses the melody in the *Orgelbüchlein*; Cantatas 9, 86, 117, 155, 186 (1716–c. 1733); and the Wedding Chorals (*Choralgesänge*, No. 89). With the exception that in the Cantatas he substitutes B for G as the first note of the last phrase of the tune (*ut supra*), Bach's text is invariable. The innovation is in Witt's text (No. 292). Having regard to Bach's invariable use elsewhere, it may be conjectured that the quaver B natural at the

---

[1] *Moravian Hymn-book*, ed. 1877, No. 19. The original hymn has fourteen stanzas, of which ii–iv, vii, viii, xi–xiv are omitted in the translation.

168   MELODIES

second beat of the final bar of the *Orgelbüchlein* Prelude belongs to the melody, and should be printed

instead of

[46]

N. xv. 109. The movement is the last of the penitential Preludes in the *Orgelbüchlein*, and one of the only two completed in that section. Bach disregards the pointedly dogmatic character of the hymn and uses its opening statement

Salvation hath come down to us

to justify a jubilant treatment of the melody. The significance of Bach's inclusion of the hymn among the penitential hymns, already pointed out in the Introduction to this volume, is enhanced when we discover him enforcing the hymn's message of comfort by associating its melody with a jubilant motive. Such a treatment of it was the more congruous in that the tune itself is an old Easter Carol.

GELOBET SEIST DU, JESU CHRIST.

Plainsong: "*Grates nunc omnes reddamus*"

Gra - tes nunc om - nes red - da - mus do - mi - no Deo,
qui su - a na - ti - vi - ta - te nos li - ber - a -
vit de di - a - bo - li ca po - tes - ta - te.
Hu - ic o - por - tet ut ca - na - mus cum an - ge - lis:
Sem - per glo - ri - a in ex - cel - sis!

Melody: "*Gelobet seist du, Jesu Christ*"   Anon. 1524

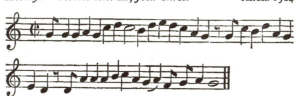

    i. Now blessed be Thou, Christ Jesu;
       Thou art man borne, this is true:
       The aungels made a mery noyse,
       Yet have we more cause to rejoyse.
                      Kirieleyson.

ii. The blessed Sonne of God onely
   In a crybbe full poore dyd lye:
   With oure poore flesh and oure poore bloude
   Was clothed that everlastynge good.
                              Kirieleyson.

iii. He that made heaven and earth of nought
   In oure flesh hath oure health brought;
   For oure sake made He hymselfe full small,
   That reigneth Lorde and Kynge over all.
                              Kirieleyson.

iv. Eternall lyght doth now appeare
   To the worlde both farre and neare;
   It shyneth full cleare even at mydnyght,
   Makynge us chyldren of His lyght.
                              Kirieleyson.

v. The Lorde Christ Jesu, God's Sonne deare,
   Was a gest and a straunger here;
   Us for to brynge from mysery,
   That we might lyve eternally.
                              Kirieleyson.

vi. Into this worlde ryght poore came He,
   To make us ryche in mercye:
   Therefore wolde He oure synnes forgeve,
   That we with Hym in heaven myght lyve.
                              Kirieleyson.

vii. All this dyd He for us frely,
   For to declare His great mercy:
   All Christendome be mery therfore,
   And geve Hym thankes evermore.
                              Kirieleyson.

Martin Luther (1483-1546)   Tr. *Bishop Myles Coverdale*[1].

[1] *Remains*, p. 562. The original hymn has seven stanzas.

Luther's hymn, "Gelobet seist du, Jesu Christ," was published in 1524, in Johann Walther's Hymnbook. Words and melody are derived from the Christmas Sequence, "Grates nunc omnes reddamus," the plainsong of which is printed *supra*. Its simplification was accomplished, presumably, by Walther himself. Outside the Organ movements *infra* Bach uses the tune in Cantatas 64, 91 (1723?–*c*. 1740); *Christmas Oratorio* (1734), Nos. 7, 28; *Choralgesänge*, No. 107. His melodic text follows Witt (No. 19) and is invariable, except in one detail. In one Organ movement (N. xviii. 37) B natural replaces C as the sixth note of the melody. The variant is found in an early text (1535), but is not in Witt.

There are four Organ movements upon the melody:

[47]

N. xv. 15. The movement is the third of the Christmas Preludes in the *Orgelbüchlein*. Bach treats the tidings of Christ's birth in another mood than that which distinguishes the first Christmas Prelude, "Puer natus in Bethlehem." The latter exhibits exuberant joy. In the present movement the rhythm expresses restrained adoration. It already has been remarked in "Alle Menschen müssen sterben" and occurs again in "Herr Christ, der ein'ge Gottes-Sohn" (N. xv. 9).

[48]

N. xviii. 37. An Organ accompaniment of the melody. Griepenkerl (P. v. 102) printed it from MSS. in the handwriting of Johann Christian Kittel and Johann Gottfried Walther. Both are now in the Berlin Royal Library. Krebs, too, preserved a sketch of it.

In B.G. xl. 158, a "Variant" of the accompaniment is printed from a Krebs MS. in the Berlin Royal Library.

[49]

N. xviii. 38. The movement is a Fughetta upon the first line of the melody. A copy of it is in the Kirnberger, and others exist in the Schicht, Schelble, and Hauser MSS.

[50]

N. xviii. 39. The movement is among the miscellaneous Preludes. Apparently only a single MS. of it exists. It is in the Royal Library, Berlin, and is described as faulty and comparatively modern. Griepenkerl printed the movement in 1847 from a copy "written by Cantor Kegel." Presumably it and the Berlin MS. are one and the same. The treatment is formal.

GOTTES SOHN IST KOMMEN.

Melody: "Gottes Sohn ist kommen"   Anon. 1531

i. Once He came in blessing,
   All our ills redressing,
   Came in likeness lowly,
   Son of God most holy,
   Bore the Cross to save us,
   Hope and freedom gave us.

ii. Still He comes within us,
    Still His voice would win us
    From the sins that hurt us;
    Would to Truth convert us
    From our foolish errors,
    Ere He comes in terrors.

iii. Thus if thou hast known Him,
     Not ashamed to own Him,
     Nor dost love Him coldly,
     But wilt trust Him boldly,
     He will now receive thee,
     Heal thee, and forgive thee.

* * *

v. But through many a trial,
   Deepest self-denial,
   Long and brave endurance,
   Must thou win assurance
   That His own He makes thee,
   And no more forsakes thee.

* * *

174 MELODIES

 ix. He who thus endureth
  Bright reward secureth.
  Come then, O Lord Jesus,
  From our sins release us.
  Let us here confess Thee,
  Till in heaven we bless Thee.
Johann Roh (d. 1547) Tr. *Catherine Winkworth*[1].

GOTT, DURCH DEINE GÜTE.

 i. God of grace and mercy,
  Glance in pity on me;
  Heart and mind and spirit,
  Keep them through Thy merit.
  Satan every hour
  Waiteth to devour.

 ii. Christ to earth Who camest,
  And Thine own reclaimest,
  Hold us in Thy keeping,
  Faithful to Thy teaching;
  Lead us to the far land
  Where Thy Father's halls stand.

 iii. Blessed Holy Spirit,
  Of Thy gracious merit
  Pardon our offences,
  Guide aright our senses;
  That we soon may greet Thee
  And be ever near Thee.
Johann Spangenberg (1484-1550) Tr. *C. S. T.*[2]

In the *Orgelbüchlein* Bach attaches the titles of two hymns, Johann Roh's "Gottes Sohn is kommen," and Johann Spangenberg's "Gott, durch deine

---

[1] *Chorale Book for England*, No. 26. The original has nine stanzas, of which iv, vi, vii, viii are omitted in the translation.

[2] The original hymn has three stanzas.

Güte," to a tune that originally belonged to neither of them, being that of the Latin hymn, "Ave ierarchia Celestis et pia." Its earliest printed form is in Michael Weisse's *Ein New Gesengbuchlen* (Jung Bunzlau, 1531), where it is set to Weisse's hymn, "Menschenkind, merk eben." In 1544, simultaneously but in different Hymn-books, Roh and Spangenberg appropriated the tune to their repective hymns.

Johann Roh's Christmas hymn, "Gottes Sohn ist kommen," first appeared in the second German Hymn-book of the Bohemian Brethren (*Ein Gesangbuch der Brüder inn Behemen und Merherrn*), published at Nürnberg in 1544, with the tune (*supra*).

Johann Roh, by birth a Bohemian, styled himself "Cornu" in Latin, "Horn" in German. In 1518 he was appointed preacher to the community of the Bohemian Brethren at Jung Bunzlau and, in 1532, became Bishop. He died at Jung Bunzlau in 1547.

Johann Spangenberg's hymn appears first among his *Alte und Newe Geistliche Lieder und Lobgesenge, von der Geburt Christi unsers Herrn, Für die Junge Christen* (Erfurt, 1544), with the melody. The hymn, accordingly, has Advent associations, though it is addressed to the Three Persons of the Trinity and directed to be sung after the Sermon.

Spangenberg was born at Hardegsen, Hanover, in 1484. After studying at Erfurt University he became preacher at Stolberg. In 1524 he was appointed pastor in St Blasius' Church, Nordhausen, and thence in 1546 passed to Eisleben as Superintendent. He died there in 1550.

Bach uses the melody in the Organ movements *infra*, and *Choralgesänge*, No. 115. His text is not invariable. In the *Choralgesänge* he follows the 1531 text. In the *Orgelbüchlein*, where the sharpened fourth note of the melody is noticeable, he exactly follows Witt (No. 5), who substitutes B for F flat as the first note of the final phrase (*supra*). N. xviii. 42, on the other hand, agrees with the *Choralgesänge* text, the fourth line of the tune suffering some compression for metrical reasons.

The three Organ movements on the melody are in triple measure. Bach thereby enhances the appropriate resemblance between the Advent tune's opening phrase and that of the Christmas Carol "In dulci jubilo."

[51]

N. xv. 5. The *Orgelbüchlein* Advent movement bears the titles both of Roh's and Spangenberg's hymns. But Bach wrote it moved by the thought of redemption which Roh's first stanza suggests. Hence the quaver joy rhythm.

[52]

N. xviii. 41. A short Fughetta, among the miscellaneous Preludes, on the first line of the melody.

GOTTES SOHN IST KOMMEN

Three MSS. of it exist, one of them in the Kirnberger, another in the Voss, collection.

[53]

N. xviii. 42. Spitta points out[1] that the earliest form of Organ Choral, contrapuntal and without a fixed subject or episodic interludes, occurs in Bach's use only in the present movement and "Vater unser im Himmelreich" (N. xix. 12). In both a few introductory bars imitate the first line of the melody. A copy of "Vater unser" (N. xix. 12) is among the Walther MSS., a fact upon which Spitta concludes[2] that it was written at Weimar. Probably the present movement must be assigned to the same period. The MS. of it is in Andreas Bach's MS. Griepenkerl printed it for the Peters Edition from a copy "communicated by C. F. Becker."

HELFT MIR GOTT'S GÜTE PREISEN.

Melody: "*Helft mir Gott's Güte preisen*"
Wolfgang Figulus 1575 [1569]

[1] Vol. I. 605. [2] *Ibid.* 654.

i. Come, let us All, with Fervour,
On whom Heaven's Mercies shine,
To our Supreme Preserver
In tuneful Praises join.
Another Year is gone;
Of which the tender Mercies
(Each pious Heart rehearses)
Demand a grateful Song.

ii. Tell o'er, with true Devotion,
The Wonders of His Grace;
Let no polluting Notion
Our Gratitude deface.
But still remember well,
That this Year's Renovation
Renews our Obligation
To fight 'gainst Sin and Hell.

iii. His Grace is still preserving
Our Peace in Church and State;
His Love is never swerving,
In Spite of Satan's Hate.
Dispensed with open Hand,
His Blessings on this Nation
Still ward off Desolation,
And save a sinful Land.

iv. 'Tis His eternal Kindness
That spares us from the Rod.
Though long our wilful Blindness
Has sore provoked our God
To pour His Vengeance down;
Yet still He Grace provides us;
And still His Mercy hides us
From His own dreadful Frown.

v. The Source of all Compassion
Pities our feeble Frame,
When turning from Transgression
We come in Jesu's Name
Before His holy Face;
Then every sinful Motion
Is cast into the Ocean
Of never-failing Grace.

vi. To Christ our Peace is owing:
Through Him Thou art appeased.
Through Him Thy Love's still flowing:
O! wilt Thou then be pleased,
Through Christ, Thy Grace to send,
In all its Strength and Beauty,
To keep us in our Duty,
Till these frail days shall end.

Paul Eber (1511-69)   Tr. *John Christian Jacobi*[1].

[1] *Psalmodia Germanica*, p. 10. The original hymn has six stanzas.

180 MELODIES

Two tunes are associated with Eber's New Year hymn and were published with it in 1575 [1569] by Wolfgang Figulus, Cantor in the Fürstenschule at Meissen. The first of them is practically identical with the contemporary "Von Gott will ich nicht lassen[1]" and derived from the same secular song, "Ich ging einmal spazieren," to whose melody Ludwig Helmbold wrote "Von Gott will ich nicht lassen." The second tune, presumably by Figulus himself, is printed *supra* in a four-part setting by him. Its Tenor, it will be observed, very closely fits the first melody. Bach uses it in the *Orgelbüchlein* and Cantatas 16, 28, 183 (*c.* 1724–*c.* 1736).

Though Bach's use of the tune extends from his Weimar to his later Leipzig period, his text of the tune shows little variation. To himself must be attributed the improving change of the fifth note of the melody (*supra*) from B flat to C natural. Witt's (No. 56) text, which Bach otherwise follows closely in the *Orgelbüchlein*, has B flat and Zahn (No. 5267) does not reveal any anticipation of Bach's emendation. For the close of lines 2 and 4 of the melody (the last three notes before the middle double-bar *supra*), and for lines 6 and 7, Bach generally follows Schein's (1627) text, which for lines 6 and 7 reads

[1] See it in *Bach's Chorals*, Part I. 63.

In the four places in which he uses the phrase Bach only once (in Cantata 28) (c. 1736) adopts Schein's B flat as its fifth note. Elsewhere he writes D, as in the *Orgelbüchlein*, and as he found it in Witt.

[54]

N. xv. 39.. The movement is the first of the New Year Preludes in the *Orgelbüchlein*. Besides the formula of jubilation which Bach introduces, his emphasis of the first four notes of the *cantus* will be remarked. The device has been noticed already in the Prelude "Dies sind die heil'gen zehn Gebot[i]." Schweitzer supposes[1] that Bach, unlike his predecessors, did not introduce motives derived from the melody as being musically effective, but only when he desired to emphasize the associated words of the hymn. In the present case, the repeated opening phrase creates the impression of a multitude of voices reiterating the prayer "Help me to sing God's praises." The movement becomes, in effect, a joyous peal of gratitude ringing in the New Year[2].

[1] Vol. II. 67.
[2] See also Sec. 59 *infra*.

Herr Christ, der ein'ge Gottes-Sohn.

Melody: "Herr Christ, der ein'ge Gottes-Sohn"

Anon. 1524

   i. Christ is the only Sonne of God,
      The Father Eternall:
      We have in Jesse founde this rod,
      God and Man naturall;
      He is the mornynge star;
      His beames sendeth He out farre
      Beyonde other starres all.

          *   *   *

  iii. Let us increase in love of The,
      And in knowlege also;
      That we, belevynge stedfastly,
      May in spirite serve The so,
      That we in our hartes may savoure
      Thy mercy and Thy favoure,
      And to thyrst after no mo.

  iv. Thou only maker of all thynge,
      Thou everlastynge lyght,
      From ende to ende all rulynge,
      By Thyne owne godly myght;
      Turne Thou oure hartes unto The,
      And lyghten them with the veritie,
      That they erre not from the ryght.

HERR CHRIST, DER EIN'GE GOTTES-SOHN

    v. Awake us, Lorde, we praye The;
       Thy Holy Spirite us geve,
       Which maye oure olde man mortifie,
       That oure new man maye lyve.
       So wyll we alwaye thanke The,
       That shewest us so great mercye,
       And oure synnes dost forgeve.
Elisabethe Cruciger d. (1535)   Tr. *Bishop Myles Coverdale*[1].

HERR GOTT, NUN SEI GEPREISET.

  i. O God in heaven we praise Thee
     And yield Thee gratitude
     For all Thy generous bounty,
     For all our daily food,
     For all the love showered on us,
     For all the grace poured on us,
     By Thee, our loving Lord.

 ii. And if these gifts of plenty
     Our appetites should tempt,
     Should draw our service from Thee,
     And bring us to contempt;
     O still in mercy spare us,
     Nor from Thy pity tear us,
     Through Jesus Christ Thy Son.

iii. And as Thou hast our members,
     Refresh also our soul,
     Expel all vile distempers,
     In Christ make us all whole;
     So shall we, ill declining,
     Our wills to Thine resigning,
     Live ever in Thy sight.
Anon.   Tr. *C. S. T.*[2]

[1] *Remains*, p. 553. The original hymn has five stanzas, of which Coverdale (corrected above) reverses the order of iii and iv.
[2] The original hymn has three stanzas.

Elisabethe Cruciger's Christmas hymn, "Herr Christ, der ein'ge Gottes-Sohn," was published, with the melody, in Walther's Hymn-book (1524). The tune appears to be an adaptation, probably by Walther himself, of the secular melody "Ich hört ein Fräulein klagen[1]." It occurs in the Organ movements *infra* and Cantatas 22, 96, 132, 164 (1715– *c.* 1740). Bach's text is practically invariable. For the seventh note of the second line of the melody *supra* he always prefers A to F. In that particular he follows Witt's text (No. 17).

The melody is found in two Organ movements:

[55]

N. xv. 9. The movement is one of the Advent Preludes in the *Orgelbüchlein*. Bach gives the alternative title of the anonymous "Herr Gott, nun sei gepreiset" (published in Babst's Hymn-book, 1553), to which the tune is set in Witt's Hymn-book. The hymn, however, a Grace after Meat, is included by Witt among his "Tisch-Gesänge," its stanzas have no connexion with the Christmas festival and certainly were not in Bach's mind[2], though Walther's(?) melody was associated with them since 1609. The rhythmic motive which Bach introduces into the

---

[1] See *Bach's Chorals*, Part II. 186, for the tune.

[2] Why Schweitzer, II. 63, quotes the movement by this secondary title is not clear. He thereby associates a motive of "beatific peace" with thanksgiving for food and drink!

HERR CHRIST, DER EIN'GE GOTTES-SOHN

Pedal expresses joyful adoration of the God-Child, to whose birth the Advent season looks forward.

[56]

N. xviii. 43. A Fughetta upon the first line of the melody. The second line is introduced at the eleventh bar. The movement is among the miscellaneous Preludes. Four MSS. of it exist, one of which, in Kittel's hand, concludes with a simple four-part setting of the melody (printed in P. v. 107).

HERR GOTT DICH LOBEN WIR.

Lord God, Thee praise do we.
Lord, we give thanks to Thee.
Thee, Father, eternal God,
Earth praises, far and broad.
All angels and heaven's host,
All that in Thy service boast,
The cherubim and seraphim,
Sing Thee ever with lofty hymn:
Holy is our Lord God!
Holy is our Lord God!
Holy is our Lord God, the God of Sabaoth.
Thy godlike might and lordship go
Wide over heaven and earth below.
To Thee the holy twelve do call,
And Thy beloved prophets all.
The precious martyrs, with one voice,
Praise Thee, O Lord, with mighty noise.
From all Thy worthy Christendom
Every day Thy praises come.
Thee God, the Father, on highest throne,
Thy true and only-begotten Son,

The holy Comforter always,
With service true they thank and praise.
Thou, King of Glory, Christ, alone
Art the Father's eternal Son;
Did'st not the Virgin's womb despise,
That so the human race might rise;
Thou on the might of Death didst tread,
And Christians all to heaven hast led.
Thou sittest now at God's right hand,
With honours all in Thy Father's land.
The hour shall come when Thou shalt yet
Judge of the dead and living sit.
Now to Thy servants help afford,
Ransomed with Thy dear blood, O Lord.
Let us in heaven have our dole,
And with the holy be ever whole.
Thy folk, Lord Jesus Christ, advance,
And bless Thine own inheritance.
Them watch and ward, Lord, every day;
Eternally them raise, we pray.
Daily, Lord God, we honour Thee,
And praise Thy name continually.
O God of truth, keep us this day
From every sin and evil way.
Be gracious to us, Lord, we plead,
Be gracious to us in all need.
Show unto us Thy pitying grace,
For all our hope in Thee we place.
Dear Lord, our hope is in Thy name;
Let us be never put to shame.

Martin Luther (1483–1546) Tr. *George Macdonald*[1].

Luther's version of the "Te Deum laudamus"
was published first in Klug's Hymn-book (1535

---

[1] *Exotics*, p. 112.

HERR GOTT DICH LOBEN WIR

[1529]). The melody is a simplified form of the Latin plainsong. Bach introduces portions of it into Cantatas 16, 119, 120, and 190 (1720–30), and treats it as a whole in the Organ movement *infra*:

[57]

N. xviii. 44. The movement is a complete five-part accompaniment to the hymn for congregational singing, and may be compared with a four-part setting of it in the *Choralgesänge*, No. 133. The source of the text of the movement is an old MS. which belonged to Johann Nikolaus Forkel (1749–1818).

HERR GOTT, NUN SCHLEUSS DEN HIMMEL AUF.

Melody: "*Herr Gott, nun schleuss den Himmel auf*"
Johann Michael Altenburg 1620

Witt's reconstruction 1715

i. Lord God, now open wide Thy heaven,
   My parting hour is near;
   My course is run, enough I've striven,
   Enough I've suffered here;
   Weary and sad
   My heart is glad
   That she may lay her down to rest;
   Now all on earth I can resign,
   But only let Thy heaven be mine.

ii. As Thou, Lord, hast commanded me,
    Have I with perfect faith
    Embraced my Saviour, and to Thee
    I calmly look in death;

With willing heart
I hence depart,
I hope to stand before Thy face :
Yes, all on earth I can resign,
If but Thy heaven at last be mine.

iii. Then let me go like Simeon
In peace with Thee to dwell,
For I commend me to Thy Son,
And He will guard me well,
And guide me straight
To the golden gate :
And in this hope I calmly die ;
Yes, all on earth I can resign,
If but Thy heaven may now be mine.

Tobias Kiel (1584–1626)   Tr. *Catherine Winkworth*[1].

Tobias Kiel's "Herr Gott, nun schleuss den Himmel auf," was first published in the first Part of Johann Michael Altenburg's *Christliche, Liebliche Und Andechtige, Newe Kirchen und Hauss Gesänge* (Erfurt, 1620), with a five-part setting of the melody (*supra*).

Kiel was born at Ballstädt, near Gotha, in 1584. Educated at Jena, he became pastor at Ballstädt and died there in 1626. The hymn was written for the Feast of the Purification, but was also in use for the Dying, in which mood Bach treats it.

Johann Michael Altenburg, the composer of the melody, was born at Alach, near Erfurt, in 1584. His life was spent in and round Erfurt as teacher

---

[1] *Lyra Germanica* (second series, London, 1868), p. 232. The original hymn has three stanzas.

and pastor. He died there in 1640. He was a good musician and at one time was precentor in Erfurt. Bach's version of the melody is a combination of the descant and Quinta vox of Altenburg's five-part setting. Bach, however, was not the author of the reconstruction. In the Gotha *Cantional* of 1646 the positions of the descant and Quinta vox of 1620 are reversed, the latter becoming the melody. Witt (No. 81), in 1715, formed a new melody by piecing together parts of the original descant and Quinta vox[1]. His version passed into the Hymn-books of Telemann (1730), König (1738), and Freylinghausen (1741). His variation of the second phrase seemingly is his own. Bach uses the tune only in the *Orgelbüchlein*.

[58]

N. xv. 53. The movement represents the Feast of the Purification in the *Orgelbüchlein*. Bach depicts the faltering footsteps of the aged Simeon (stanza iii) by means of a syncopated and halting Pedal rhythm. His addition of a "second" or Quinta vox to the *cantus* was clearly suggested by the history of the tune. It is taken from Witt's four-part setting of the melody, excepting the first note of the eighteenth and last note of the twenty-second bars, which are not congruous to Witt's figuring.

[1] The arrows are introduced into the setting *supra* to show the method of the reconstructed melody.

HERR JESU CHRIST, DICH ZU UNS WEND'.

Melody: "Herr Jesu Christ, dich zu uns wend'" Anon. 1648

* The accidental is not found in the 1651 text.

i. Lord Christ, reveal Thy holy face,
And send the Spirit of Thy grace,
To fill our hearts with fervent zeal,
To learn Thy truth, and do Thy will.

ii. Lord, lead us in Thy holy ways,
And teach our lips to tell Thy praise;
Revive our hope, our faith increase,
To taste the sweetness of Thy grace:

iii. Till we with angels join to sing
Eternal praise to Thee, our King;
Till we behold Thy face most bright,
In joy and everlasting light.

iv. To God the Father, God the Son,
And God the Spirit, Three in One,
Be honour, praise, and glory given
By all on earth and all in heaven.

? Duke William II of Saxe-Weimar
(1598-1662)   Tr. *John Christian Jacobi*[1].

The hymn, "Herr Jesu Christ, dich zu uns wend'," was first published (stanzas i–iii) in Johann Niedling's *Lutherisch Hand-Büchlein* (Altenburg, 1648). It was repeated, with the melody (*supra*)

[1] *Moravian Hymn-book*, ed. 1877, No. 733. The original hymn has four stanzas.

and the fourth stanza, in the *Cantionale Sacrum* (Gotha, 1651). The hymn is attributed, on inconclusive evidence, to William II, Duke of Saxe-Weimar. He was born in 1598, studied music, among other subjects, at Jena, fought in the Thirty Years' War on the Protestant side, and died in 1662. The hymn is entitled "Frommer Christen Hertzens-Seufftzerlein umb Gnade und Beystand des Heiligen Geistes, bey dem Gottesdienst vor den Predigten" (A heartfelt petition of pious Christians for grace and the help of the Holy Spirit, during Divine Service before the sermon). It was in use in Saxony on all Sundays and festivals.

The melody (*supra*) attached to the hymn in 1651 is found three years earlier in an octavo volume published at Görlitz, entitled *Pensum sacrum, Metro-Rhythmicum, CCLXVII Odis...denuo expansum expensumque Opera et Studio Tobiae Hauschkonii* (1648), whose Appendix contains eighty melodies, without texts, suitable for the Latin odes in the volume. Among them (No. 45) is the melody printed *supra*. It occurs among several old hymn tunes, and, no doubt, dates from an older period than the volume in which it first appears. Bach's text of the melody is invariable and follows the 1648 text except in the *Choralgesänge*, No. 139, where he follows Witt (No. 240) in a variation of the end of the second phrase of the tune.

HERR JESU CHRIST, DICH ZU UNS WEND' 193

Probably it is not an unrelated coincidence that the number of Bach's Organ movements upon the melody equals the number of stanzas of the hymn. Their differing moods and appropriateness to a particular stanza support the assumption that Bach had the text of the hymn before him and followed it closely. The four movements are discussed in the order of their assumed association with the hymn text:

[59]

N. xv. 99. Throughout the *Orgelbüchlein*, Schweitzer supposes[1], Bach employs a motive derived from the Choral only "when there is a meaning in the repetition of the words." If that is so, he brings out conspicuously here the words "Herr Jesu Christ" in imitation throughout the movement, an emphasis of the initial invocation which would not appear to be demanded[2].

[60]

N. xviii. 50. The movement, one of the miscellaneous Preludes, is quiet and reflective in mood. The undulations of melodic treatment permit the conjecture that Bach had in mind the words of the second stanza:

Lord, lead us in Thy holy ways.

Eight MSS. of the movement are extant, in the Kirnberger and Voss Collections and elsewhere.

[1] Vol. II. 67.   [2] See also Sec. 54 *supra*.

[61]

N. xvii. 26. The movement is one of the *Eighteen Chorals*, a Trio upon the melody, jubilant in mood and attuned to the third stanza of the hymn :

> Till we with angels join to sing
> Eternal praise to Thee, our King;
> Till we behold Thy face most bright,
> In joy and everlasting light.

Spitta points out[1] that Bach follows Pachelbel here in forming a theme out of the opening phrase of the *cantus* and, after developing it adequately, bringing in the complete melody on the Pedal. A Fugue upon "Allein Gott in der Höh' sei Ehr'" (N. xviii. 7) shows similar treatment.

Peters' Edition (P. vi. 107, 108) prints two older readings of the movement, the first of which exists in a MS. in Oley's hand, and the second is among Johann Ludwig Krebs' MSS. The Berlin Royal Library has a third MS. of the movement (B.G. xxv. (2) 160) of recent and minor authority.

[62]

N. xviii. 52. An Organ accompaniment of the tune. Parry suggests[2] that the movement, like others of its kind[3], was written for the instruction

---

[1] Vol. I. 615.   [2] *Op. cit.* 502.
[3] See "Allein Gott" (N. xviii. 4), "Gelobet seist du" (N. xviii. 37), "In dulci jubilo" (N. xviii. 61), "Lobt Gott, ihr Christen" (N. xviii. 74), "Herr Gott dich loben wir" (N. xviii. 44), and "Vom Himmel hoch" (N. xix. 19).

HERR JESU CHRIST, DICH ZU UNS WEND' 195

of "some insufficiently discreet or experienced performer." It is not extravagant to hold the movement inspired by the fourth stanza of the hymn:

> Be honour, praise, and glory given
> By all on earth and all in heaven.

The MS. of the movement is among the Kellner MSS. in the Berlin Royal Library.

HERZLICH THUT MICH VERLANGEN.

Melody: "Herzlich thut mich verlangen"
Hans Leo Hassler 1601

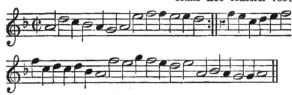

i. My heart is filled with longing
To pass away in peace;
For woes are round me thronging,
And trials will not cease.
O fain would I be hasting
From thee, dark world of gloom,
To gladness everlasting;
O Jesus, quickly come!
                Tr. *Catherine Winkworth*[1].

* * *

iv. Though worms destroy my body
Within its earth-bound grave,
Yet Christ one day shall call me
And from the tomb me save.

[1] *Chorale Book for England*, App. IV. The original hymn has eleven stanzas.

> Then, clothed in radiant glory,
> Before my God I'll sing
> Of His great love the story.
> O Death, where is thy sting!
> Christoph Knoll (1563-1650)　　　Tr. C. S. T.

Christoph Knoll's funerary hymn, "Herzlich thut mich verlangen," was first printed in 1605. Eight years later (1613) it was attached to the tune *supra*. The melody had been published four years before Knoll's hymn was written. Its composer, Hans Leo Hassler, set it in 1601 to a secular song, "Mein G'müt ist mir verwirret von einer Jungfrau zart." It is known, however, through its association with three well-known hymns—Knoll's "Herzlich thut mich verlangen" (1613), Cyriacus Schneegass' "Ach Herr, mich armen Sünder" (1620), and Gerhardt's "O Haupt voll Blut und Wunden" (1656), to which it was attached at the dates indicated. Bach uses the tune in association with all three hymns, in the Organ movement *infra*; Cantatas 25, 135, 153, 159, 161 (1715-*c.* 1740); *St Matthew Passion* (1729), Nos. 21, 23, 53, 63, 72; *Christmas Oratorio* (1734), Nos. 5, 64; *Choralgesänge*, Nos. 157, 158.

Bach's text of the *cantus* is almost invariable. He regularly substitutes C for G as the penultimate note of the melody. For the fourth note in the fourth phrase (the fifth note in line 2 *supra*) he very rarely (only in Cantatas 153, 161 (1715-24), *St Matthew Passion*, No. 72, and N. xviii. 53) follows the text of

1601; elsewhere he substitutes B flat for D. For both innovations there is early sanction; for the first, a text of 1694; for the second, a text of 1679. Witt (No. 253) adopts the first of them, but rejects the second. Bach occasionally introduces poignant variations of the original text in the second phrase of the melody (notes 8-13 *supra*). In No. 72 of the *St Matthew Passion*, No. 5 of the *Christmas Oratorio*, and the Organ movement *infra*, by a turn of the phrase he conveys an impression of wistfulness which, in the two Oratorios, certainly was suggested by the words. The fact affords a clue to the interpretation of the single Organ movement in which the melody occurs:

[63]

N. xviii. 53. The movement's poetic basis is found in the first stanza of Knoll's hymn. Bach's treatment of the melody of the second line of the stanza is inspired by the word "verlangen." As Sir Hubert Parry points out[1], Bach breaks up the melody into short phrases each one of which becomes a sigh of tender aspiration:

> My heart is filled with longing
> To pass away in peace.

The movement matches those in the *Orgelbüchlein* as an example of Bach's poetic and pictorial treatment. Hence Schweitzer's conjecture that Bach

[1] *Op. cit.* 503.

MELODIES

neglected the melody in that work—it is among its unwritten movements (No. 73)—on the ground that it "could only be developed as pure music[1]," is untenable. Spitta[2] holds the movement to have been composed during the Weimar period. Copies of it are among the Krebs and Walther MSS.

HEUT' TRIUMPHIRET GOTTES SOHN.

Melody: "Heut' triumphiret Gottes Sohn"
Bartholomäus Gesius 1601

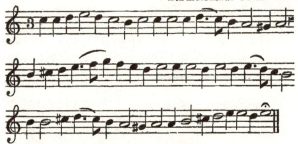

i. To-day God's only-gotten Son
Arose from death, and triumph won,
   Alleluya, Alleluya,
In mighty pomp and rich array;
His therefore be the praise alway.
   Alleluya, Alleluya.

ii. Lo! Death is crushed—nay, Death must die,
By Jesus smitten hip and thigh.
   Alleluya, Alleluya.
Like armoured knight, with skilful thrust
Christ made His foeman lick the dust.
   Alleluya, Alleluya.

[1] Vol. I. 287.   [2] Vol. I. 654.

iii. Almighty Lord of great and small,
    Redeemer of poor sinners all,
            Alleluya, Alleluya,
    Grant us, for great Thy mercy is,
    To reign with Thee in endless bliss.
            Alleluya, Alleluya.

                *   *   *

v. We hymn Thee, Christ, our living Head,
   Hereafter Judge of quick and dead.
            Alleluya, Alleluya.
   At doomsday spare us, mighty King,
   That we may always say and sing
            Alleluya, Alleluya.

vi. To God the Father on His Throne,
    To Jesus Christ, His Son alone,
            Alleluya, Alleluya.
    To God the Holy Paraclete,
    Be laud and glory infinite.
            Alleluya, Alleluya.

? Caspar Stolshagius (1591)   Tr. *G. R. Woodward*[1].

The Easter hymn, " Heut' triumphiret Gottes Sohn," appeared first in the *Kinderspiegel* (Eisleben, 1591) of Caspar Stolshagius, Lutheran pastor at Iglau, in Moravia. Whether he wrote it cannot be stated positively. It is also attributed to Jakob Ebert and Basilius Förtsch.

The melody (*supra*) is found in association with the hymn in Bartholomäus Gesius' *Geistliche deutsche Lieder*, published in 1601 at Frankfort a. Oder,

[1] *Songs of Syon* (London, 1910), No. 50. The original hymn has six stanzas, of which iv is omitted in the translation.

where Gesius at that time was Cantor. The tune appears in 1601 for the first time and certainly was composed by Gesius himself.

Bach uses the melody in the Organ movement *infra, Choralgesänge*, No. 171, but employs different melodic texts. In the *Choralgesänge* the fourth and last phrases of the tune do not follow the original. In the Organ movement, excepting the last three bars, which are an added "Alleluya," he follows the 1601 text and Witt, who also (No. 145) has three concluding "Alleluyas":

[64]

N. xv. 94. The movement is the last of the Easter Preludes in the *Orgelbüchlein*, instinct with the triumph of the festival[1]. The Pedal subject, as Schweitzer points out[2], is almost ferocious in its representation of the risen Christ spurning his foes as though He were treading the wine-press. In Cantata 43, written for Ascension Day (1735), the Aria "'Tis He Who all alone hath trodden well the wine-press" has a similar masterful subject[3].

[1] The Prelude is wrongly associated with Ascensiontide in the Novello Edition.
[2] Vol. II. 63.
[3] See Novello's Edition, *God goeth up with shouting*, p. 22.

Hilf Gott, dass mir's gelinge.

Melody: "Hilf Gott, dass mir's gelinge" — Anon. 1545

i. Help, God, the formar of all thing,
That to Thy gloir may be my dyte;
Be baith at end and beginning,
That I may mak ane sang perfyte
Of Jesus Christis Passioun,
Sinnaris onlie Saluatioun,
As witnes is Thy word in write.
* * *
iii. Jesus, the Fatheris word allone,
Discendit in ane Virgin pure,
With meruellis greit and mony one,
And be Judas, that fals tratour,
That Lamb for sober summe was sauld,
And gaif His lyfe, for cause He wald
Redeme all sinfull Creature.
* * *
viii. That Prince on Croce thay lyftit on hicht
For our Redemptioun, that thocht sa lang:
He said, I thrist, with all my micht,
To saif mankynde fra panis strang.
He that all warldis was beforne
Come downe of Marie to be borne,
For our trespas on Croce He hang.
ix. Than He His heid culd inclyne,
As wrytis Johne, and gaif the Gaist,
And of the Croce taine was syne,
And laid in graue; bot sune in haist
Leuand He rais, on the thrid day,
And to His Apostillis did say,
To thame appeirand maist and leist.
x. And syne He did His Apostillis teiche
Throw all the warld for to pas,
And till all Creature for to preiche,
As thay of Him instructit was.
Quha bapteist is, and will beleue,
Eternall deide sall nocht thame greue,
Bot salbe sauit mair and les.
* * *

xii. Ane confortour to us He did send,
Quhilk from the Father did proceid,
To gyde us trewlie to the end,
In inwart thocht and outward deid.
Call on the Lord, our gyde and lycht,
To leide us in His Law full rycht,
And be our help in all our neid.

xiii. Pray for all men in generall,
Suppose thay wirk us richt or wrang:
Pray for zour Prince in speciall.
Thocht thay be Just or Tyranis strang,
Obey; for sa it aucht to be.
In presoun for the veritie,
Ane faithfull brother maid this sang[1].

Heinrich Müller (1527)   Tr. *Gude and Godlie Ballatis*[2].

This hymn or ballad of the Passion was written by Heinrich Müller—the initial letters of its thirteen stanzas spell "Heinrich Müler." The last two lines of the last stanza repeat his name, and state that the hymn was written by him in prison[1]. He appears to have been a Lutheran of Nürnberg, imprisoned, *circa* 1527, by the Duke of Saxony. Released in 1539, he conducted a school at Annaberg until about 1580. The ballad was published as a broadsheet in 1527 and was included in the Rostock Hymn-book of 1531. Luther thought

[1]   Hat Heinrich Müller gesungen
      In dem Gefängniss sein.

[2] P. 42. The original hymn has thirteen stanzas, all of which are translated in the *Ballatis*. The translator interpolates a stanza between v and vi of the German.

so highly of it that he introduced it into Valentin Babst's *Geistliche Lieder* (Leipzig, 1545), the last Hymn-book issued under his supervision. The first of the three melodies (*supra*) was attached to it there. The author of the tune is not known. It is found in many forms in the late sixteenth and early seventeenth century Hymn-books and probably is of secular origin. The earliest approximation to the form in which Bach knew it is found in 1573 (*supra*). From 1601 the first half of the tune definitely took the form Bach uses. For the second part of the melody he is not consistent. In the *Orgelbüchlein* he follows the 1573 text (the F sharp that ends his sixth line is as old as 1609). In the *Choralgesänge*, No. 172, he prefers Crüger's (1653) text (*supra*). Witt's (No. 94) has peculiarities which Bach does not repeat.

[65]

N. xv. 76. The animation of this movement, one of the Passiontide Preludes in the *Orgelbüchlein*, is hardly congruous to the mood of Müller's hymn. Influenced by the character of the melody, Bach would appear not to have looked beyond the words "ditty" and "perfect song" in the first stanza. The incessant stream of semiquaver triplets appears to be called into being by the word "fröhlich":

> Dass ich mög fröhlich heben an
> Von deinem Wort zu singen.

The low F sharp on the Pedal in the last bar is an emendation by Bach himself. In the Mendelssohn Autograph he wrote

ICH HAB' MEIN SACH' GOTT HEIMGESTELLT.
Melody: "*Ich weiss mir ein Röslein hübsch und fein*"
Anon. 1589

[1] Spitta, I. 651.

i. My cause is God's, and I am still,
Let Him do with me as He will;
Whether for me the race is won,
Or scarce begun,
I ask no more—His will be done!
* * *
xi. My sins are more than I can bear,
Yet not for this will I despair;
I know to death and to the grave
The Father gave
His dearest Son, that He might save.
* * *
xiii. To Him I live and die alone,
Death cannot part Him from His own;
Living or dying, I am His
Who only is
Our comfort, and our gate of bliss.
xiv. This is my solace, day by day,
When snares and death beset my way,
I know that at the morn of doom
From out the tomb
With joy to meet Him I shall come.
* * *
xvi. Then I shall see God face to face,
I doubt it not, through Jesu's grace,
Amid the joys prepared for me!
Thanks be to Thee
Who givest us the victory!
* * *
xviii. Amen, dear God! now send us faith,
And at the last a happy death;
And grant us all ere long to be
In heaven with Thee,
To praise Thee there eternally.

Johannes Leon (d. 1597)   Tr. *Catherine Winkworth*[1].

[1] *Chorale Book for England,* No. 127. The original hymn has eighteen stanzas, of which ii–x, xii, xv, xvii are omitted in the translation.

ICH HAB' MEIN SACH' GOTT HEIMGESTELLT 207

Johannes Leon's hymn, "Ich hab' mein Sach' Gott heimgestellt," was first published in *Psalmen, geistliche Lieder und Kirchengesäng* (Nürnberg, 1589). The author was born at Ohrdruf, near Gotha, and after service as an army chaplain became pastor at Königsee and Wölfis. He died at Wölfis in 1597. Associated with Leon's hymn are two melodies, both of which are used by Bach, and are traced to the same origin, a four-part setting (*supra*) of the secular song "Ich weiss mir ein Röslein hübsch und fein," published by Johann Rhau in 1589. The Tenor of the setting becomes the melody of Leon's hymn in a Hymn-book dated 1609[1] and in Witt (No. 317). Bach introduces it into the orchestral accompaniment of Cantata 106 (1711). Meanwhile, the descant melody of the 1589 four-part setting also became attached to Leon's hymn in David Wolder's Hymn-book, published in 1598. Bach uses this tune in the Organ movements *infra*, and there is a four-part setting of it among the *Choralgesänge*, No. 182. Bach's text is practically invariable. The D natural which he substitutes for F natural as the fourth note of the melody (*supra*) has early (1611) sanction. His variant of the opening of the second line of the stanza (notes 3-5 of line 2 *supra*) follows a reconstruction of the melody which

[1] It is printed in *Bach's Chorals*, Part II. 344.

became the accepted form of the tune in Hymnbooks after 1601, when it first appears.

[66]

N. xviii. 54. The movement treats in fugue the five phrases of the *cantus*. MSS. of the movement are among the Kirnberger and Oley MSS. and four other copies are extant. The B.G. Edition ascribes it confidently to Bach's early period, and Spitta[1] attributes it to Walther. There does not appear to be any close relation between it and the stanzas of the hymn. Five of the six MSS. of it conclude with a plain four-part harmonization of the tune, having a certain amount of free figure work. It is omitted from the Novello Edition, and printed in P. vi. 77.

[67]

N. xviii. 58. The two arrangements come from different sources. The first (A) is found in Kirnberger's, Voss', and three other MSS. The second (B) occurs in a much later (1836) text and is misleadingly described in the B.G. Edition as a " Variant " of A. Both settings are plain four-part harmonizations of the tune, of greater simplicity than that appended to No. 66 *supra*.

---

[1] Vol. i. 656.

209

ICH RUF' ZU DIR, HERR JESU CHRIST.

Melody: "Ich ruf' zu dir, Herr Jesu Christ"
Anon. 1535

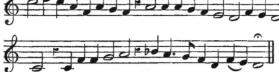

i. Lord, hear the voice of my complaint,
To Thee I now commend me,
Let not my heart and hope grow faint,
But deign Thy grace to send me.
True faith from Thee, my God, I seek,
The faith that loves Thee solely,
Keeps me lowly,
And prompt to aid the weak,
And mark each word that Thou dost speak.

ii. Yet more from Thee I dare to claim,
Whose goodness is unbounded;
Oh let me ne'er be put to shame,
My hope be ne'er confounded;
But e'en in death still find Thee true,
And in that hour, else lonely,
Trust Thee only,
Not aught that I can do,
For such false trust I sore should rue.

iii. Oh grant that from my very heart
My foes be all forgiven;
Forgive my sins and heal their smart,
And grant new life from heaven;

T. B. C.

Thy word, that blessed food, bestow,
Which best the soul can nourish;
Make it flourish
Through all the storms of woe
That else my faith might overthrow.

iv. Then be the world my foe or friend,
Keep me to her a stranger,
Thy steadfast soldier to the end,
Through pleasure and through danger.
From Thee alone comes such high grace,
No works of ours obtain it,
Or can gain it;
Our pride hath here no place,
'Tis Thy free promise we embrace.

v. Help me, for I am weak; I fight,
Yet scarce can battle longer;
I cling but to Thy grace and might,
'Tis Thou must make me stronger.
When sore temptations are my lot,
And tempests round me lower,
Break their power.
So, through deliverance wrought,
I know that Thou forsak'st me not!

Johannes Agricola (1492-1566)   Tr. *Catherine Winkworth*[1].

Johannes Agricola's hymn, "Ich ruf' zu dir, Herr Jesu Christ," was published, along with the anonymous melody (*supra*) in Klug's Hymn-book in 1535 [1529]. The tune is also used by Bach in the *Orgelbüchlein* and Cantatas 177, 185 (1715-32). His text of it is invariable and follows Witt's (No. 299).

[1] *Chorale Book for England*, No. 116. The original hymn has five stanzas.

ICH RUF' ZU DIR, HERR JESU CHRIST 211

[68]

N. xv. 111. The movement is the only completed number in the "Christian Life and Experience" section of Part II of the *Orgelbüchlein*. It may be conjectured that, when he wrote it, Bach had before him particularly the first stanza of the hymn. His treatment of the melody of the first two lines of the stanza conveys a wistfulness of appeal that may have been suggested by the words

> Lord, hear the voice of my complaint,
> To Thee I now commend me.

Underneath this petition the Pedal asserts a firm and confident rhythm which seems to express the

> True faith from Thee, my God, I seek

of the fifth line, and may be compared with the steadfast procession of Pedal crotchets in the "Credo in unum Deum" of the B minor Mass, which symbolizes the unshakable solidarity of the Church's faith.

IN DICH HAB' ICH GEHOFFET, HERR.

Melody: "*Erstanden ist uns Jesus Christ*"   Anon. 1555

Melody: *"In dich hab' ich gehoffet, Herr"*

Seth Calvisius 1581

i. In Thee, Lord, have I put my trust,
Leave me not helpless in the dust,
Let not my hope be brought to shame,
But still sustain,
Through want and pain,
My faith that Thou art aye the same.

ii. Incline a gracious ear to me,
And hear the prayers I raise to Thee,
Show forth Thy power and haste to save!
For woes and fear
Surround me here;
Oh swiftly send the help I crave!

iii. My God and Shield, now let Thy power
Be unto me a mighty tower,
Whence I may freely, bravely, fight
Against the foes
That round me close,
For fierce are they and great their might.

iv. Thy Word hath said, Thou art my Rock,
The Stronghold that can fear no shock,
My help, my safety, and my life,
Howe'er distress
And dangers press;
What then shall daunt me in the strife?

IN DICH HAB' ICH GEHOFFET, HERR

v. The world for me hath falsely set
Full many a secret snare and net,
Dark lies, delusions sweet and vain;
Lord, hear my prayers,
And break these snares,
And make my path before me plain.

vi. With Thee, Lord, would I cast my lot;
My God, my God, forsake me not,
O faithful God, for I commend
My soul to Thee.
Deliver me,
Both now and when this life must end.

Adam Reissner (1496–c. 1575)   Tr. *Catherine Winkworth*[1].

Adam Reissner's hymn, "In dich hab' ich gehoffet, Herr," based on Psalm 31, was first published in 1533[2]. In the sixteenth century two tunes attached themselves to it, both of which Bach uses.

[69]

N. xv. 113. The movement is the second in the "In Time of Trouble" section of the *Orgelbüchlein*. It is described as "alio modo," *i.e.* the melody Bach uses is different from that to which the hymn is set in Witt (No. 606). Bach's tune, a pre-Reformation Easter melody, occurs in a fifteenth century MS. now in the Royal Library, Berlin, set to the hymn "Christ ist erstanden" or "Christus ist erstanden."

---
[1] *Chorale Book for England*, No. 120. The original hymn has seven stanzas, of which the last is omitted in the translation.

[2] See *Bach's Chorals*, Part I. 17.

It is found in print, set to the latter hymn, in 1536. In 1555 Valentin Triller, describing it as old and well-known, set it to the Easter hymn "Erstanden ist uns Jesus Christ." Five years later, with an altered last line, the tune was attached to Reissner's "In dich hab' ich gehoffet, Herr," in the Strasbourg *Gros Kirchen Gesangbuch* (1560). The Easter associations of the tune throw light upon Bach's treatment of it in this movement.

[70]

N. xviii. 59. The second of the two melodies is used in this Fughetta. The tune (*supra*) by Seth Calvisius, one of Bach's predecessors in the Cantorate of St Thomas', Leipzig, was first published in association with Reissner's hymn in 1581. Elsewhere Bach uses it in the *St Matthew Passion* (1729), No. 38; *Christmas Oratorio* (1734), No. 46; Cantatas 52, 106 (1711–c. 1730); *Choralgesänge*, No. 212. His melodic text is practically invariable and shows marked divergencies from the 1581 form. His first phrase is found in Witt (No. 606). His closing cadence is in Schein (1627). He differs from Witt in his treatment of phrases 4 and 5, and his version is not traceable in Zahn. Perhaps it is his own. Only in the Fughetta (N. xviii. 59) does he follow the original and Witt in those phrases, with a single variation—B flat for A as the first note of phrase 5 (the second note of line 3 *supra*).

IN DICH HAB' ICH GEHOFFET, HERR

In this movement, as in No. 69 *supra*, Bach's exegesis of Reissner's hymn does not travel beyond the first line of stanza i. It exhibits a mood of confidence and trust which this happy Fughetta reflects. Copies of it are among the Kirnberger, Voss, and Oley MSS.

IN DIR IST FREUDE.

Melody: "*O Gott, mein Herre*"   G. G. Gastoldi 1609

Melody: "*In dir ist Freude*"   Witt's version 1715

i. In Thee is gladness
   Amid all sadness,
   Jesus, Sunshine of my heart!
   By Thee are given
   The gifts of heaven,
   Thou the true Redeemer art!
   Our souls Thou wakest,
   Our bonds Thou breakest,
   Who trusts Thee surely
   Hath built securely,
   He stands for ever: Hallelujah!
   Our hearts are pining
   To see Thy shining,
   Dying or living
   To Thee are cleaving,
   Nought can us sever: Hallelujah!
ii. If He is ours
    We fear no powers,
    Nor of earth, nor sin, nor death;
    He sees and blesses
    In worst distresses,
    He can change them with a breath!
    Wherefore the story
    Tell of His glory
    With heart and voices;
    All heaven rejoices
    In Him for ever: Hallelujah!
    We shout for gladness,
    Triumph o'er sadness,
    Love Thee and praise Thee,
    And still shall raise Thee
    Glad hymns for ever: Hallelujah!

? Johann Lindemann (c. 1550–1634)
                    Tr. *Catherine Winkworth*[1].

[1] *Chorale Book for England*, No. 156. The original hymn has two stanzas.

The hymn, "In dir ist Freude," is found first in Johann Lindemann's *Amorum Filii Dei decades duae*, published, perhaps at Erfurt, in 1598. It is there entitled "Liebe zu Jesu" (A hymn of love for Jesus), the collection of twenty hymns being described in the subtitle as "Weyhenachten Gesenglein" (Little Christmas Songs). The hymn, which appears without any indication of its authorship, has been attributed to Lindemann himself, but cannot positively be regarded as his.

Lindemann was born at Gotha *circa* 1550, and from 1571 or 1572 to 1631 held a post there which he describes on his title-page as "Der Kirchen und Schulen zu Gotha Cantor und Musicus" (Cantor and Musicus of the Churches and Schools at Gotha). He died after 1634. The hymn passed into general use as a Christmas hymn.

The melody (*supra*), which at least from 1663 has been regarded as proper to the hymn, is by Giovanni Giacomo Gastoldi. He was born at Caravaggio *circa* 1556, and was successively Capellmeister at Mantua and Milan (1592). He died at Milan in 1622.

In 1591 Gastoldi published at Venice a set of "Balletti." Among them is one entitled "L'innamorato: A lieta vita: à 5," which, in 1609, was inserted as a hymn tune in David Spaiser's *Vier und zwainzig Geystliche Lieder, Sambt ihren aignen*

Welsch- und Teutschen Melodeyen. The tune is set there to Spaiser's hymn, "O Gott, mein Herre," whose eight-lined stanza the tune exactly fitted. In 1663, if not earlier[1], it was attached to Lindemann's (?) hymn in Nikolaus Stenger's *Christlich-Neu-vermehrt und gebessertes Gesangbuch* (Erfurt), each half of the tune being repeated in order to fit the sixteen-lined stanza.

It is worthy of remark that three of Gastoldi's dance measures (1591) passed into use as hymn tunes, and Spaiser included them all in his volume. One of them—"A lieta vita"—eventually was attached to "In dir ist Freude"; the other two also were set to Lindemann's (?) texts: "Viver lieto voglio" to "Jesu, wollst uns weisen"; and "Questa dolce sirena" to "Wohlauf, ihr Musicanten."

Bach treats the melody in a single Organ movement:

[71]

N. xv. 45. The New Year Prelude pulses with joy, the *basso ostinato* being particularly animated. The trills in the last eight bars, Schweitzer supposes[2], "correspond to the 'Alleluia' of the text." In fact

---

[1] According to Winkworth (Index, p. xi) the association is found in the Gotha *Cantionale Sacrum* of 1646. If so, Witt's reconstruction of the tune is the more noteworthy in relation to Bach's treatment of the melody.

[2] Vol. II. 69.

the "Hallelujah" falls only in the last bar of the movement.

The *cantus* is not clearly laid out in the movement. The first statement of the first half of the tune begins at bar 4 of the middle stave on page 45 of the Novello Edition and ends on bar 5 of the third stave. The repetition of the first half begins at bar 4 of the middle stave on page 46 and ends at the first bar on page 47. The first statement of the second half of the tune begins at bar 3 of the middle stave of page 47 and ends at the first bar of the second stave on page 48. The second statement of the second half begins at the second bar of the middle stave of page 48. Bach follows Witt's (No. 62) text, which differs materially from the original[1].

The Prelude, as Spitta points out[2], is a free handling of the melody in the manner of Böhm. Its brilliant executive requirements are somewhat foreign to the collection in which it occurs. Spitta therefore concluded that "undoubtedly" it is of an earlier date than the other contents of the *Orgelbüchlein*. But Bach's evident reliance on Witt's text affords a reason for challenging Spitta's inference.

[1] A harmonization of the 1609 melody is in the *Chorale Book for England*, No. 156.
[2] Vol. I. 603.

In Dulci Jubilo.

Melody: "*In dulci jubilo*" Anon. 1535

   i. *In dulci jubilo*,
     Now lat us sing with myrth and jo.
     Our hartis consolatioun
     Lyis *in praesepio*,
     And schynis as the Sone,
     Matris in gremio;
     Alpha es et O,
     Alpha es et O.

  ii. *O Jesu parvule!*
     I thrist sore efter The,
     Confort my hart and mynde;
     O puer optime,
     God of all grace sa kynde,
     Et princeps gloriae,
     Trahe me post te,
     Trahe me post te.

IN DULCI JUBILO 221

   iii. *Ubi sunt gaudia*
      In ony place bot thair,
      Quhair that the Angellis sing
      Nova cantica,
      Bot and the bellis ring
      In regis curia;
      God gif I war thair,
      God gif I war thair.
Anon.   Tr. *Gude and Godlie Ballatis*[1].

The mediaeval Christmas hymn, "In dulci jubilo," a macaronic partly German, partly Latin, dates from the early part of the fifteenth century, or earlier. It is found in various forms, of from three to eight stanzas in length. The ancient melody of the hymn was printed for the first time in Joseph Klug's *Geistliche Lieder zu Wittenberg* (Wittenberg, 1535 [1529]).

Besides a four-part setting of it in *Choralgesänge*, No. 215, the melody is treated in two Organ movements. Witt (No. 36), it may be remarked, has B natural for the fifth and thirteenth notes of the tune (*supra*):

[72]

N. xv. 26. The Christmas movement is a canon on the octave between the Bass and Treble, against a florid background in Bach's characteristic "joy" rhythm. In the original Autograph the Pedal part

[1] *Scottish Text Society* (1897), p. 53. The translation is of a three-stanza version dated 1550.

is written for an 8ft. stop and is carried up to F sharp. A Pedal of that natural compass was unusual then and remains unusual now. Spitta infers[1] that Bach used the Weimar Castle 4ft. Cornet stop on the Pedals. But in a movement of very similar construction, "Gottes Sohn ist kommen" (N. xv. 5), where the Pedal is carried up to F natural, Bach's own direction is "Ped. Tromp. 8 F." In N. xv. 26 the Pedal is transposed down an octave.

[73]

N. xviii. 61. A brilliant treatment of the melody, inspired, it is impossible to doubt, by the third stanza of the hymn, a vision of the heavenly halls:

> Quhair that the Angellis sing
> *Nova cantica,*
> Bot and the bellis ring
> *In regis curia.*

If, as certainly was the case, the movement was designed to accompany the congregational singing of the hymn, we can understand, though not be tempted to associate ourselves with, the complaint of the Arnstadt Consistory against Bach, February 21, 1706: "Charge him with having been hitherto in the habit of making surprising *variationes* in the chorals, and intermixing divers strange sounds, so

---

[1] Vol. I. 602.

that thereby the congregation were confounded[1]."
It is in the Christmas hymns particularly—judging by the examples that survive—that Bach painted the glorious pictures which their melodies summoned before his responsive mind.

Of this movement Spitta writes finely[2]: "The first lines are brought out in majestic five-part harmony below the notes of the melody. But from the third line the flood of ornate imagery which is poured in among them can no longer be held back. It spreads out under cover of the upper part, becomes visible during the pauses between the sections, sometimes makes its way to the highest part, overspreading the melody for a little space; then, hurried on into triplets, it surges from the depths with added force, and returns to calm only on the last line but one, where the master restores the peace that ruled at the beginning, and builds up at last a seven-part harmony on the tonic pedal, which is held through several bars. As we contemplate such a piece as this, some dim idea steals over us of the form it must have assumed under Bach's fingers, when, wrapt in the ecstasy of religious inspiration, he called up visions of celestial palaces, appearing and vanishing in an instant, and golden cloud-castles, the sublime and visionary birthplace of these sacred voices and pious melodies."

[1] Spitta, I. 315.   [2] *Ibid.* 596.

224 MELODIES

The movement comes to us through a MS. once in the possession of Johann Christian Kittel[1], who died in 1809. He was the last of Bach's pupils. Krebs also preserved a sketch of it.

B.G. xl. 158 prints a "Variant" of the movement from a Krebs MS. in the Royal Library, Berlin. It is significant of their purpose that these examples of the art of accompanying survive generally in the collections of Bach's pupils.

JESU, MEINE FREUDE.

(1) Witt has C♯.   (2) Witt has F♮.

i. Jesu, priceless treasure,
Source of purest pleasure,
Truest Friend to me;
Ah! how long I've panted,
And my heart hath fainted,
Thirsting, Lord, for Thee!
Thine I am, O spotless Lamb,
I will suffer nought to hide Thee,
Nought I ask beside Thee.

[1] Peters, v. 103.

JESU, MEINE FREUDE

ii. In Thine arm I rest me,
Foes who would molest me
Cannot reach me here;
Though the earth be shaking,
Every heart be quaking,
Jesus calms my fear;
Sin and hell in conflict fell
With their bitter storms assail me;
Jesus will not fail me.

* * *

iv. Wealth, I will not heed thee,
For I do not need thee,
Jesus is my choice;
Honours, ye may glisten,
But I will not listen
To your tempting voice;
Pain or loss, nor shame nor cross,
E'er to leave my Lord shall move me,
Since He deigns to love me.

v. Farewell, thou who choosest
Earth, and heaven refusest,
Thou wilt tempt in vain;
Farewell, sins, nor blind me,
Get ye all behind me,
Come not forth again:
Past your hour, O Pride and Power;
Worldly life, thy bonds I sever,
Farewell now for ever!

vi. Hence, all fears and sadness,
For the Lord of gladness,
Jesus, enters in;
They who love the Father,
Though the storms may gather,
Still have peace within;

> Yea, whate'er I here must bear,
> Still in Thee lies purest pleasure,
> Jesu, priceless treasure!

Johann Franck (1618–77) Tr. *Catherine Winkworth*.

Johann Franck's hymn, "Jesu, meine Freude," was published, to Johann Crüger's melody (*supra*), in 1653. Bach uses it in Cantatas 12, 64, 81, 87 (*c.* 1723–35?), and a Motett (1723). A collation of his texts proves Bach to have used at different times three forms of the melody. In the Organ movements *infra* and, as far as it goes, in a fragment upon the melody in his son Friedemann's *Clavierbüchlein* (P. v. 112) he follows Witt's (No. 337) version of the 1653 text. In the Motett, Cantata 81, and *Choralgesänge*, No. 195, he prefers a version of the second and penultimate phrases of the tune not found in print, according to Zahn (No. 8032), before 1730. As the Motett and Cantata were composed in 1723–24, this version of the melody may be attributed to Bach himself, a deduction supported by the circumstance that it is printed for the first time in the Hymn-book (1730) of his Leipzig contemporary Georg Philipp Telemann. In Cantatas 64 and 87, the latter of which is assigned conjecturally to 1735, Bach employs a third form, whose source is not disclosed, the first part of which reverts to his earlier pre-Leipzig use.

[1] *Chorale Book for England*, No. 151. The original hymn has six stanzas, of which iii is omitted in the translation.

The melody is treated in two Organ movements:

[74]

N. xv. 31. The movement is among the Christmas pieces of the *Orgelbüchlein*, an act of personal devotion to the Child Saviour. Bach sets the melody in the significant rhythm which has been considered in the Preludes, " Alle Menschen " and " Herr Christ, der ein'ge Gottes-Sohn."

[75]

N. xviii. 64. The movement is a Fantasia, which Schweitzer[1] regards as a youthful work. It does not seem to be related to any particular stanza of the hymn. There are resemblances, however, between the $\frac{3}{8}$ section and Bach's setting of stanza v in the Motett on the hymn. Seven MSS. of it are extant in the Kirnberger, Voss, Fischhof, and other Collections. A variant reading is in B.G. xl. 155, from the Schelble-Gleichauf MSS.

JESUS CHRISTUS, UNSER HEILAND, DER DEN TOD.

Melody: "Jesus Christus, unser Heiland"

? Johann Walther 1524

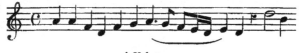

[1] Vol. I. 293.

228   MELODIES

i. Jesus Christ, our Saviour true,
   He who Death overthrew,
   Is up arisen,
   And sin hath put in prison.
                    Kyrieleison.

ii. Born Whom Mary sinless hath,
    Bore He for us God's wrath,
    Hath reconciled us—
    Favour God doth now yield us.
                    Kyrieleison.

iii. Death and sin, and life and grace,
All in His hands He has.
He can deliver
All who seek the life-giver.
Kyrieleison.

Martin Luther (1483-1546)   Tr. *George Macdonald*[1].

Luther's Easter hymn, "Jesus Christus, unser Heiland, Der den Tod überwand," was first published in 1524, in Walther's Wittenberg Hymn-book and in the Erfurt *Enchiridion*. In Walther's book it is set to the first and second melodies printed *supra*. Both are the Tenor of a four-part setting probably composed by Walther himself. In the *Enchiridion* only the second tune is found. The hymn was repeated in Klug's Hymn-book, 1535 [1529], but with a new melody, the third of those printed *supra*, which has displaced the earlier ones. Its source is not determined.

Bach uses the Klug melody in the Organ movement *infra* and *Choralgesänge*, No. 207. With one trifling exception—the substitution of G for A as the second note of the first and fourth phrases of the melody (*supra*) in the *Choralgesänge*—his two melodic texts are identical and conform to Witt's version (No. 144). Bach's (and Witt's) closing cadence dates back to 1585.

---

[1] *Exotics*, p. 54. The original hymn has three stanzas.

MELODIES

[76]

N. xv. 81. The movement is the second of the Easter Preludes in the *Orgelbüchlein*. The assertive, jubilant figure in the accompaniment expresses the triumph of which the first stanza of the hymn sings.

JESUS CHRISTUS, UNSER HEILAND, DER VON UNS.
Melody: "Jesus Christus, unser Heiland"

Martin Luther 1524

i. Christ Jesus, our Redeemer born,
Who from us did God's anger turn,
Through His sufferings sore and main,
Did help us all out of hell-pain.

ii. That we never should forget it,
Gave He us His flesh, to eat it,
Hid in poor bread, gift divine,
And, to drink, His blood in the wine.

iii. Who will draw near to that table
Must take heed, all he is able.
Who unworthy thither goes,
Thence death instead of life he knows.

iv. God the Father praise thou duly,
   That He thee would feed so truly,
   And for ill deeds by thee done
   Up unto death has given His Son.

v. Have this faith, and do not waver,
   'Tis a fool for every craver
   Who, his heart with sin opprest,
   Can no more for its anguish rest.

vi. Such kindness and such grace to get,
   Seeks a heart with agony great.
   Is it well with thee? take care,
   Lest at last thou shouldst evil fare.

vii. He doth say, Come hither, O ye
   Poor, that I may pity show ye.
   No physician th' whole man will,
   He makes a mockery of his skill.

viii. Hadst thou any claim to proffer,
   Why for thee then should I suffer?
   This table is not for thee,
   If thou wilt set thine own self free.

ix. If such faith thy heart possesses,
   And the same thy mouth confesses,
   Fit guest then thou art indeed,
   And so the food thy soul will feed.

x. But bear fruit, or lose thy labour:
   Take thou heed thou love thy neighbour;
   That thou food to him mayst be,
   As thy God makes Himself to thee.

Martin Luther (1483–1546)   Tr. *George Macdonald*[1].

The hymn is a translation, by Martin Luther, of the Eucharistic "Jesus Christus, nostra salus,"

[1] *Exotics*, p. 103. The original hymn has ten stanzas.

generally described as "St Johannes Hussen Lied," though Hus's authorship is doubtful. Luther's hymn was published in Walther's *Geystliche gesangk Buchleyn* (Wittenberg, 1524) and in *Enchiridion oder eyn Handbuchlein* (Erfurt, 1524), in both cases with the tune (*supra*). The hymn is described as "St John Hus's hymn improved." In fact only the first of its ten stanzas is based on the Latin. Luther and his musical helper, Johann Walther, appear to have discarded the old melody of the Latin hymn. The 1524 tune is attributed, without strong evidence, to Luther himself. When the hymn was repeated in Joseph Klug's *Geistliche Lieder* (Wittenberg, 1535), a tune was substituted for that of 1524, which also bears no resemblance to the Latin melody.

In *Choralgesänge*, No. 206, and the Organ movements *infra* Bach uses the 1524 melody, his text of which is invariable. His version of the second and third phrases differs from the original and is found in Witt (No. 320).

The 1524 melody appears to have been very dear to Bach. The Organ movements on it number four; two of them in the third part of the *Clavierübung*, and the other two among the *Eighteen Chorals*.

[77]

N. xvi. 74. The most striking feature of this *Clavierübung* Fantasia is the arresting "step" motive

JESUS CHRISTUS, UNSER HEILAND   233

which paces throughout it, a musical exegesis of the hymn. The striding and confident theme inculcates stedfast faith in the power of the sacrament to forgive sin. " Bach wishes," writes Schweitzer[1], " to illustrate the Lutheran dogma of the Communion. We know that Luther was opposed to the rationalism of Zwingli, who regarded the sacramental words as symbolical and the whole celebration as a simple ceremony of remembrance. To Luther the essence of the doctrine of the sacrament was faith in a real change in the elements, in virtue of which the Communion gives remission of sins." Bach shared Luther's conviction and expresses his confidence in a theme spaced extraordinarily widely. The tremendous "step" motive in the "Sanctus" of the B minor Mass may be compared with it, in which the adoration of men and angels is built upon a theme that strides in octaves and arches the heavens. In the present movement Bach clearly had the fifth stanza of Luther's hymn before him:

> Have this faith, and do not waver,
> 'Tis a fool for every craver
> Who, his heart with sin opprest,
> Can no more for its anguish rest.

[78]
N. xvi. 80. The second of the *Clavierübung* movements is in strong contrast to its predecessor.

[1] Vol. II. 61.

Fugal in form, and based on the first phrase of the melody only, it is contemplative in mood, and seems to follow No. 77 as the ninth stanza of the hymn is the corollary of the fifth:

> If such faith thy heart possesses,
> And the same thy mouth confesses,
> Fit guest then thou art indeed,
> And so the food thy soul will feed.

[79]

N. xvii. 74. When, eight or nine years after the *Clavierübung* was published, Bach included two movements upon the melody among the *Eighteen Chorals*, he approached the hymn from a different standpoint. He probably felt that the first of the *Clavierübung* movements sacrificed art to dogmatics. The first of the movements in the "Eighteen" is a Communion Prelude; alone of the four it is marked "sub communione." It is one of two Preludes—"O Lamm Gottes" (N. xvii. 32) being the other—in which Bach illustrates in their sequence the lines of the hymn text. In the present movement he selects from each of the four lines of the first stanza a particular word for illustration:

> Christ Jesus, our Redeemer born,
> Who from us did God's anger turn,
> Through His sufferings sore and main,
> Did help us all out of hell-pain.

For the first thirteen bars Bach's treatment of the *cantus* is inspired by the word "Redeemer." At the fourteenth bar he introduces a rhythm which Schweitzer likens to the accompaniment of the *Arioso* "O gracious God" (No. 60) in the *St Matthew Passion*, which recalls Christ's scourging. It suggests the strokes of God's anger, from which the Redeemer's Passion rescued mankind, and persists to the twenty-sixth bar, accompanying the second phrase of the *cantus*. At bar twenty-seven chromatic scale passages picture Christ's "bitter Leiden" (sufferings sore and main). They are woven above and below the third phrase of the *cantus* and reach their climax in the thirty-seventh bar. At bar thirty-eight the fourth phrase of the *cantus* is introduced by a short figure

which typifies the Resurrection and man's rescue from the pains of Hell. "We fancy," writes Schweitzer "we can see in this affecting ending the strong arm of the Saviour drawing mankind upward[1]."

B.G. xxv. (2) 188 (P. vi. 112) prints an older text of the movement, the MS. of which formerly was in Krebs' possession.

[80]

N. xvii. 79. The movement must have been one of the last Bach revised. The MS. of it is in his

[1] Vol. II. 73. See also Spitta, I. 613. He anticipates Schweitzer's analysis.

236   MELODIES

son-in-law Altnikol's hand[1]. It is, however, one of Bach's early works. Schweitzer[2] points to the influence of Buxtehude. Spitta[3] places the composition in the first years of Bach's residence at Weimar.

It cannot be without design that Bach devotes the last nine bars of the movement to an elaboration of the fourth phrase of the *cantus*. Consequently he emphasizes the line:

   ·Did help us all out of hell-pain.

JESUS, MEINE ZUVERSICHT.

Melody: "*Jesus, meine Zuversicht*"
? Johann Crüger 1653

  i. Jesus Christ, my sure Defence
   And my Saviour, ever liveth;
   Knowing this, my confidence
   Rests upon the hope it giveth,
   Though the night of death be fraught
   Still with many an anxious thought.

[1] Altnikol married Bach's daughter Elisabeth in 1749.
[2] Vol. I. 292.   [3] Vol. I. 613.

JESUS, MEINE ZUVERSICHT

ii. Jesus, my Redeemer, lives!
I too unto life must waken;
He will have me where He is,
Shall my courage then be shaken?
Shall I fear? Or could the Head
Rise and leave its members dead?

iii. Nay, too closely am I bound
Unto Him by hope for ever;
Faith's strong hand the Rock hath found,
Grasped it, and will leave it never;
Not the ban of death can part
From its Lord the trusting heart.

* * *

vii. What now sickens, mourns, and sighs,
Christ with Him in glory bringeth;
Earthly is the seed and dies,
Heavenly from the grave it springeth;
Natural is the death we die,
Spiritual our life on high.

viii. Then take comfort, nay, rejoice,
For His members Christ will cherish;
Fear not, they will know His voice,
Though awhile they seem to perish,
When the final trump is heard,
And the deaf, cold grave is stirred.

ix. Laugh to scorn the gloomy grave,
And at death no longer tremble;
For the Lord, who comes to save,
Round Him shall His saints assemble,
Raising them o'er all their foes,
Mortal weakness, fear, and woes.

x. Only draw away your heart
Now from pleasures base and hollow;
Would ye there with Christ have part,
Here His footsteps ye must follow;
Fix your heart beyond the skies,
Whither ye yourselves would rise!
? Luise Henriette Electress of Brandenburg (1627-67)
Tr. *Catherine Winkworth*[1].

The Easter hymn, "Jesus, meine Zuversicht," attributed to Luise Henriette Electress of Brandenburg, was published, set to Johann Crüger's (?) melody, in Christoph Runge's *Geistliche Lieder und Psalmen* (Berlin, 1653)[2]. A reconstruction of the melody (*supra*) appeared in the Berlin *Praxis pietatis melica* of the same year. The melody was attributed posthumously to Crüger, though possibly only the reconstruction is by him. Bach uses the *Praxis* version invariably, in Cantata 145 (1729–30), *Choralgesänge*, No. 208, and the movement *infra*. Invariably he substitutes G for A as the third note of the second bar of the melody (*supra*), an innovation found in Freylinghausen (1704). Bach's treatment of the first bar of the second part of the tune (line 2, bar 1 *supra*) varies. Only in the Organ movement does he follow Crüger's version. As his other readings differ in that passage, they may

[1] *Chorale Book for England*, No. 59. The original hymn has ten stanzas, of which iv–vi are omitted in the translation.
[2] See *Bach's Chorals*, Part II. 412, for the Runge form.

perhaps be regarded as his own. Witt (No. 712) sets the hymn to another tune.

Luise Henriette, to whom the hymn is attributed, was born at the Hague in 1627. She was a granddaughter of William the Silent, Prince of Orange, wife (1646) of Frederick William the "Great Elector" of Brandenburg, and great-grandmother of Frederick the Great. She died in 1667.

[81]

N. xviii. 69. The movement is in the *Clavierbüchlein* which Bach made for his wife Anna Magdalena in 1722. As Spitta points out[1], it is a three-part Clavier piece, included in the *Clavierbüchlein* in order to give practice in the *fioriture*, which, it may be remarked, are not accurately printed in the Peters and Novello Editions[2]. Another MS. of the movement, a "gute alte Abschrift," is in the Berlin Royal Library.

Komm, Gott, Schöpfer, heiliger Geist.

Melody: "*Komm, Gott, Schöpfer, heiliger Geist*"

Anon. 1535

[1] Vol. I. 594 n.
[2] The second beat of the third bar should be marked ₩.

240   MELODIES

Crüger's version 1640

i. Come, God, Creator, Holy Ghost,
Visit the heart of all Thy men;
Fill them with grace, the way Thou know'st;
What Thine was, make it again.

ii. For Thou art called the Comforter,
The blessed gift of God above,
A ghostly balm, our quickener,
A living well, fire, and love.

iii. O kindle in our minds a light;
Give in our hearts love's glowing gift;
Our weak flesh, known to Thee aright,
With Thy strength and grace uplift.

iv. In giving gifts Thou art sevenfold;
The finger Thou on God's right hand;
His word by Thee right soon is told
With clov'n tongues in every land.

v. Drive far the cunning of the foe;
Thy grace bring peace and make us whole,
That we glad after Thee may go,
And shun that which hurts the soul.

vi. Teach us to know the Father right,
And Jesus Christ, His Son, that so
We may with faith be filled quite,
Spirit of both, Thee to know.

KOMM, GOTT, SCHÖPFER, HEILIGER GEIST 241

    vii. Praise God the Father, and the Son,
        Who from the dead arose in power;
        Like praise to the Consoling One,
        Evermore and every hour.
Martin Luther (1483-1546)   Tr. *George Macdonald*[1].

The words and melody of Luther's Whitsuntide hymn, "Komm, Gott, Schöpfer, heiliger Geist," are derived from the Latin "Veni Creator Spiritus," and were first published in 1524. In Klug's Hymn-book (1535 [1529]) the melody, considerably modified[2], approached the form in which it is universally known. In the Cantata "Gott der Hoffnung erfülle euch," attributed to Bach, the tune is used exactly in its 1535 form. Elsewhere, in *Choralgesänge*, No. 218, and the two Organ movements (*infra*), Bach follows a version of the melody based on Crüger's text (1640) (*supra*) invariably for the third phrase. Witt (No. 171) exactly conforms to the 1535 text.

Bach treats the melody in two Organ movements:

[82]

N. xv. 97. The movement is the only completed Prelude in the Whit-Sunday section of the *Orgelbüchlein*. The similarity of its Bass to that of the four-part setting in the *Choralgesänge* suggests that they were written in close association.

---

[1] *Exotics*, p. 56. The original hymn has seven stanzas.
[2] For the 1524 version, see *Bach's Chorals*, Part II. 479.

Spitta[1] finds the movement out of place among Preludes in which Bach undertook to treat the Pedal uniformly obbligato throughout. He regards it as the fragment of a movement conceived on a much bigger scale—in fact, an introduction to No. 83 *infra*.

An older reading of the movement is in P. vii. 86(A), whose original is in the Mendelssohn Autograph.

[83]

N. xvii. 82. The movement is among the *Eighteen Chorals* and is the *Orgelbüchlein* Prelude with the addition of another verse, in which the *cantus* is on the Pedal. Its treatment suggests that Bach had in mind Acts ii. 2, 3: "And suddenly there came a sound from heaven.....And there appeared unto them cloven tongues like as of fire."

KOMM, HEILIGER GEIST, HERRE GOTT.

Melody: "*Komm, heiliger Geist, Herre Gott*"   Anon. 1535

[1] Vol. I. 650.

KOMM, HEILIGER GEIST, HERRE GOTT 243

Cadence 1524   Cadence 1569

i. Come, holy Spirite, most blessed Lorde,
   Fulfyl our hartes nowe with Thy grace,
   And make our myndes of one accorde,
   Kyndle them with love in every place.
   O Lorde, Thou forgevest our trespace,
   And callest the folke of every countre
   To the ryght fayth and truste of Thy grace,
   That they may geve thankes and synge to Thee,
                Alleluya, Alleluya.

ii. O holy lyght, moste principall,
The worde of lyfe shewe unto us,
And cause us to knowe God over all
For our owne Father moste gracious.
Lorde, kepe us from lernyng venymous
That we folowe no masters but Christe.
He is the verite, His word sayth thus;
Cause us to set in Hym our truste.
            Alleluya, Alleluya.
iii. O holy fyre, and conforth moste swete,
Fyll our hertes with fayth and boldnesse,
To abyde by The in colde and hete,
Content to suffre for ryghteousnesse:
O Lord, geve strength to our weaknesse,
And send us helpe every houre;
That we may overcome all wyckednesse,
And brynge this olde Adam under Thy power.
            Alleluya, Alleluya.

Martin Luther (1483-1546)   Tr. *Bishop Myles Coverdale*[1].

Luther's Whitsuntide hymn, "Komm, heiliger Geist, Herre Gott," an expansion of the Latin "Veni Sancte Spiritus," was first published, with the melody, in the Erfurt and Wittenberg Hymnbooks of 1524. Klug's Hymn-book of 1535 [1529] prints an older form, with an expanded cadence for the concluding "Hallelujahs." Bach uses the 1524 form invariably for the body of the tune. In Cantatas 59 and 175 (1716-1735?) and the Motett "Der Geist hilft" (1729) he uses the cadence of the 1535 version. There is also an abbreviated treatment of the

---

[1] *Remains*, p. 542. The original hymn has three stanzas.

melody in Cantata 172 (1724-5). In the Organ movements he invariably uses the 1524 cadence (*supra*) somewhat altered, in a form which dates from 1569 (*supra*). Witt (No. 170) also prefers the 1524 text, but his cadence is quite distinct from the other versions.

There are two Organ movements upon the melody :

[84]

N. xvii. 1. The Fantasia is No. 1 of the *Eighteen Chorals*. Schweitzer[1] finds it reminiscent of Buxtehude's style, an early work retouched, no doubt, by Bach for inclusion in his final collection. The strong statement of the *cantus* and the flickering semiquavers above it seem to paint stanza ii—"He is the verite," and the tongues of fire. An earlier, perhaps the original, text is printed in P. vii. 86. Two MSS. of it are extant, one of which was formerly in Krebs' possession.

[85]

N. xvii. 10. The movement, a treatment of the *cantus* phrase by phrase, is No. 2 of the *Eighteen Chorals*. The last sixteen bars are a joyous setting of the "Hallelujahs" in Bach's characteristic idiom. An older version of the movement is in P. vii. 88. The MS. of it comes through Krebs.

[1] Vol. I. 292.

KOMMST DU NUN, JESU, VOM HIMMEL HERUNTER AUF ERDEN?

Melody: " Hast du denn, Liebster, dein Angesicht gantzlich verborgen"   Anon. 1665

i. Can it be, Jesu, from highest Heaven hither
        Thou wendest,
   E'en to this sin-laden frail earth
        Thy presence Thou lendest?
   Is it indeed,
   In my distress and dire need,
   Thee Whom Thy Father's love sendeth?

ii. Thou by Thy life-blood and Passion the curse
        hast removed,
   Laid on our first parents sinful, in Eden reproved.
   O loving heart,
   Through Thee, Who Son of Man art,
   Gone is the curse that man doomed.

iii. Death and the Devil their wiles do encompass
        me hourly;
   For my dark sins doth Hell's deepest pit
        yawn to devour me.
   Almighty one,
   Answer me, succour me, come!
   Let not the fierce flames o'erpower me!

iv. Grant me, O Jesu, fair thoughts and high
purpose to serve Thee.
Drill my weak nature, give strength to me,
quicken and nerve me.
O God of love,
Call me to glory above,
Making my song of Thee worthy.

v. Speed the way, Jesu; in Heaven above haste to
instal me,
As Thou hast promised to all that unfeignedly
call Thee;
Risen I'd be,
From Death's grim fetters all free,
'Fore Thy throne's splendour in glory!

Caspar Friedrich Nachtenhöfer (1624–85)   Tr. C. S. T.[1]

Caspar Friedrich Nachtenhöfer's hymn was first published in the Coburg Hymn-book of 1667, to the anonymous melody "Hast du denn, Liebster," which had appeared two years earlier (1665) in the Stralsund Hymn-book. Zahn (No. 1912) supposes it founded on a secular tune.

Nachtenhöfer was born at Halle in 1624, became deacon and later pastor at Meder, and eventually (1671) pastor in Coburg. He died in 1685.

Bach uses the melody in Cantatas 57, 137 (c. 1732–40), in the unfinished Cantata "Herr Gott, Beherrscher aller Dinge" (c. 1740) and in the Organ movement *infra*. All of these works belong to his later Leipzig years. But though his form of the

[1] The original hymn has five stanzas.

melody is fundamentally uniform, he treats it with a freedom which its spirited character invited.

[86]

N. xvi. 14. The movement is No. 6 of the *Schübler Chorals*, and is an adaptation of the Alto Solo on the second stanza of Joachim Neander's "Lobe den Herren, den mächtigen König der Ehren," in Cantata 137 (? 1732):

> Praise to the Lord! who o'er all things so wondrously
> reigneth,
> Shelters thee under His wings, yea so gently sustaineth;
> Hast thou not seen
> How thy desires have been
> Granted in what He ordaineth?

The accompaniment on the first Manual is a Violin Solo in the Cantata.

KYRIE, GOTT VATER IN EWIGKEIT.

Melody: "*Kyrie, Gott Vater in Ewigkeit*" 1525

KYRIE, GOTT VATER IN EWIGKEIT

"*Christe, aller Welt Trost*"

"*Kyrie, Gott heiliger Geist*"

i. O Lord the Father for evermore!
We Thy wondrous grace adore;
We confess Thy power, all worlds upholding.
Have mercy, Lord.

ii. O Christ, our Hope alone,
Who with Thy blood didst for us atone;
O Jesu! Son of God!
Our Redeemer! our Advocate on high!
Lord, to Thee alone in our need we cry,
Have mercy, Lord.

iii. Holy Lord, God the Holy Ghost!
Who of life and light the fountain art,
With faith sustain our heart,
That at the last we hence in peace depart.
Have mercy, Lord.
Anon. Tr. *Arthur T. Russell*[1].

The Litany is a recast of the "Kyrie summum bonum : Kyrie fons bonitatis," printed, apparently at Wittenberg, in 1541. The melody is a literal adaptation of the Latin plainsong. It is printed *supra* from the *Teutsch Kirchenamt* (Erfurt, 1525), where it is set to other words. Bach's melodic text, in *Choralgesänge*, No. 225, and the Organ movements *infra*, is invariable and follows the original (1525), to which Witt (No. 187) also conforms.

[87] [88]

N. xvi. 28–38. The two sets of three movements, the one long (N. xvi. 28–35), the other short (N. xvi. 36–38), are in the *Clavierübung*. Schweitzer points out[2] that the majority of the long movements in the *Clavierübung* are worked out to such excessive length as to diminish the impression they would otherwise make. The criticism does not apply to the "Kyrie." The longer set is developed in the style of Pachelbel rather than that of the

---

[1] *Psalms and Hymns*, No. 14. The original hymn has three stanzas.
[2] Vol. ii. 67.

KYRIE, GOTT VATER IN EWIGKEIT 251

Choral Fantasia, with magnificent tonal effect. The shorter set is of a different texture, written for the manuals only, and in another mood.

LIEBSTER JESU, WIR SIND HIER.
Melody: "Ja, er ists, das Heil der Welt"
Johann Rodolf Ahle 1664

Reconstruction 1687

i. Blessed Jesu, at Thy word
We are gathered all to hear Thee;
Let our hearts and souls be stirred
Now to seek and love and fear Thee,
By Thy teachings sweet and holy
Draw from earth to love Thee solely.

ii. All our knowledge, sense, and sight
Lie in deepest darkness shrouded,
Till Thy Spirit breaks our night
With the beams of truth unclouded;
Thou alone to God canst win us,
Thou must work all good within us.

iii. Glorious Lord, Thyself impart!
Light of Light from God proceeding,
Open Thou our ears and heart,
Help us by Thy Spirit's pleading,
Hear the cry Thy people raises,
Hear, and bless our prayers and praises!
Tobias Clausnitzer (1618-84)   Tr. *Catherine Winkworth*[1].

Tobias Clausnitzer's hymn, "Liebster Jesu, wir sind hier," for use before the sermon, was first published, but without a melody, in the Altdorf *Bet- und Gesang Büchlein* (1663).

Clausnitzer was born at Thum, in Saxony, in 1618. He graduated at Jena University in 1643 and became an army chaplain in Swedish service during the Thirty Years' War. Upon the conclusion of peace in 1648 he was appointed pastor at Weiden, where he died in 1684.

The melody (*supra*) of the hymn was composed by Johann Rodolph Ahle, and was published first in his *Neue Geistliche Auf die Sontage...gerichtete Andachten* (Mühlhausen, 1664). It is set there to Franz Joachim Burmeister's hymn, "Ja, er ists, das Heil der Welt." A reconstruction of the melody (*supra*) was attached to Clausnitzer's hymn in the Darmstadt *Cantional* of 1687.

Besides a four-part setting of the melody in the *Choralgesänge*, No. 228, there are five short treat-

[1] *Chorale Book for England*, No. 12. The original hymn has three stanzas.

ments of it among the Organ works. Bach's text is invariable only for the first phrase of the melody, which exactly follows the 1687 reconstruction, excepting the last note, where he substitutes C for A (*supra*). For the remaining phrases, though his text generally conforms to the 1687 reconstruction, Bach introduces into all of them variants which, generally, have their authority in Leipzig use. The five melodic texts are discussed in the sections *infra*. A peculiar intimacy distinguishes Bach's treatment of them all.

[89] [90]

P. v. 109 and N. xv. 101. The melody appears twice, among the Trinity hymns, in the *Orgelbüchlein*. It is the only tune introduced more than once into that work, and the significance of the fact has been pointed out in the Introduction to this volume. Making allowance for the free embellishments Bach introduces, the *cantus* exactly follows the reconstruction of 1687, excepting the last note of the first phrase of the tune, which is C natural intead of A. This improvement is found in Witt (No. 241), whose text Bach exactly follows. The two *Orgelbüchlein* movements differ in the smallest details, and the Novello Edition only prints the second of them; Bach distinguished it as "distinctius." The first movement, "in Canone alla Quinta," is printed in the other Editions.

[91]

N. xviii. 70. The melodic text of the movement conforms to the 1687 reconstruction, except in the third phrase, which is first found in Vetter's Hymnbook (1709). The melodic text of the *Choralgesänge* setting is identical with that of this movement, allowance being made for the free figures that embellish the latter. Both are in the key of G major. Peters printed the movement from Kittel's MS. The Dröbs MS. provides another copy.

[92]

N. xviii. 71. The melodic text of the movement conforms to the 1687 reconstruction, excepting the third phrase, whose source is not ascertained; probably it is Bach's own. The authorities for the movement are as in No. 91 *supra*.

[93]

N. xviii. 72. This is a simple four-part setting in two verses. The first half of its melodic text exactly conforms to the 1687 reconstruction. The second half of it follows Vetter. Six MSS. of the setting are extant, one of them being in the Kirnberger and another in the Krebs Collections.

Since Bach uses the 1687 or Witt form of the melody only in the *Orgelbüchlein*, while all the other settings show variants which are traceable to Vetter's Hymn-book, which was published at Leipzig

LIEBSTER JESU, WIR SIND HIER   255

a few years before Bach went there, it is a reasonable
deduction that Nos. 91, 92, 93 and the *Choralgesänge*
setting date from the Leipzig period.

LOB SEI DEM ALLMÄCHTIGEN GOTT.

Melody: "Conditor alme siderum"   Anon. 1531

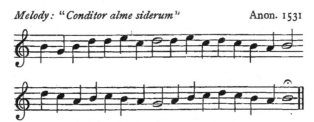

 i. To God we render thanks and praise,
  Who pitied mankind's fallen race,
  And gave His dear and only Son
  That us, as children, He might own.

 ii. He came to seek and save the lost;
  We sinned, and He would bear the cost,
  That we might share eternal bliss;
  O what unbounded love was this!

 iii. What grace, what great benevolence,
  What love, surpassing human sense:
  For this great work no angel can
  Him duly praise, much less a man.

    * * *

 v. The Word eternal did assume
  Our flesh and blood, and man become;
  The First and Last with wonder see
  Partake of human misery.

vi. For what is all the human race,
That God should show such matchless grace,
To give His Son, that we might claim
Life everlasting in His name.

vii. How wretched they who still despise
Jesus, the pearl of greatest price:
Those who neglect to hear His voice
Must perish by their own free choice.

viii. Unhappy those who turn away,
Or such as carelessly delay
To meet their Saviour, though He came
Their souls from misery to reclaim.

ix. Come, sinners, Jesus will receive
The chief of sinners: come and live:
"I'll dwell with you," our Saviour saith;
Receive Him in your hearts by faith.

x. Your crimes and self-made holiness,
Your carnal reason and distress,
Give up, and trust to Christ alone,
Who did for all your sins atone.

* * *

xiv. Thus saved by God's unbounded grace,
You'll humbly render thanks and praise,
With all the numerous ransomed host,
To Father, Son, and Holy Ghost.

Michael Weisse (1480?–1534)   Tr. *John Gambold*[1].

Michael Weisse's Advent hymn, "Lob sei dem allmächtigen Gott," was first published in *Ein New Gesengbuchlen* (Jung Bunzlau, 1531), the earliest

---

[1] *Moravian Hymn-book*, ed. 1877, No. 31. The original hymn has fourteen stanzas, of which iv, xi–xiii are omitted in the translation.

LOB SEI DEM ALLMÄCHTIGEN GOTT 257

Hymn-book of the Bohemian Brethren, of which he was editor. Its melody (*supra*) is that of the Latin Advent hymn, "Conditor alme siderum." The melody is treated in two Organ movements. The source of Bach's variations of the 1531 text is not ascertained. In Witt (No. 15) the hymn is set to the melody "Vom Himmel hoch da komm ich her.

[94]

N. xv. 11. The movement is the last of the Advent Preludes in the *Orgelbüchlein*. The imminence of Christmas, rather than the text of the hymn, moves Bach to an expression of fervent devotion by means of a characteristic rhythm (cf. N. xv. 9, 31).

[95]

N. xviii. 73. A brief Fughetta, for the manuals, upon the first line of the *cantus* stated in free form. A copy of the movement is among the Kirnberger MSS. There are three other MSS. of it in the Berlin Royal Library, one of them in Forkel's Collection.

LOBT GOTT, IHR CHRISTEN ALLE GLEICH.

Melody: "*Lobt Gott, ihr Christen alle gleich*"
Nikolaus Herman 1554

    i. Let all together praise our God
       Upon His lofty throne;
       He hath His heavens unclosed to-day,
       And given to us His Son.

          *   *   *

   iii. He lays aside His majesty,
       And seems as nothing worth,
       And takes on Him a servant's form,
       Who made both heaven and earth.

          *   *   *

   vi. Behold the wonderful exchange
       Our Lord with us doth make!
       Lo! He assumes our flesh and blood!
       We of His heaven partake!

          *   *   *

  viii. The glorious gates of Paradise
       The cherub guards no more;
       This day again those gates unfolds!
       With praise our God adore!

Nikolaus Herman (*c.* 1485-1561)   Tr. *Arthur T. Russell*[1].

[1] *Psalms and Hymns*, No. 52. The original hymn has eight stanzas, of which ii, iv, v, vii are omitted in the translation.

LOBT GOTT, IHR CHRISTEN ALLE GLEICH 259

The words and melody of the Christmas hymn, "Lobt Gott, ihr Christen alle gleich [allzugleich]," by Nikolaus Herman, were first published together in 1560. The tune (*supra*) had appeared six years earlier in association with another hymn by Herman. In both hymns the fourth line of the stanza is repeated. Bach uses the melody in Cantatas 151 and 195 (?*c.* 1726–40), *Choralgesänge*, Nos. 233, 234, and in the two movements *infra*. His text generally differs from that of 1554 in phrases 2 and 4. His version of both is adumbrated in texts dated 1576 and 1592. Excepting his treatment of the second phrase (the last six notes of line 1 *supra*) Bach's version of the melody is invariable. In the *Orgelbüchlein* and Cantatas 151 and 195 he adopts the 1554 form, which is also that of Witt (No. 32), but always begins the second phrase on G (not A *ut supra*). The source of his variation of that line elsewhere is not ascertained. An unimportant modification of the closing cadence occurs in Cantata 195 (?*c.* 1726).

[96]

N. xv. 29. The movement, in the Christmas section of the *Orgelbüchlein*, expresses the jubilation of earth at the angels' Christmas message. Bach introduces into the movement, therefore, a characteristic rhythm of joy.

[97]

N. xviii. 74. A brilliant Organ accompaniment of the melody, inspired by stanza viii, more literally translated thus:

> Wide open stands the once closed door
> Of beauteous Paradise;
> The Angel guardeth it no more.
> To God be thanks and praise.

Bach buries the second phrase of the *cantus* under harmonies soaring heavenward followed by a downward rush of whirling notes, typifying dispersal of the forces that hitherto barred the Gate of Life.

A copy of the movement is in the Dröbs MS. A so-called "variant," which comes from the Krebs MSS., is printed in B.G. xl. 159. The second phrase of the melody is in a form Bach does not use elsewhere.

MEINE SEELE ERHEBT DEN HERREN.

The association of "Tonus Peregrinus" with the *Magnificat* dates at least from the sixteenth century. Bach invariably associates the two, in the Organ movements *infra*, Cantata 10, and the Latin *Magnificat* (No. 10). There are two harmonizations of the melody in *Choralgesänge*, Nos. 120, 121.

MEINE SEELE ERHEBT DEN HERREN 261

[98]

N. xvi. 8. The movement, the fourth of the *Schübler Chorals*, is an arrangement of the fifth movement of Cantata 10 (*c*. 1740), an Alto-Tenor Duetto to the words, "He remembering His mercy hath holpen His servant Israel." In the Cantata the *cantus* is played by the Oboes and Tromba in unison. In the *Magnificat* (? 1723) Bach introduces the melody obbligato in the same verse of the Canticle. In the present movement the care-free subject sung by the two voices displays the mood of ransomed Israel.

[99]

N. xviii. 75. Spitta points out[1], in regard to this sublime Fugue, that in it Bach illustrates the Pachelbel form at its highest expression, prefacing the melody, treated with brilliant counterpoint, by a Fugue constructed on the first line of it. A Fugue of ninety-seven bars on the manuals precedes the *cantus firmus*' "ponderous foundation-stones" on the Pedals. The Fugue on "Allein Gott in der Hoh' sei Ehr" (N. xviii. 7) may be compared with it. Griepenkerl printed the movement for Peters "from a single copy, in my collection," his Preface to P. vii. states. The B.G. Edition quotes two MSS., one of which is in the Amalienbibliothek, the other being a copy by Grell.

[1] Vol. I. 606.

Mit Fried' und Freud' ich fahr' dahin.

Melody: "*Mit Fried' und Freud' ich fahr' dahin*"
? Martin Luther 1524

* In later texts a ♭ here.

i. In peace and joy I now depart,
   According to God's will,
   For full of comfort is my heart,
   So calm and sweet and still;
   So doth God His promise keep,
   And death to me is but a sleep.

ii. 'Tis Christ hath wrought this work for me,
    Thy dear and only Son,
    Whom Thou hast suffered me to see,
    And made Him surely known
    As my Help when trouble's rife,
    And even in death itself my Life.

iii. For Thou in mercy unto all
     Hast set this Saviour forth;
     And to His kingdom Thou dost call
     The nations of the earth
     Through His blessed wholesome Word,
     That now in every place is heard.

iv. He is the heathens' saving Light,
And He will gently lead
Those who now know Thee not aright,
And in His pastures feed;
While His people's joy He is,
Their Sun, their glory, and their bliss.

Martin Luther (1483-1546)   Tr. *Catherine Winkworth*[1].

Martin Luther's free rendering of the *Nunc dimittis* was first published, with the melody, in Walther's Wittenberg Hymn-book (1524). It is probable that the tune was composed by Luther himself.

Besides the *Orgelbüchlein* movement (*infra*) Bach uses the melody in Cantatas 83, 95, 106, 125 (1711– *c.* 1740), and *Choralgesänge*, No. 249. His text differs from the original form (*supra*) only in the substitution of B flat for B natural as the second note of the third line *supra*, and of B natural for A natural as the first note of the second line *supra*. In both particulars he conforms to Witt's text (No. 80).

[100]

N. xv. 50. The movement is one of two Preludes for the Purification in the *Orgelbüchlein*. It illustrates the first line of the aged Simeon's song:

In peace and joy I now depart.

Bach therefore accompanies the *cantus* throughout with the rhythm 𝅘𝅥𝅯𝅘𝅥𝅯𝅘𝅥𝅯 𝅘𝅥𝅯𝅘𝅥𝅯𝅘𝅥𝅯 expressive of

---

[1] *Chorale Book for England*, No. 81. The original hymn has four stanzas.

joy. The sturdy and reliant Pedal figure represents the confidence in God's promise with which Simeon faces the unknown journey.

NUN DANKET ALLE GOTT.

Melody: "*Nun danket alle Gott*" Johann Crüger 1648

 i. Now thank we all our God,
  With heart and hands and voices,
  Who wondrous things hath done,
  In Whom His world rejoices;
  Who from our mother's arms
  Hath blessed us on our way
  With countless gifts of love,
  And still is ours to-day.

 ii. O may this bounteous God
  Through all our life be near us,
  With ever joyful hearts
  And blessed peace to cheer us;
  And keep us in His grace,
  And guide us when perplexed,
  And free us from all ills
  In this world and the next.

iii. All praise and thanks to God
   The Father now be given,
   The Son, and Him Who reigns
   With Them in highest Heaven,
   The One Eternal God,
   Whom earth and Heaven adore;
   For thus it was, is now,
   And shall be evermore.

Martin Rinkart (1586–1649)   Tr. *Catherine Winkworth*[1].

Martin Rinkart's hymn, "Nun danket alle Gott," was first published in 1648, with the melody (*supra*). The latter, published anonymously in 1648, was attributed to Crüger in 1653. It has been assigned also to Rinkart himself and to Luca Marenzio.

In addition to the Organ movement *infra*, Bach uses the melody in Cantatas 79, 192 (*c.* 1732–5), the Wedding Chorals (No. 3), and *Choralgesänge*, No. 257. His text is invariable. His versions of the second and last lines of the melody differ from the 1648 form and are found in Witt (No. 386).

[101]

N. xvii. 40. The movement, the seventh of the *Eighteen Chorals*, is both a splendid exercise in the Pachelbel form and a jubilant musical expression of the triumphant hymn[2].

---

[1] *Hymns Ancient and Modern*, No. 379. The original hymn has three stanzas.

[2] See *supra*, p. 81.

NUN FREUT EUCH, LIEBEN CHRISTEN G'MEIN.

Melody: "*Nun freut euch, lieben Christen g'mein*"
Anon. 1535

Melody: "*Wach auf, wach auf, du schöne*"   Anon. 1555

1. Dear Christians, let us now rejoice,
   And dance in joyous measure;
   That, of good cheer, and with one voice,
   We sing in love and pleasure
   Of what to us our God hath shown,
   And the sweet wonder He hath done:
   Full dearly hath He wrought it.

ii. Forlorn and lost in death I lay,
   A captive to the devil.
   My sin lay heavy, night and day,
   For I was born in evil.
   I fell but deeper for my strife,
   There was no good in all my life,
   For sin had all possessed me.

iii. My good works they were worthless quite,
   A mock was all my merit;
   My free will hates God's judging light,
   To all good dead and buried.
   Even to despair me anguish bore,
   That nought but death lay me before;
   I must go down to hell-fire.

iv. Then God was sorry on His throne
   To see such torment rend me;
   His tender mercy He thought on,
   His good help He would send me.
   He turned to me His father-heart;
   Ah! then was His no easy part,
   For of His best it cost Him.

v. To His dear Son He said: Go down;
   Things go in piteous fashion;
   Go down, My heart's exalted crown,
   Be the poor man's salvation.
   Lift him from out sin's scorn and scathe,
   Strangle for him that cruel Death,
   And take him to live with Thee.

vi. The Son He heard obediently,
   And by a maiden mother,
   Pure, tender—down He came to me,
   For He would be my brother.
   Secret He bore His strength enorm,
   He went about in my poor form,
   For He would catch the devil.

vii. He said to me: Hold thou by Me,
    Thy matters I will settle;
    I give Myself all up for thee,
    And I will fight thy battle.
    For I am thine, and thou art Mine,
    And My house also shall be thine;
    The enemy shall not part us.

viii. He will as water shed My blood,
    My life he from Me reave will;
    All this I suffer for thy good—
    To that with firm faith cleave well.
    My Life doth swallow up that Death;
    My innocence bears thy sins, He saith,
    So henceforth thou art happy.

ix. To Heaven unto My Father high
    From this life I am going;
    But there thy Master still am I,
    My spirit on thee bestowing,
    Whose comfort shall thy trouble quell,
    Who thee shall teach to know Me well,
    And in the truth shall guide thee.

x. What I have done, and what have said,
    Shall be thy doing, teaching,
    That so the kingdom of God may spread—
    All to His glory reaching.
    And take heed what men bid thee do,
    For that corrupts the treasure true;
    With this last word I leave thee.

Martin Luther (1483-1546)   Tr. *George Macdonald*

[1] *Exotics*, p. 80. The original hymn has ten stanzas.

Es ist gewisslich an der Zeit.

i. 'Tis sure that awful time will come,
   When Christ, the Lord of glory,
   Shall from His throne give men their doom,
   And change things transitory:
   This will strike dumb each impious jeer,
   When all things are consumed by fire,
   And heaven and earth dissolved.

ii. The wakening trumpet all shall hear,
    The dead shall then be raised,
    And 'fore the judgment-seat appear,
    On the right and left hand placed:
    Those in the body at that time
    Shall, in a manner most sublime,
    Endure a transmutation.

    * * *

iv. Woe, then, to him that hath despised
    God's word and revelation,
    And here done nothing but devised
    His lust's gratification;
    Then, how confounded will he stand,
    When he must go, at Christ's command,
    To everlasting torment.

v. When all with awe shall stand around
   To hear their doom allotted,
   O may my worthless name be found
   In the Lamb's book unblotted:
   Grant me that firm, unshaken faith,
   That Thou, my Saviour, by Thy death
   Hast purchased my salvation.

vi. Before Thou shalt as Judge appear,
    Plead as my Intercessor,
    And on that awful day declare
    That I am Thy confessor;

Then bring me to that blessed place,
Where I shall see with open face
The glory of Thy kingdom.

vii. O Jesus, shorten the delay,
And hasten Thy salvation,
That we may see that glorious day
Produce a new creation:
Lord Jesus, come, our Judge and King,
Come, change our mournful notes, to sing
Thy praise for ever: Amen.

Bartholomäus Ringwaldt (1532–c. 1600)
Tr. *John Christian Jacobi*[1].

The melody, "Nun freut euch, lieben Christen g'mein," generally known as "Luther's Hymn," is said to have been written down by the Reformer after hearing a travelling artisan sing it. Its original is the secular song "Wach auf, wach auf, du schöne," whose melody (*supra*) Valentin Triller in 1555 (*Ein Schlesich singebüchlein aus Göttlicher schrifft*) appropriated to his hymn "Merk auf, merk auf, du schöne." Luther's melody is also associated with Bartholomäus Ringwaldt's Advent hymn, "Es ist gewisslich an der Zeit" (1582). In the Organ movement (*infra*) the names of both hymns are attached to the tune. It occurs also in the *Christmas Oratorio* (1734), No. 59, Cantata 70 (1716), and *Choralgesänge*, No. 262.

[1] *Moravian Hymn-book*, ed. 1877, No. 1215. The original hymn has seven stanzas.

Bach's text of the melody is invariable and differs, as to the third and fourth phrases (line 2 of the 1535 melody *supra*), from the 1535 form. His variants are found in late sixteenth century texts and also in Witt (No. 293). The third phrase of the tune in *Hymns Ancient and Modern*, No. 52, it may be noted, occurs in a 1598 text. The melody is treated in a single Organ movement:

[102]

N. xviii. 80. The semiquaver subject suggests that Bach had before him particularly the first stanza of Luther's hymn. But it cannot be stated positively that the addition of " Es ist gewisslich an der Zeit " to the title of the movement is without significance. Bach occasionally gives a festive treatment to the Advent tunes in anticipation of Christmas. Ringwaldt's hymn has a particular relation to the Second Advent, and it is not improbable that Bach had in mind here its last stanza.

Four copies of the movement survive, in the Fischhof and Oley MSS. P. vii. 91 prints a variant reading. Two MSS. of it are extant, one of them in a volume of Organ Chorals attributed to Bach, in the Berlin Royal Library, another in Schelble's hand.

Nun komm, der Heiden Heiland.

Melody: "Veni Redemptor gentium"   Anon. 1531

Ve-ni Re-demp-tor gen-ti-um, ost-en-de par-tum vir-gi-nis, mi-re-tur om-ne sae-cu-lum, ta-lis de-cet par-tus De-um.

   i. Come, Saviour of nations wild,
      Of the maiden owned the Child,
      Fill with wonder all the earth,
      God should grant it such a birth.

  ii. Not of man's flesh or man's blood,
      Only of the Spirit of God,
      Is His Word a man become,
      Of woman's flesh the ripened bloom.

 iii. Maiden she was found with child,
      Chastity yet undefiled;
      Many a virtue from her shone,
      God was there as in His throne.

 iv. From His chamber of content,
      Royal hall so pure, He went;
      Good by kind, in hero's grace,
      Forth He comes to run His race.

  v. From the Father came His road,
      And returns again to God;
      Unto hell His road went down,
      Up then to the Father's throne.

NUN KOMM, DER HEIDEN HEILAND

vi. Thou, the Father's form express,
Get Thee victory in the flesh,
That Thy godlike power in us
Make weak flesh victorious.

vii. Shines Thy manger bright and clear,
Sets the night a new star there;
Darkness thence must keep away,
Faith dwells ever in the day.

viii. Honour unto God be done;
Honour to His only Son;
Honour to the Holy Ghost,
Now, and ever, ending not.

Martin Luther (1483-1546)   Tr. *George Macdonald*[1].

Luther's Advent or Christmas hymn, "Nun komm, der Heiden Heiland," a translation of St Ambrose's (?) "Veni Redemptor gentium," was published in 1524, with the melody[2], a simplification of that of the Latin hymn (*supra*), a reconstruction which may be attributed to Luther or Johann Walther.

Besides the Organ works *infra*, the melody occurs in Cantatas 36, 61, and 62 (1714–*c.* 1740). Bach's text is invariable, with the exception that in the *Eighteen Chorals* and their variants he writes G sharp for G natural as the fourth note of bar 1 and second note of bar 4 *supra*. The modification is not found in Witt (No. 4). It produces the interval

---
[1] *Exotics*, p. 39. The original hymn has eight stanzas.
[2] See it in *Bach's Chorals*, Part II. 208.

of a diminished fourth, which is very significant of suffering (cf. the "Crucify" theme in the *St Matthew Passion* and the first Chorus of Cantata 61 (1714), where the rhythm of majesty is given to the strings while the Saviour's suffering is, by this means, suggested by the voices).

There are five Organ movements on the melody —one in the *Orgelbüchlein*, three among the *Eighteen Chorals*, and one among the miscellaneous Preludes.

[103]

N. xv. 3. The movement is the first of the Advent Preludes in the *Orgelbüchlein*. It breathes a certain wistfulness of petition, a reiterated " Now, come."

[104] [105] [106]

N. xvii. 46, 49, 52. The three movements are the ninth, tenth, and eleventh numbers of the *Eighteen Chorals*. As they exist in a text of Walther's they must be assigned to the Weimar period. Spitta[1] regards them as having been composed by Bach " as a connected whole." Their tonality is identical. The first is in the Buxtehude form and the phrases of the *cantus* are unusually prolonged. The second is a Trio, which needs nothing but a freely invented

[1] Vol. I. 618.

NUN KOMM, DER HEIDEN HEILAND 275

theme to place it in the category of the Choral Fantasia. It therefore forms a bridge between the first and the third, which is a Choral Fantasia. They illustrate the hymn as a whole rather than any particular stanza. Older readings of all are in P. vii. 92, 93, 94, 96 from the Kirnberger, Krebs, and Walther Collections. Of P. vii. 93 the Autograph is in the Berlin Royal Library.

[107]

N. xviii. 83. A Fughetta, on the first phrase of the melody, among the miscellaneous Preludes. Copies of the movement are in the Kirnberger and Schelble-Gleichauf MSS. in the Berlin Royal Library.

O GOTT, DU FROMMER GOTT.

Melody: "Gross ist, O grosser Gott"   Anon. 1646

* A Lüneburg text of 1665 has a ♯.

i. O God, Thou faithful God,
   Thou Fountain ever flowing,
   Without Whom nothing is,
   All perfect gifts bestowing;
   A pure and healthy frame
   O give me, and within
   A conscience free from blame,
   A soul unhurt by sin.

ii. And grant me, Lord, to do,
    With ready heart and willing,
    Whate'er Thou shalt command,
    My calling here fulfilling,
    And do it when I ought,
    With all my strength, and bless
    The work I thus have wrought,
    For Thou must give success.

iii. And let me promise nought
     But I can keep it truly,
     Abstain from idle words,
     And guard my lips still duly;
     And grant, when in my place
     I must and ought to speak,
     My words due power and grace,
     Nor let me wound the weak.

iv. If dangers gather round,
    Still keep me calm and fearless;
    Help me to bear the cross
    When life is dark and cheerless;
    To overcome my foe
    With words and actions kind;
    When counsel I would know,
    Good counsel let me find.

O GOTT, DU FROMMER GOTT

v. And let me be with all
   In peace and friendship living,
   As far as Christians may.
   And if Thou aught are giving
   Of wealth and honours fair,
   Oh this refuse me not,
   That nought be mingled there
   Of goods unjustly got.

vi. And if a longer life
    Be here on earth decreed me,
    And Thou through many a strife
    To age at last wilt lead me,
    Thy patience in me shed,
    Avert all sin and shame,
    And crown my hoary head
    With pure untarnished fame.

vii. Let nothing that may chance
     Me from my Saviour sever;
     And, dying with Him, take
     My soul to Thee for ever;
     And let my body have
     A little space to sleep
     Beside my fathers' grave,
     And friends that o'er it weep.

viii. And when the Day is come,
      And all the dead are waking,
      Oh reach me down Thy hand,
      Thyself my slumbers breaking;
      Then let me hear Thy voice,
      And change this earthly frame,
      And bid me aye rejoice
      With those who love Thy name.

ix. To Thee, God Father, laud
Be now and evermore;
O God the Son receive
The love our full hearts store;
God Holy Ghost, Thy fame
From day to day increase;
O blessed Three in One
Thy praises ne'er shall cease.

Johann Heermann (1585–1647)   Tr. *Catherine Winkworth*[1].

Johann Heermann's hymn, "O Gott, du frommer Gott," entitled "Ein täglich Gebet" (A daily prayer), was first published, but not to the above melody, in his *Devoti Musica Cordis* (Leipzig, 1630), in eight stanzas. A posthumous ninth stanza[2] was added to the hymn in the Hanover *Neue Musikalische Kreutz-Trost- Lob- und Dank Schuhle* (Lüneburg, 1659).

The melody (*supra*) is found for the first time in the *New Ordentlich Gesang-Buch* (Hanover, 1646), set to Johann Heermann's hymn, "Gross ist, O grosser Gott." A widespread and erroneous impression that Bach composed it arose, presumably, from the fact that his harmonized version of the melody is found in Schemelli's Hymn-book (1736) (Erk, No. 103). Elsewhere it occurs only in the Organ works. His version of the last two phrases of the tune is not uniform. In the Organ Partite *infra* it approximates significantly to a Hamburg text of 1690. Witt (No. 527) uses another melody.

[1] *Chorale Book for England*, No. 115. The original hymn has only eight stanzas.

[2] The translation of it *supra* is by the present writer.

O GOTT, DU FROMMER GOTT 279

[108]

N. xix. 44. The melody is treated in a series of nine Partite, or Variations. Spitta is convinced that they were written in Lüneburg, or under the direct influence of Böhm, in the first decade of the eighteenth century[1], a conclusion supported by the strong Hanoverian associations which attach to Bach's melodic text and to the added ninth stanza. Schweitzer also holds them to be the product of Bach's earliest youth, on the ground of the awkward harmonization of the melody and the optional use of the Pedal[2]. Parry finds in them an air of ingenuous simplicity that proves them to be very early compositions[3]. It is the more interesting to find the youthful Bach illustrating in some of them the text of the hymn, the number of whose stanzas corresponds with the number of Partite.

Partita I may be regarded either as an introduction to stanza i, or perhaps as a broad expression of the opening line

O Gott, du frommer Gott,

the word "frommer" summoning the picture of a Personality strong, reliable, unwavering.

The second stanza hardly invites pictorial treatment. Bach would appear, as Spitta notes, to be copying Böhm's habit of extending the *cantus*.

[1] Vol. I. 211.   [2] Vol. I. 282.   [3] P. 505.

Stanza iii, like its predecessor, does not appear to have drawn the juvenile Bach to attempt illustration.

In *Partita* IV Bach's youthful eye caught the words "Gieb das ich meinen Feind...überwind" (Help me to overcome my foe); the left hand sounds a triumphant rhythm.

In *Partita* V the general atmosphere of "Fried und Freundschaft" (peace and friendship), of which the corresponding stanza speaks, draws from Bach one of his characteristic joy motives in the animated semiquaver passages which accompany the *cantus*.

Stanza vi, with its reference to "meine graue Haar" (my hoary head), summons to Bach's mind instantly the picture of an old man with halting footsteps groping his way to the grave. The same idea is expressed by similar means in "Herr Gott, nun schleuss den Himmel auf" (N. xv. 53) and "Da Jesus an dem Kreuze stund" (N. xv. 67).

In *Partita* VII, by prolonged descending passages in the first four bars and at the close of the movement, Bach illustrates the word "Grab":

> And let my body have
> A little space to sleep
> Beside my fathers' grave.

By similar means a quarter of a century later, in the last number of the *St Matthew Passion*, he

O GOTT, DU FROMMER GOTT

pictured the lowering of the dead Christ to the tomb.

In *Partita* VIII, in chromatic passages, Bach pictures the torture of the dead awaiting judgment.

Partita IX is built throughout upon the rhythm of fervent adoration elsewhere found in "Herr Christ, der ein'ge Gottes-Sohn" (N. xv. 9) and "Lob sei dem allmächtigen Gott" (N. xv. 11).

The MS. from which the Partite were published by Griepenkerl in 1846 belonged to Johann Nikolaus Forkel (1749-1818). Another MS. is in the Collection of Bach's pupil Krebs, and bears the inscription "J. S. B." Naumann mentions a third copy by F. Roitzsch in Dehn's Collection, inscribed "da Giov. Bast. Bach."

O Lamm Gottes unschuldig.

Melody: "*O Lamm Gottes unschuldig*"   Anon. 1598

282   MELODIES

    i. O Lamb of God, most stainless!
       Who on the Cross didst languish,
       Patient through all Thy sorrows,
       Though mocked amid Thine anguish;
       Our sins Thou bearest for us,
       Else had despair reigned o'er us:
       Have mercy upon us, O Jesu!

    ii. O Lamb of God, most stainless!
       Who on the Cross didst languish,
       Patient through all Thy sorrows,
       Though mocked amid Thine anguish;
       Our sins Thou bearest for us,
       Else had despair reigned o'er us:
       Have mercy upon us, O Jesu!

    iii. O Lamb of God, most stainless!
       Who on the Cross didst languish,
       Patient through all Thy sorrows,
       Though mocked amid Thine anguish;
       Our sins Thou bearest for us,
       Else had despair reigned o'er us:
       Grant us Thy peace to-day, O Jesu!

Nikolaus Decius (d. 1541)   Tr. *Catherine Winkworth*[1].

There are two forms of the ancient melody of the "Agnus Dei" adapted by Nikolaus Decius to his translation of that hymn: the original published in 1542, and a later version published in 1545[2]. The latter is in use particularly in North Germany and Bach uses it with textual variations, chiefly in the fourth phrase of the tune. It occurs in the *St Matthew*

[1] *Chorale Book for England*, No. 46. The original hymn has three stanzas.
[2] Both are printed in *Bach's Chorals*, Part I. 1, and Part II. 495.

O LAMM GOTTES UNSCHULDIG 283

Passion (1729), No. 1, *Choralgesänge*, No. 285, and the two Organ movements *infra*. In the second of them (No. 110) Bach's melodic text approximates to a reconstruction of the 1545 version found in an Eisleben Hymn-book of 1598 (*supra*). The melody occurs in two Organ movements:

[109]

N. xv. 58. The movement is the first of the Passiontide Preludes in the *Orgelbüchlein*. The *cantus* is accompanied by a sequence of sobbing notes slurred in pairs. In Bach's unvarying idiom they depict mental pain in contradistinction to the chromatic sequence by which he represents physical suffering. Bach's melodic text conforms closely to Witt's (No. 104).

[110]

N. xvii. 32. The Prelude, the sixth of the *Eighteen Chorals*, is a setting of the three stanzas of the hymn. In Verses 1 and 2 Bach does not attempt word painting. But at bar 19 (N. xvii. 37) of Verse 3, anticipating the melodic phrase of the line

Our sins Thou bearest for us,

Bach introduces a subject clearly based on it

which, upon the entry of the *cantus* (N. xvii. 38, bar 4),

accompanies it with increasing urgency of self-accusation until the words

> Else had despair reigned o'er us

are heard in the *cantus* (N. xvii. 38, bar 10). Chromatic sequences, entering at the $\frac{3}{2}$ bar, express in poignant harmonies the agony of the Saviour's death. With the entry of the last phrase of the *cantus* (N. xvii. 39, bar 1) and its petition

> Grant us Thy peace to-day, O Jesu!

the threnody is stilled, and undulating quaver sequences remind us, as Schweitzer comments[1], of the angelic proclamation of "Peace on earth" in some of the Christmas Preludes. The final ascending cadence may be pictured as the Heavenward flight of the angelic messengers.

P. vii. 97 prints an older reading of the movement. The MS. of it is among the Krebs MSS.

O MENSCH, BEWEIN' DEIN' SÜNDE GROSS.

Melody: "*Es sind doch selig alle*" Matthäus Greitter 1525

[1] Vol. II. 72.

is painted by Bach in his chromatic "grief" motive. The concluding bars, as Sir Hubert Parry remarks[1], "show how fully Bach realised the highest capacities of harmony."

PUER NATUS IN BETHLEHEM.

Melody: "*Puer natus in Bethlehem*"   Anon. 1553

    i. A Child is born *in Bethlehem ;
       Exult for joy, Jerusalem!
                Allelujah, Allelujah!
    ii. Lo, He who reigns *above the skies
       There, in a manger lowly, lies.
                Allelujah, Allelujah!
    iii. The ox and ass *in neighbouring stall
       See in that Child the Lord of all.
                Allelujah, Allelujah!
    iv. And kingly pilgrims, *long foretold,
       From East bring incense, myrrh, and gold,
                Allelujah, Allelujah!
    v. And enter with *their offerings,
       To hail the new-born King of Kings.
                Allelujah, Allelujah!
    vi. He comes, *a maiden mother's Son,
       Yet earthly father hath He none;
                Allelujah, Allelujah!

[1] *Op. cit.* 556.

vii. And, from *the serpent's poison free,
   He owned our blood and pedigree.
   Allelujah, Allelujah!

viii. Our feeble flesh *and His the same,
   Our sinless kinsman He became,
   Allelujah, Allelujah!

ix. That we, *from deadly thrall set free,
   Like Him, and so like God, should be.
   Allelujah, Allelujah!

x. Come then, and on *this natal day,
   Rejoice before the Lord and pray.
   Allelujah, Allelujah!

* * *

xii. And to *the Holy One in Three
   Give praise and thanks eternally.
   Allelujah, Allelujah!

Traditional   Tr. *Hamilton Montgomerie MacGill*[1].

The melody of the fourteenth century Christmas Carol "Puer natus in Bethlehem" ("Ein Kind geborn zu Bethlehem") exists in two forms. Of the original there is a text printed in 1543[2]. The second (*supra*), found in 1553, is the descant of a four-part setting in which the original (1543) tune appears as the Tenor. Bach uses it in Cantata 65 (1724) and a single movement *infra*. His text is

[1] *Songs of the Christian Creed and Life* (London, 1876), No. 35. The original hymn is in twelve stanzas, of which xi is omitted in the translation. To fit the melody the first line of every stanza must be repeated from the word marked *.

[2] See it on p. 308 *infra*.

invariable, except that in the latter he substitutes F sharp for F natural as the ninth note of the second line *supra*. Otherwise his text conforms to Witt's (No. 35).

The 1543 melody, with slight modifications, is that of the Christmas hymn, "Vom Himmel kam der Engel Schaar," and is used by Bach in the *Orgelbüchlein* for that Carol. (See No. 126 *infra*.)

[112]

N. xv. 13. The movement is the first of the Christmas Preludes in the *Orgelbüchlein*. Though the hymn stands there as a general introduction to the festival, its central incident is the visit of the three Kings from the East and their homage. Bach seemingly sets himself to paint stanza iv. While the quaver passages express the visitors' joy at the fruition of their long quest, he distinguishes the three Wise Men individually on the Pedal. In bars 1–4 the bearer of incense approaches the manger. The first two Pedal notes mark his deep obeisance to the Infant. In bars 5–7 the myrrh giver performs his duty in a similar manner. In bars 8–11 the bearer of gold makes his obeisance and gift. In the last six bars (bar 12—end) the Three Kings withdraw, making obeisance at every step, and their deepest curtsey as they leave the Presence.

The "programme" might be rejected as extravagant but for Bach's naïve habit of literalness. An alternative interpretation of the movement as a lullaby is not supported by the character of the music.

Schmücke dich, O liebe Seele.

Melody: "*Schmücke dich, O liebe Seele*"

Johann Crüger 1649

i. Deck thyself, my soul, with gladness,
Leave the gloomy haunts of sadness,
Come into the daylight's splendour,
There with joy thy praises render
Unto Him Whose grace unbounded
Hath this wondrous banquet founded.
High o'er all the heavens He reigneth,
Yet to dwell with thee He deigneth.

ii. Hasten as a bride to meet Him,
And with loving reverence greet Him,
For with words of life immortal
Now He knocketh at thy portal;

Haste to ope the gates before Him
Saying, while thou dost adore Him
"Suffer, Lord, that I receive Thee,
And I never more will leave Thee."

* * *

iv. Ah how hungers all my spirit
For the love I do not merit!
Oft have I, with sighs fast thronging,
Thought upon this food with longing,
In the battle well-nigh worsted,
For this cup of life have thirsted,
For the Friend, who here invites us,
And to God Himself unites us.

v. Now I sink before Thee lowly,
Filled with joy most deep and holy,
As with trembling awe and wonder
On Thy mighty works I ponder,
How, by mystery surrounded,
Depths no man hath ever sounded
None may dare to pierce unbidden
Secrets that with Thee are hidden.

* * *

vii. Sun, who all my life dost brighten,
Light, who dost my soul enlighten,
Joy, the sweetest man e'er knoweth,
Fount, whence all my being floweth,
At Thy feet I cry, my Maker,
Let me be a fit partaker
Of this blessed food from heaven,
For our good, Thy glory, given.

* * *

ix. Jesus, Bread of Life, I pray Thee,
Let me gladly here obey Thee;
Never to my hurt invited,
Be Thy love with love requited;

SCHMÜCKE DICH, O LIEBE SEELE

> From this banquet let me measure,
> Lord, how vast and deep its treasure;
> Through the gifts Thou here dost give me
> As Thy guest in heaven receive me.

Johann Franck (1618-77)   Tr. *Catherine Winkworth*[1].

Johann Franck's Eucharistic hymn, "Schmücke dich, O liebe Seele," was first published, with Johann Crüger's melody (*supra*), in 1649. Bach uses the melody in Cantata 180 (*c.* 1740) and in the movement *infra*. His text of it is practically invariable. Of his variation of bars 4 and 5 (*supra*) Zahn does not reveal an earlier instance. Witt's text (No. 308) did not guide him.

[113]

N. xvii. 22. The movement is the fourth of the *Eighteen Chorals* and, as is invariably the case when the words of the hymn stirred Bach to deep emotion, the *cantus* is treated very freely. He retards, embellishes, and emphasizes it as if to make it interpret the Holy of Holies of his thoughts. The intimacy which characterizes Bach's treatment of the melody is inspired by the lines of the last stanza:

> Jesus, Bread of Life, I pray Thee,
> ....
> Be Thy love with love requited.

---

[1] *Chorale Book for England*, No. 93. The original hymn has nine stanzas, of which iii, vi, viii are omitted in the translation.

292 MELODIES

Schumann once wrote to Mendelssohn, who had played the movement to him, that around the *cantus* " hung winding wreaths of golden leaves, and such blissfulness was breathed from within it, that you yourself [Mendelssohn] avowed that if life was bereft of all hope and faith, this one Choral would renew them for you. I was silent and went away dazed into God's acre, feeling acutely pained that I could lay no flower on his urn[1]."

B.G. xl. 181 prints a movement on the melody whose genuineness is doubtful. The text of the second part of the tune differs conspicuously from that which Bach uses elsewhere. Five MSS. of it are extant in the Schelble, Hauser, and other Collections. It is also attributed to Gottfried August Homilius (1714–85).

SEI GEGRÜSSET, JESU GÜTIG.

Melody: "*Sei gegrüsset, Jesu gütig*"
? Gottfried Vopelius 1682

[1] Quoted in Parry, *Bach*, p. 539.

SEI GEGRÜSSET, JESU GÜTIG 293

Witt's version 1715

i. Jesu, Saviour, heed my greeting,
Kind and gentle is Thy being:
Long the torture Thou hast suffered,
Deep the insults to Thee offered.
Let me all Thy love inherit
And meet death in Thy sure merit.

ii. Jesu, master, dearest treasure,
Christ, my Saviour, my heart's pleasure,
Hands and pierced Side, O show me,
Give me grace in Heaven to know Thee.
Let me all Thy love inherit
And meet death in Thy sure merit.

iii. On my sins look Thou with pity,
Christ, Who bearest all men's frailty;
Faints my heart, my soul doth languish,
Thou alone canst heal my anguish.
Let me all Thy love inherit
And meet death in Thy sure merit.

iv. O Thou fountain ever flowing,
Gracious comfort e'er bestowing,
When Death lays his hand upon me
Help me to be loyal to Thee.
Let me all Thy love inherit
And meet death in Thy sure merit.

v. Sweet refreshment floweth freely
   To Thy children stayed upon Thee;
   On Thy Passion firm relying
   Nought I fear the test of dying.
   Let me all Thy love inherit
   And meet death in Thy sure merit.

Christian Keimann (1607-62)   Tr. *C. S. T.*[1]

Christian Keimann's hymn, "Sei gegrüsset, Jesu gütig," was first published in Martin Janus' *Passionale Melicum* (Görlitz, 1663). In the Wolfenbüttel Hymn-book of 1672 its stanzas are printed alternately with those of the Passiontide prayer, " Salve Jesu, summe bonum," attributed to St Bernard of Clairvaulx. There does not appear to be reasonable ground for holding Keimann's hymn a version of the Latin. Two stanzas, improbably by Keimann, were added to his original five in the Gotha *Geistlichen Gesang-Büchlein* of 1666.

The melody (*supra*) is first found in Gottfried Vopelius' *Neu Leipziger Gesangbuch* (Leipzig, 1682), where it is set to Keimann's hymn. It is one of fourteen new anonymous melodies in that work, in all probability by Vopelius himself, one of Bach's predecessors (d. 1715) as Cantor of St Nicolas' Church, Leipzig. His name is not attached to "Sei gegrüsset," perhaps because the first half of the tune is practically identical with a melody set to E. C.

[1] The original hymn has five stanzas.

Homburg's "Grossfürst hoher Cherubinen," composed by Werner Fabricius and published in 1659. As Fabricius was a former Organist of St Nicolas' his tune must have been familiar to Vopelius. There is a four-part setting of Vopelius' melody in *Choralgesänge*, No. 307. Bach uses it elsewhere in the Organ works, where also his own is uniform with Witt's (No. 125) text, though he writes D for B as the penultimate note of bar 8 (*supra*).

[114]

N. xix. 55. A set of Partite or Choral Variations on the melody. There are eleven movements. Schweitzer[1] asserts inaccurately that the hymn has eleven stanzas, and infers that the numerical correspondence of movements and stanzas is intentional. In fact the original hymn contained five stanzas, and occasionally is found in a seven-stanza form. In eleven stanzas it is not known.

The allegation of an artistic relation between the stanzas and Bach's Partite is also rejected upon an analysis of the Variations.

Spitta divides the eleven movements into three groups which, he gives grounds for supposing, Bach wrote at different times. They are as follows[2]:

[1] Vol. I. 282.
[2] Spitta follows the order of the Peters Edition, in which Partite 6 and 7 are transposed. The Novello and B.H. Editions follow the B.G. Edition in printing Peters' 6 as 7 and his 7 as 6. The references to the Partite *supra* are to the Novello Edition.

O MENSCH, BEWEIN' DEIN' SÜNDE GROSS

i. O man, thy grievous sin bemoan,
For which Christ left His Father's throne,
From highest heaven descending.
Of Virgin pure and undefiled
He here was born, our Saviour mild,
For sin to make atonement.
The dead He raised to life again,
The sick He freed from grief and pain,
Until the time appointed
That He for us should give His Blood,
Should bear our sins' o'erwhelming load,
The shameful Cross enduring.

Sebald Heyden (1494-1561)   Tr. *Rodney Fowler*[1].

Matthäus Greitter's melody, published in 1525, was from *circa* 1584 attached to Sebald Heyden's Passiontide hymn, " O Mensch, bewein' dein' Sünde gross." Bach uses it in the *St Matthew Passion* (1729), No. 35, *Choralgesänge*, No. 286, and the movement *infra*. His text is practically uniform and close to that of 1525. The B naturals which replace B flat as the penultimate notes of bars 1 and 2 *supra* are in Witt (No. 96) and elsewhere. In the *Orgelbüchlein* Bach writes B natural as the third note of bar 7.

[111]

N. xv. 69. The movement is among the Passiontide Preludes in the *Orgelbüchlein*. It is written upon the first stanza of the hymn, whose last line

The shameful Cross enduring

---

[1] *St Matthew Passion*, No. 35, Novello's Edition. The original hymn has twenty-three stanzas.

Group I. Partite 1, 2, 3, 4, 6, Spitta concludes, were written at about the period in which the Partite on "O Gott, du frommer Gott" and "Christ, der du bist der helle Tag" were composed. He instances, in proof, their restriction to the manuals and general resemblance to Böhm's models. They display the true Partita form, in which the *cantus* is completely or partially absorbed by the ornament.

Group II. Variations 5, 7, 9, 10, 11 are all *Orgelchoräle*, similar in form to the type that predominates in the *Orgelbüchlein*. All but one of them (Variation V) have an *obbligato* pedal.

Group III. Variation 8.

If Spitta is correct, the Partite were composed by Bach at three periods, in two of which he set himself to produce five movements on the melody. The hymn itself has five stanzas. But there is no evidence of any intimate relation between them and the Partite. The hymn, in fact, is the prayer of a dying man, of uniform mood throughout, and affording none of the pictorial vistas which Bach's warm imagination so readily explored.

Griepenkerl published the Variations for Peters in 1846 partly from Johann Ludwig Krebs' MS., partly from a copy in the possession of Carl Ferdinand Becker, a Leipzig organist and Bach enthusiast. The former contains only Partite 1, 2, 4, 10. The latter places Partita 7 before Partita 6. The Voss, Westphal, Forkel MSS., among others, contain copies.

VALET WILL ICH DIR GEBEN.

Melody: "Valet will ich dir geben"

Melchior Teschner 1614

i. Farewell, henceforth for ever,
All empty, worldly, joys;
Farewell, for Christ my Saviour
Alone my thoughts employs:
In Heaven's my conversation,
Where the redeemed possess
In Him complete salvation,
The gift of God's free grace.

ii. Counsel me, dearest Jesus,
According to Thy heart;
Heal Thou all my diseases,
And every harm avert:
Be Thou my consolation
While here on earth I live,
And at my expiration
Me to Thyself receive.

iii. May in my heart's recesses
Thy name and Cross always
Shine forth, with all their graces,
To yield me joy and peace:
Stand 'fore me in that figure
Wherein Thou bar'st for us
Justice in all its rigour,
Expiring on the Cross.

iv. Thou diedst for me—oh hide me
When tempests round me roll ;
Through all my foes, oh guide me,
Receive my trembling soul :
If I but grasp Thee firmer,
What matters pain when past?
Hath he a cause to murmur
Who reaches Heaven at last?

v. Oh write my name, I pray Thee,
Now in the book of life ;
So let me here obey Thee,
And there, where joys are rife,
For ever bloom before Thee,
Thy perfect freedom prove,
And tell, as I adore Thee,
How faithful was Thy love.

Valerius Herberger (1562-1627)
Tr. *L. T. Nyberg* (i-iii), *Catherine Winkworth* (iv-v)[1].

Valerius Herberger's funerary hymn, "Valet will ich dir geben," was published, with the melody (*supra*), in 1614. The familiar tune is by Melchior Teschner, and bears a close resemblance to "Sellenger's Round." Bach uses it in the *St John Passion* (1723), No. 28, Cantata 95 (? 1732), *Choralgesänge*, No. 314, and the two Organ movements *infra*. His text is practically invariable. The substitution of C natural for A as the eleventh note of the first phrase of the tune is found in a Gotha text of 1648

---

[1] *Moravian Hymn-book*, ed. 1877, No. 1182: *Chorale Book for England*, No. 137. The original hymn has five stanzas. The last two lines of each are repeated to the melody.

and Witt (No. 722). Excepting N. xix. 2, Bach always writes G for E as the eighth note of the last phrase. The innovation dates from 1668. Bach's second phrase is quite distinct from Witt's.

[115]

N. xix. 2. The movement, perhaps, is a treatment of the first stanza of the hymn, the ascending final cadence being inspired by the words:

> In Heaven's my conversation,
> Where the redeemed possess
> In Him complete salvation,
> The gift of God's free grace.

Two MSS. of the movement are in the Berlin Royal Library, both of them of secondary authority.

An older reading of the movement is in P. vii. 100. The fact that it is found in Walther's Collection, where it is inscribed "J. S. B.," is good evidence that the Prelude belongs to the Weimar period.

[116]

N. xix. 7. The movement has the rhythm of a funeral march. But the mood is joyful and reflects that of the second half of stanza i rather than its opening valediction. Three MSS. of the Prelude exist, one of them in Dröbs' hand.

VATER UNSER IM HIMMELREICH.

Melody: " *Vater unser im Himmelreich* " Anon. 1539

  i. Our Father in the heaven Who art,
Who tellest all of us in heart
Brothers to be, and on Thee call,
And wilt have prayer from us all,
Grant that the mouth not only pray,
From deepest heart oh help its way.

 ii. Hallowed be Thy name, O Lord;
Amongst us pure oh keep Thy word,
That we too may live holily,
And keep in Thy name worthily.
Defend us, Lord, from lying lore;
Thy poor misguided folk restore.

iii. Thy kingdom come now here below,
And after, up there, evermo.
The Holy Ghost His temple hold
In us with graces manifold.
The devil's wrath and greatness strong
Crush, that he do Thy Church no wrong.

 v. Thy will be done the same, Lord God,
On earth as in Thy high abode;

VATER UNSER IM HIMMELREICH

  In pain give patience for relief,
  Obedience in love and grief;
  All flesh and blood keep off and check
  That 'gainst Thy will makes a stiff neck.
v. Give us this day our daily bread,
  And all that doth the body stead;
  From strife and war, Lord, keep us free,
  From sickness and from scarcity;
  That we in happy peace may rest,
  By care and greed all undistrest.
vi. Forgive, Lord, all our trespasses,
  That they no more may us distress,
  As of our debtors we gladly let
  Pass all the trespasses and debt.
  To serve make us all ready be
  In honest love and unity.
vii. Into temptation lead us not.
  When the evil spirit makes battle hot
  Upon the right and the left hand,
  Help us with vigour to withstand,
  Firm in the faith, armed 'gainst a host,
  Through comfort of the Holy Ghost.
viii. From all that's evil free Thy sons—
  The time, the days are wicked ones.
  Deliver us from endless death;
  Comfort us in our latest breath;
  Grant us also a blessed end,
  Our spirit take into Thy hand.
ix. Amen! that is, let this come true!
  Strengthen our faith ever anew,
  That we may never be in doubt
  Of that we here have prayed about.
  In Thy name, trusting in Thy word,
  We say a soft Amen, O Lord.

Martin Luther (1483–1546) Tr. *George Macdonald*[1].

[1] *Exotics*, p. 91. The original hymn has nine stanzas.

Luther's versification of the Lord's Prayer, "Vater unser im Himmelreich," was first published, with an anonymous melody (*supra*), in 1539. Fr. Zelle[1] supposes the tune in origin a "Bergmannslied." Bach uses it in Cantatas 90, 101, 102 (1731–*c.* 1740), *Choralgesänge*, No. 316, *St John Passion* (1723), No. 5, and four Organ movements *infra.* Excepting a single detail, his melodic text is invariable and conforms to the original: in the three Cantatas, the *Orgelbüchlein*, and N. xvi. 61 he substitutes B for G sharp as the thirteenth note of the second line *supra*. Witt (No. 232) has G sharp there.

[117]

N. xv. 105. The movement is in the Catechism section of the second part of the *Orgelbüchlein*. It stands for " Prayer," and Bach illuminates it by enforcing the intimate and rapt spirit in which prayer should be offered. The rhythm he employs on the Pedal to express blissful adoration has already been remarked in the Preludes "Alle Menschen müssen sterben," "Jesu, meine Freude," and others.

[118] [119]

N. xvi. 53, 61. These two *Clavierübung* movements, a long one and a short one, illustrate the ordinance of Prayer. Of the first and longer one

---

[1] *Die Singerweisen der ältesten evangelischen Zeit*, p. 54.

Bach's programme is not patent. Schweitzer[1] finds the word "Father" prominent in it; it does not seem to be more so than any other. Spitta, remarking[2] that the melody appears against three parts in counterpoint in canon on the octave, speculates that Bach thereby intended to symbolize the childlike obedience with which the Christian appropriates the prayer prescribed by Christ Himself. The device would appear unduly complicated for the conveyance of that impression. It is, on the whole, safer to draw attention to the fact that the simple, unadorned *cantus* (in canon on the octave) is a thread in a larger fabric woven by (1) an exceptionally embellished presentment of the *cantus* (in canon on the fifth), and (2) a Pedal part markedly contrasted in character. Conjecturally, the plain *cantus* is the Prayer of Prayers, Christ's own utterance. The embellished, ruminative version of the *cantus* expresses the intimate spirit of prayer; and the firm, reliant Pedal part typifies the faith without which prayer is vain.

In the shorter movement the *cantus* is unadorned and, alone among the *Clavierübung* Choral movements, is presented without interludes. P. v. 109 prints a variant reading from a Hauser MS.

[1] Vol. II. 68.   [2] Vol. III. 216.

[120]

N. xix. 12. The movement, a solemn prayer, is an early work of the Weimar period, similar in form to "Gottes Sohn ist kommen" (No. 53 *supra*). The MS. of it is in the Walther Collection of Choral Preludes.

In addition to the above movement, B.G. xl. 183, 184 prints two of doubtful authenticity. Both are among the Kirnberger MSS. and are attributed to Georg Böhm, of Lüneburg, Bach's contemporary there, who died *circa* 1734.

VOM HIMMEL HOCH DA KOMM ICH HER.

Melody: "*Vom Himmel hoch da komm ich her*"

? Martin Luther 1539

i. From heaven above to earth I come
To bear good news to every home;
Glad tidings of great joy I bring,
Whereof I now will say and sing.

ii. To you this night is born a Child
Of Mary, chosen mother mild;
This little Child, of lowly birth,
Shall be the joy of all your earth.

VOM HIMMEL HOCH DA KOMM ICH HER

iii. 'Tis Christ, our God, Who far on high
Hath heard your sad and bitter cry;
Himself will your Salvation be,
Himself from sin will make you free.

iv. He brings those blessings, long ago
Prepared by God for all below;
Henceforth His kingdom open stands
To you, as to the angel bands.

v. These are the tokens ye shall mark—
The swaddling clothes and manger dark;
There shall ye find the young Child laid,
By Whom the heavens and earth were made.

vi. Now let us all with gladsome cheer
Follow the shepherds, and draw near
To see this wondrous gift of God,
Who hath His only Son bestowed.

vii. Give heed, my heart, lift up thine eyes!
Who is it in yon manger lies?
Who is this Child, so young and fair?
The blessed Christ-child lieth there.

viii. Welcome to earth, Thou noble guest,
Through Whom e'en wicked men are blest!
Thou com'st to share our misery,
What can we render, Lord, to Thee?

ix. Ah Lord, Who hast created all,
How hast Thou made Thee weak and small,
That Thou must choose Thy infant bed
Where ass and ox but lately fed!

x. Were earth a thousand times as fair,
Beset with gold and jewels rare,
She yet were far too poor to be
A narrow cradle, Lord, for Thee.

xi. For velvets soft and silken stuff
 Thou hast but hay and straw so rough,
 Whereon Thou King, so rich and great,
 As 'twere Thy heaven, art throned in state.

xii. Thus hath it pleased Thee to make plain
 The truth to us poor fools and vain,
 That this world's honour, wealth, and might
 Are nought and worthless in Thy sight.

xiii. Ah! dearest Jesus, Holy Child,
 Make Thee a bed, soft, undefiled,
 Within my heart, that it may be
 A quiet chamber kept for Thee.

xiv. My heart for very joy doth leap,
 My lips no more can silence keep;
 I too must raise with joyful tongue
 That sweetest ancient cradle-song—

xv. Glory to God in highest heaven,
 Who unto man His Son hath given!
 While angels sing with pious mirth
 A glad New Year to all the earth.

Martin Luther (1483-1546)   Tr. *Catherine Winkworth*[1].

Luther published his Christmas hymn, "Vom Himmel hoch da komm ich her," in Schumann's Hymn-book (1539) with a tune which is generally attributed to himself. Bach uses it in the *Christmas Oratorio* (1734), Nos. 9, 17, 23, and in the Organ movements *infra*. His text is invariable and conforms to the original except in one detail: for the fifth note of the last phrase he takes the melody up

---

[1] *Chorale Book for England*, No. 30. The original hymn has fifteen stanzas.

VOM HIMMEL HOCH DA KOMM ICH HER

to D (*supra*). The emendation dates from 1629 and is found in Witt's text (No. 21).

[121]

N. xv. 21. In the Christmas group of the *Orgelbüchlein* the hymn records the Angelic annunciation of the new-born Christ. By ascending and descending scale passages Bach indicates the presence of the heavenly host.

[122]

N. xix. 14. The movement is a Fughetta, for the manuals, on the first two phrases of the melody. In more vivid colours Bach paints again the *Orgelbüchlein* picture. The brilliant scale passages not only represent the ascending and descending angels, but sound joyous peals from many belfries ringing in the Saviour's birth. Five copies of the movement, an early work, are extant, one of them in the Kirnberger Collection, another in the Schicht MSS.

[123]

N. xix. 16. A Fugue on the melody, phrase by phrase, without attempt at pictorial treatment. There are seven texts of the movement, a youthful work, in the Kirnberger, Schelble, and other collections.

[124]

N. xix. 19. An Organ accompaniment of the melody exhibiting the same pictorial treatment as in

Nos. 121 and 122. A MS. of the movement survives in Kittel's handwriting, and another in Dröbs'. A variant reading is in B.G. xl. 159, printed from Krebs' MS. in the Berlin Royal Library.

[125]

N. xix. 73. The Canonic Variations upon the melody have been discussed already in the Introduction[1]. They are five in number and exhibit the pictorial treatment already remarked in Nos. 121, 122, 124.

Besides the Autograph (Berlin Royal Library), copies of the Variations are in the Westphal, Forkel, Dröbs, Schelble, and Schicht MSS.

VOM HIMMEL KAM DER ENGEL SCHAAR.

Melody: "*Puer natus in Bethlehem*" Anon. 1543

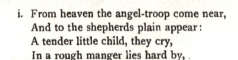

i. From heaven the angel-troop come near,
And to the shepherds plain appear:
A tender little child, they cry,
In a rough manger lies hard by,.

[1] See p. 75 *supra*.

VOM HIMMEL KAM DER ENGEL SCHAAR

ii. In Bethlehem, David's town of old,
  As Prophet Micah has foretold;
  'Tis the Lord Jesus Christ, I wis,
  Who of you all the Saviour is.
iii. And ye may well break out in mirth,
  That God is one with you henceforth;
  For He is born your flesh and blood—
  Your brother is the eternal Good.
iv. What can death do to you, or sin?
  The true God is to you come in.
  Let hell and Satan raging go—
  The Son of God's your comrade now.
v. He will nor can from you go hence;
  Set you in Him your confidence.
  Let many battle on you make,
  Defy them—He cannot forsake.
vi. At last you must approval win,
  For you are now of God's own kin.
  For this thank God, ever and aye,
  Happy and patient all the day.

Martin Luther (1483-1546)   Tr. *George Macdonald*[1].

Martin Luther's Christmas Carol, "Vom Himmel kam der Engel Schaar," was first published in Joseph Klug's *Geistliche Lieder zu Wittemberg* (Wittenberg, 1543). The melody (*supra*) with which it is familiarly associated is proper to the Carol "Puer natus in Bethlehem," published in the same Hymn-book, and is found as the Tenor of a four-part setting in which the 1553 melody of the Carol[2] appears as the descant. Zahn (No. 192a) seems to

[1] *Exotics*, p. 48. The original hymn has six stanzas.
[2] See *supra*, p. 286.

imply that the conversion of the 1543 melody to the use of "Vom Himmel kam der Engel Schaar" first appears in Vulpius (1609). The hymn, in fact, had two earlier melodies of its own, both of which are reconstructions of Latin hymns: one of them (1593) being developed from "A solis ortus cardine," and the other (1598) from "Puer nobis nascitur." Bach uses the melody only in the Organ movement *infra*. His distinctive first phrase (varying notes 1–8 *supra*) is in Witt (No. 22).

[126]

N. xv. 23. The movement is one of the Christmas Preludes in the *Orgelbüchlein*. The brilliant scale passages represent the descending and ascending angels. The Pedal notes, too, provide a ladder. Had Bach Jacob's vision in his mind?

VON GOTT WILL ICH NICHT LASSEN.
Melody: "*Von Gott will ich nicht lassen*"
Anon. 1572 [1571]

* See page 313.

i. From God shall nought divide me,
   For He is true for aye,
   And on my path will guide me,
   Who else should often stray;
   His ever-bounteous hand
   By night and day is heedful,
   And gives me what is needful,
   Where'er I go or stand.

   * * *

iii. If sorrow comes, He sent it,
   In Him I put my trust;
   I never shall repent it,
   For He is true and just,
   And loves to bless us still;
   My life and soul, I owe them
   To Him Who doth bestow them,
   Let Him do as He will.

iv. Whate'er shall be His pleasure
   Is surely best for me;
   He gave His dearest treasure
   That our weak hearts might see
   How good His will t'ward us;
   And in His Son He gave us
   Whate'er could bless and save us—
   Praise Him Who loveth thus!

v. Oh praise Him, for He never
   Forgets our daily need;
   Oh blest the hour whenever
   To Him our thoughts can speed;
   Yea, all the time we spend
   Without Him is but wasted,
   Till we His joy have tasted,
   The joy that hath no end.

vi. For when the world is passing
   With all its pomp and pride,
   All we were here amassing
   No longer may abide;
   But in our earthly bed,
   Where softly we are sleeping,
   God hath us in His keeping,
   To wake us from the dead.

* * *

viii. Then though on earth I suffer
   Much trial, well I know
   I merit ways still rougher,
   And 'tis to heaven I go;
   For Christ I know and love,
   To Him I now am hasting,
   And gladness everlasting
   With Him this heart shall prove.

ix. For such His will Who made us;
   The Father seeks our good;
   The Son hath grace to aid us,
   And save us by His blood;
   His Spirit rules our ways,
   By Faith in us abiding,
   To heaven our footsteps guiding;
   To Him be thanks and praise.

Ludwig Helmbold (1532–98)   Tr. *Catherine Winkworth*[1].

Ludwig Helmbold's hymn, "Von Gott will ich nicht lassen," was written *circa* 1563 to a secular melody, "Ich ging einmal spazieren," and was published along with it in 1572 [1571]. Its relation to Paul Eber's "Helft mir Gott's Güte preisen" has

[1] *Chorale Book for England*, No. 140. The original hymn has nine stanzas, of which ii and vii are omitted in the translation.

VON GOTT WILL ICH NICHT LASSEN 313

been discussed already[1]. It occurs in Cantatas 11, 73, 107 (*c.* 1725–35), the doubtful "Lobt ihn mit Herz und Munde," *Choralgesänge*, Nos. 324–326, and the Organ movement *infra*. Zahn (No. 5264*b*) does not reveal an earlier example of Bach's distinctive variation of the opening phrase. It is not in Witt (No. 542). Bach's text of the fifth (notes 9–13 of the second line *supra*) invariably contains one foot more than the original, an elongation of the line due to the addition of a syllable—"Er reicht mir seine Hand" for "Reicht mir seine Hand."

[127]

N. xvii. 43. The movement is the eighth of the *Eighteen Chorals*. By means of a characteristic rhythm of joy, Bach, as in the Prelude "In dich hab' ich gehoffet, Herr," expresses complete trust in and loyalty to God. The impression of intense feeling is conveyed by his ruminative treatment of the melody in the opening bars. Below these expressions of intimate feeling the Pedal *canto fermo* marches with unfaltering assurance in God's goodness. An older text of the movement is in P. vii. 102. Two MSS. of it exist, one of them in Krebs' hand.

[1] See *Bach's Chorals*, Part I. 63.

Wachet auf, ruft uns die Stimme.

Melody: "*Wachet auf, ruft uns die Stimme*"
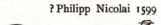

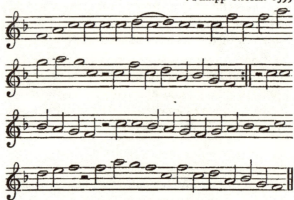

i. Wake, awake, for night is flying,
   The watchmen on the heights are crying;
   Awake, Jerusalem, at last!
   Midnight hears the welcome voices,
   And at the thrilling cry rejoices:
   Come forth, ye virgins, night is past!
   The Bridegroom comes, awake,
   Your lamps with gladness take;
   Hallelujah!
   And for His marriage feast prepare,
   For ye must go to meet Him there.

ii. Zion hears the watchmen singing,
    And all her heart with joy is springing,
    She wakes, she rises from her gloom;
    For her Lord comes down all-glorious,
    The strong in grace, in truth victorious;
    Her Star is risen, her Light is come!

WACHET AUF, RUFT UNS DIE STIMME

Ah! come, Thou blessed Lord,
O Jesus, Son of God,
Hallelujah!
We follow till the halls we see
Where Thou hast bid us sup with Thee.

iii. Now let all the heavens adore Thee,
And men and angels sing before Thee,
With harp and cymbal's clearest tone;
Of one pearl each shining portal,
Where we are with the choir immortal
Of angels round Thy dazzling throne;
Nor eye hath seen, nor ear
Hath yet attained to hear
What there is ours,
But we rejoice, and sing to Thee
Our hymn of joy eternally.

Philipp Nicolai (1556-1608) Tr. *Catherine Winkworth*[1].

Philipp Nicolai's hymn, with the melody (*supra*), was published in 1599. Its opening line is identical with "O Lamm Gottes[2]" and, according to Christian Huber (1682), the tune appeared in Balthasar Musculus' *Cithara sacra, c.* 1591, some years before its association with Nicolai's hymn. It would seem, therefore, that, as in the case of "Wie schön leuchtet der Morgenstern," Nicolai adapted older material.

Bach uses the tune in Cantata 140 (1731) and in the Organ movement *infra*.

---

[1] *Chorale Book for England*, No. 200. The original hymn has three stanzas.
[2] See *Bach's Chorals*, Part II. 495.

[128]

N, xvi. 1. The Prelude is the first of the *Schübler Chorals*, a rearrangement of the fourth movement of Cantata 140. In the latter the *cantus* is assigned to the Tenor and the *obbligato* (" dextra" manual) to the Violins and Viola in unison. The movement is a setting of the second stanza of the hymn. The happy, smooth-running *obbligato* illustrates the words:

> Zion hears the watchmen singing,
> And all her heart with joy is springing.

WENN WIR IN HÖCHSTEN NÖTHEN SEIN.

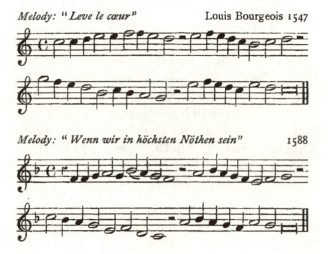

Melody: "*Leve le cœur*" Louis Bourgeois 1547

Melody: "*Wenn wir in höchsten Nöthen sein*" 1588

WENN WIR IN HÖCHSTEN NÖTHEN SEIN

i. When in the hour of utmost need
We know not where to look for aid,
When days and nights of anxious thought
Nor help nor counsel yet have brought,

ii. Then this our comfort is alone,
That we may meet before Thy throne,
And cry, O faithful God, to Thee,
For rescue from our misery,

iii. To Thee may raise our hearts and eyes,
Repenting sore with bitter sighs,
And seek Thy pardon for our sin,
And respite from our griefs within :

iv. For Thou hast promised graciously
To hear all those who cry to Thee,
Through Him Whose name alone is great,
Our Saviour and our Advocate.

v. And thus we come, O God, to-day,
And all our woes before Thee lay,
For tried, forsaken, lo! we stand,
Perils and foes on every hand.

vi. Ah! hide not for our sins Thy face,
Absolve us through Thy boundless grace,
Be with us in our anguish still,
Free us at last from every ill ;

vii. That so with all our hearts we may
Once more our glad thanksgivings pay,
And walk obedient to Thy word,
And now and ever praise the Lord.

Paul Eber (1511–69)   Tr. *Catherine Winkworth*[1].

[1] *Chorale Book for England*, No. 141. The original hymn has seven stanzas.

Vor deinen Thron tret' ich hiemit.

i. Before Thy throne, my God, I stand,
Myself, my all, are in Thy hand;
Turn to me Thine approving face,
Nor from me now withhold Thy grace.

ii. O God, my Father, Thou hast laid
Thy likeness on me, whom Thou'st made;
In Thee is all my being here,
With Thee beside me nought I fear.

iii. How oft and with what gracious speed
Hast thou solaced me in my need,
When but a step did intervene
Between me and the dark unseen!

iv. My very self I owe to Thee;
With love's fond care Thou holdest me;
Thou art a Friend most leal and true,
Beneath whose care shall nought me rue.

v. O Son of God, through Thy dear Blood
Have I escaped from Hell's dark flood:
'Tis Thou hast paid the price decreed,
And of God's wrath my soul relieved.

vi. Should Sin and Satan hold me thrall,
Should heart grow faint and fears appal,
Sure still Thou dost behind me stand
To stay my God's avenging hand.

vii. Thou interced'st for me above,
My Friend, my Saviour. 'Tis Thy love,
And through Thy saving grace alone,
My soul hath its salvation won.

viii. O Holy Spirit, power divine,
Fill full this erring heart of mine.
Of good repute whate'er there be
In me is found, it comes from Thee.

WENN WIR IN HÖCHSTEN NÖTHEN SEIN

ix. To Thee, most precious gift, I owe,
That God the Father's love I know,
Whose blessed word and sacrament
Sustain me till this life be spent.

x. Through Thee I scorn temptation's hour,
Nor faint when troubles o'er me lower;
Thou dost my heart with solace fill
And cheerful make me do God's will.

xi. Wherefore I thank Thee, Heavenly Three,
Now evening's shadows fall on me,
For all the grace Thou dost bestow,
For all the joy my soul doth know.

xii. I pray that by Thy gracious hand
My life may ever be o'erspanned,
My soul and body, honour, place,
Stand sure beneath Thy sheltering grace.

xiii. Grant me a pure and upright heart,
To ever play an honest part;
An open faith and constancy,
Purged clean of false hypocrisy.

xiv. Release me from sin's heavy debt,
Thy face with pardon toward me set;
Enkindle faith and constancy
And soon to heaven welcome me.

xv. Grant that my end may worthy be,
And that I wake Thy face to see,
Thyself for evermore to know.
Amen, Amen, God grant it so!

? Bodo von Hodenberg (1604-50)   Tr. *C. S. T.*[1]

---

[1] The original hymn has fifteen stanzas. In the eleventh stanza the words "morning," "mid-day," "evening" are alternatives in the second line.

Paul Eber's "Wenn wir in höchsten Nöthen sein," for use in time of trouble, is founded upon a hymn by his former master at Nürnberg, Joachim Camerarius:

> In tenebris nostrae et densa caligine mentis,
> Cum nihil est toto pectore consilii,
> Turbati erigimus, Deus, ad Te lumina cordis
> Nostra, tuamque fides solius erat opem.
> Tu rege consiliis actus, Pater optime, nostros,
> Nostrum opus ut laudi serviat omne Tuae.

Eber's hymn was first printed as a broadsheet at Nürnberg *circa* 1560, and later in the Dresden *New Betbüchlein* (1566).

The melody (*supra*) is by Louis Bourgeois. It appeared first in the French Psalter of 1547: *Pseaulmes cinquante de David, Roy et prophete, traduictz en uers francois par Clement Marot et mis en musique par Loys Bourgeoys, à quatre parties* (Lyons, 1547). It is set there to the hymn on the Ten Commandments, "Leve le cœur, ouvre l'oreille." The tune was attached to Eber's hymn by Franz Eler, in his *Cantica sacra* (Hamburg, 1588). There are harmonizations of the melody in *Choralgesänge*, Nos. 358, 359. The tune does not occur in Bach elsewhere than in the Organ works *infra*. His text is invariable. Witt's (No. 656) is uniform with it.

[129]

N. xv. 115. A short movement of nine bars in the "In Time of Trouble" section of the *Orgel-*

büchlein. It will be noticed that Bach constantly states and inverts the opening four notes of the *cantus*,

The effect, as Schweitzer notes[1], is that the three lower parts constantly voice the urgency of their "utmost need," while over their lament the melody flows along "like a divine song of consolation, and in a wonderful final cadence seems to silence and compose the other parts." The *cantus* itself is treated in Bach's most intimate and reflective manner, as though he sought to convey through its short phrases the utmost of the intense feeling that filled his own soul.

[130]

N. xvii. 85. The movement is the last of the *Eighteen Chorals*. During Bach's last illness he continued to revise his Organ Preludes, a work upon which he had been engaged for some time. He was almost blind and passed his days in a darkened room. Paul Eber's hymn had brought comfort to many in their distress, and to its melody Bach turned in the last weeks of his life. His strength no longer being equal to the effort, he dictated to

[1] Vol. II. 71.

Altnikol, his son-in-law, this movement upon a melody he had treated years before in the *Orgelbüchlein*. "In the dark chamber," writes Schweitzer finely[1], "with the shades of death already falling round him, the master made this work, that is unique even among his creations. The contrapuntal art that it reveals is so perfect that no description can give any idea of it. Each segment of the melody is treated in a fugue, in which the inversion of the subject figures each time as the counter-subject. Moreover, the flow of the parts is so easy that after the second line we are no longer conscious of the art, but are wholly enthralled by the spirit that finds voice in these G major harmonies. The tumult of the world no longer penetrated through the curtained windows. The harmonies of the spheres were already echoing round the dying master. So there is no sorrow in the music; the tranquil quavers move along on the other side of all human passion; over the whole thing gleams the word 'Transfiguration.'"

But it was not Paul Eber's hymn that Bach employed to disclose the spirit of his music. His was no cry of distress, but the simple faith of a devout nature facing eternity, and ready to meet it, with the words of a prayer of daily use upon his lips. Bach bade Altnikol inscribe the music with

[1] Vol. 1. 224.

the title "Vor deinen Thron tret' ich hiemit." The hymn was first published by Justus Gesenius and David Denicke in the *New Ordentlich Gesang-Buch* (Hanover, 1646), and is entitled "Am Morgen, Mittag und Abend kan man singen" (For use morning, mid-day, and evening). Its authorship is attributed, on certain grounds, to Bodo von Hodenberg, who was born at Celle in 1604 and died in 1650 at Osterode, where he then was Landrost. The Novello Edition (xv. 114; xvii. 185) quotes Hodenberg's (?) hymn as "Vor deinen Thron tret' ich *allhier*." Fischer-Tümpel (ii. 410) does not sanction this form. The hymn had its proper melody (Zahn, No. 669) since 1695, but neither hymn nor melody was in general use: the former is not in the *Unverfälschter Liedersegen* (Berlin, 1851).

"Death," writes Sir Hubert Parry[1], "had always had a strange fascination for Bach, and many of his most beautiful compositions had been inspired by the thoughts which it suggested. And now he met it, not with repinings or fear of the unknown, but with the expression of exquisite peace and trust. Music had been his life. Music had been his one means of expressing himself, and in the musical form which had been most congenial to him he bids his farewell; and only in the last bar of all for

[1] *Johann Sebastian Bach*, 542.

a moment a touch of sadness is felt, where he seems to look round upon those dear to him and to cast upon them the tender gaze of sorrowing love."

The foundation of the movement is the *Orgelbüchlein* Prelude (*supra*), minus its elaborate ornamentation of the *cantus*, and with the addition of the astonishing interludes on which Schweitzer's commentary already has been quoted.

WER NUR DEN LIEBEN GOTT LÄSST WALTEN.

Melody: "*Wer nur den lieben Gott lässt walten*"
Georg Neumark 1657

i. If thou but suffer God to guide thee,
   And hope in Him through all thy ways,
   He'll give thee strength, whate'er betide thee,
   And bear thee through the evil days.
   Who trusts in God's unchanging love
   Builds on the rock that nought can move.

ii. What can these anxious cares avail thee,
    These never-ceasing moans and sighs?
    What can it help, if thou bewail thee
    O'er each dark moment as it flies?
    Our cross and trials do but press
    The heavier for our bitterness.

WER NUR DEN LIEBEN GOTT LÄSST WALTEN

iii. Only be still and wait His leisure
In cheerful hope, with heart content
To take whate'er thy Father's pleasure
And all-deserving love hath sent,
Nor doubt our inmost wants are known
To Him Who chose us for His own.

iv. He knows the time for joy, and truly
Will send it when He sees it meet,
When He hath tried and purged thee throughly
And finds thee free from all deceit ;
He comes to thee all unaware
And makes thee own His loving care.

v. Nor think amid the heat of trial
That God hath cast thee off unheard,
That He whose hopes meet no denial
Must surely be of God preferred ;
Time passes and much change doth bring,
And sets a bound to everything.

vi. All are alike before the Highest.
'Tis easy to our God, we know,
To raise thee up, though low thou liest,
To make the rich man poor and low ;
True wonders still by Him are wrought
Who setteth up and brings to nought.

vii. Sing, pray, and keep His ways unswerving,
So do thine own part faithfully,
And trust His word; though undeserving,
Thou yet shalt find it true for thee—
God never yet forsook at need
The soul that trusted Him indeed.

Georg Neumark (1621-81)   Tr. *Catherine Winkworth*[1].

[1] *Chorale Book for England*, No. 134. The original hymn has seven stanzas.

Georg Neumark's consolatory hymn, "Wer nur den lieben Gott lässt walten," was first published, words and melody (*supra*), in 1657. Bach uses the tune in Cantatas 21, 27, 84, 88, 93, 166, 179, 197 (1714– c. 1740); *Choralgesänge*, No. 367; and the movements *infra*. His text is invariable. The E flat for E natural as the third note of the second phrase dates from 1682. In the second half of the tune he invariably writes A for B flat as the first note, and C for B flat as the seventh note of the second line *supra*, while his closing phrase differs from the original. In all these details he follows Witt (No. 553).

There are four Organ movements on the melody:

[131]

N. xv. 117. The movement is the last of the "In Time of Trouble" section of the *Orgelbüchlein*, and is placed there by Bach in order to end upon a note of confidence. For that reason he introduces the rhythm of joy which the thought of God's nearness and watchfulness ever roused in him (cf. "In dich hab' ich gehoffet, Herr," and "Von Gott will ich nicht lassen"). The movement particularly illustrates the first stanza:

> Who trusts in God's unchanging love
> Builds on the rock that nought can move.

[132]

N. xvi. 6. The movement, No. 3 of the *Schübler Chorals*, is an arrangement of a setting of the fourth

WER NUR DEN LIEBEN GOTT LÄSST WALTEN 327

stanza of Neumark's hymn in Cantata 93 (? 1728)[1]. In the Cantata the *cantus* is played by Violins and Violas in unison, while the part allotted to the "dextra" manual is a *Duetto* for Soprano and Alto. The "sinistra" manual plays the original *Continuo*. As in the *Orgelbüchlein* movement Bach uses the rhythm of joy:

> He knows the time for joy, and truly
> Will send it when He sees it meet.

[133]

N. xix. 21. The movement stands in contrast to the others upon the melody, not in mood, but in the means by which Bach expresses it. The animated semiquaver passages accompanying the *cantus* express whole-hearted joy. In the B.G. Edition the movement ends with a simple four-part setting of the melody. It is not reproduced in the Novello Edition, but will be found in P. v. 57. Copies are among Kirnberger's, Voss', Westphal's, Fischhof's, and Forkel's MSS.

[134]

N. xix. 22. This short, intimate movement is found in Wilhelm Friedemann's (1720) and Anna Magdalena's (1722) *Clavierbüchlein*. It is also among the Kirnberger, Oley, and Schelble MSS. Bach probably gave it to his son and wife as an exercise in playing *fioriture*. But, as in "Wenn wir in höchsten

[1] See *Bach's Chorals*, Part II. 321.

Nöthen sein," his reflective treatment of the *cantus* reveals the intimacy of its appeal to his religious feelings. The movement is extracted from a longer one, printed in P. v. 111. The latter includes the *cantus*, as in N. xix. 22, with a prelude of nine bars; an interlude of two bars between lines $\left.{1\atop 3}\right\}$ and $\left.{2\atop 4}\right\}$ of the melody; an interlude of five bars before the second part of the tune; and a postlude of four bars to conclude it. No doubt the movement was written for Church use, and Spitta[1] attributes it to the early years of the Arnstadt period, in view of its evidence of Böhm's influence. There are two MSS. of the movement, one in Schelble's hand, the other in a collection of Organ Chorals attributed to Bach, in the Berlin Royal Library.

WIE SCHÖN LEUCHTET DER MORGENSTERN.

Melody: " *Wie schön leuchtet der Morgenstern* "

? Philipp Nicolai 1599

[1] Vol. I. 313.

WIE SCHÖN LEUCHTET DER MORGENSTERN

Melody: "Jauchzet dem Herren, alle Land"   Anon. 1538

i. O Morning Star! how fair and bright
Thou beamest forth in truth and light!
O Sovereign meek and lowly,
Thou Root of Jesse, David's Son,
My Lord and Bridegroom, Thou hast won
My heart to serve Thee solely!
Holy art Thou,
Fair and glorious, all victorious,
Rich in blessing,
Rule and might o'er all possessing.

* * *

iii. Thou Heavenly Brightness! Light Divine!
O deep within my heart now shine,
And make Thee there an altar!
Fill me with joy and strength to be
Thy member, ever joined to Thee
In love that cannot falter;
Toward Thee longing
Doth possess me; turn and bless me;
For Thy gladness
Eye and heart here pine in sadness.

iv. But if Thou look on me in love,
　　There straightway falls from God above
　　A ray of purest pleasure ;
　　Thy word and Spirit, flesh and blood,
　　Refresh my soul with heavenly food.
　　Thou art my hidden treasure ;
　　Let Thy grace, Lord,
　　Warm and cheer me. O draw near me ;
　　Thou hast taught us
　　Thee to seek since Thou hast sought us !
　　　　　　*　　*　　*
vii. Here will I rest, and hold it fast,
　　The Lord I love is First and Last,
　　The End as the Beginning !
　　Here I can calmly die, for Thou
　　Wilt raise me where Thou dwellest now,
　　Above all tears, all sinning :
　　Amen ! Amen !
　　Come, Lord Jesus, soon release us.
　　With deep yearning,
　　Lord, we look for Thy returning !
Philipp Nicolai (1556–1608)　　Tr. *Catherine Winkworth*[1].

Philipp Nicolai's hymn was first published, with the melody, in 1599. The tune (*supra*) is a reconstruction of older material. The first half is taken, with the alteration of two notes, from the first, second, and concluding phrases of the melody (*supra*) to which Psalm 100, "Jauchzet dem Herren, alle Land," is set in Wolff Köphel's Psalter, published in 1538. The concluding phrase of Nicolai's tune also is modelled on that original. The opening phrase of

[1] *Chorale Book for England*, No. 149. The original hymn has seven stanzas, of which ii, v, vi are omitted in the translation.

the second part of his tune (line 7 of the hymn) is identical with one in the old Carol "Resonet in laudibus," whose opening phrase, moreover, bears close similarity to "Jauchzet dem Herren," a fact, perhaps, which drew Nicolai's attention to it. The tune occurs in Cantatas 1, 36, 37, 49, 61, 172 (1714–c. 1740); *Choralgesänge*, No. 375; and the movement *infra*. Bach's text is invariable for the first part of the melody and follows the original, except for the substitution of A for C as the first note of the third phrase, as in Witt (No. 479). For the second part of the tune Bach either keeps to the original, as in Witt (No. 479), Cantata 172 (1724–5), and the Organ movement; or follows Crüger (1640) in substituting A and B flat for G and A as the sixth and seventh notes of line 3 *supra*, as in Cantatas 1 and 36 (*c.* 1730–40); or adopts Vopelius' (1682) text there, as in *Choralgesänge*, No. 375.

[135]

N. xix. 23. The movement seems to be inspired by the third stanza of the hymn :

> Fill me with joy and strength to be
> Thy member, ever joined to Thee.

Bach's Autograph (four leaves of small quarto) is in the Royal Library, Berlin. Spitta assigns it to the Arnstadt period[1].

[1] Vol. I. 254.

B.G. xl. 164 prints another, but incomplete (23 bars), movement on the melody, the Autograph of which is in the Berlin Royal Library.

Wir Christenleut'.

Melody: " Wir Christenleut'"

Caspar Fuger the younger 1593

i. We Christians may
   Rejoice to-day,
   When Christ was born to comfort and to save us;
   Who thus believes
   No longer grieves,
   For none are lost who grasp the hope He gave us.

ii. O wondrous joy!
    That God most high
    Should take our flesh, and thus our race should honour;
    A virgin mild
    Hath borne this Child,
    Such grace and glory God hath put upon her.

iii. Sin brought us grief,
     But Christ relief,
     When down to earth He came for our salvation;
     Since God with us
     Is dwelling thus,
     Who dares to speak the Christian's condemnation?

iv. Then hither throng,
With happy song,
To Him Whose birth and death are our assurance;
Through Whom are we
At last set free
From sins and burdens that surpassed endurance.

v. Yes, let us praise
Our God and raise
Loud hallelujahs to the skies above us.
The bliss bestowed
To-day by God
To ceaseless thankfulness and joy should move us.

Caspar Fuger (d. *c.* 1592)   Tr. *Catherine Winkworth*[1].

The Christmas hymn, " Wir Christenleut'," was written by Caspar Fuger, whose son (?), also named Caspar, wrote the melody to it. The tune (*supra*), which is certainly as old as 1589, was published with the hymn in 1593. Bach uses it in Cantatas 40, 110, 142 (*c.* 1712–*c.* 1734); *Christmas Oratorio* (1734), No. 35; and the Organ movements *infra*. His text is invariable and follows the original. Witt's (No. 33) text is uniform with it.

The melody is treated in two of the Organ Chorals :

[136]

N. xv. 36. The movement concludes the Christmas section of the *Orgelbüchlein*. Bach's reason for placing it there is revealed in his treatment of the

[1] *Chorale Book for England*, No. 34. The original hymn has five stanzas. The first line of each is repeated to the melody.

melody. He is not moved by the hymn's invitation to rejoice over the Christmas story, but by the blessings which result to mankind from it. They are stated in the latter half of the first stanza: "He whose faith stands fast to the Incarnation shall never be confounded." To bring out this interpretation of the hymn Bach sets the *cantus* upon a broadly-spaced figure on the Pedals, which, frequently repeated, typifies the Christian's confident faith in the Incarnation as the instrument of his salvation.

[137]

N. xix. 28. The movement, a direct and happy treatment of the Christmas tune, conveys none of the symbolism of the *Orgelbüchlein* Prelude. Copies of it are in the Kirnberger, Oley, Schicht, and Schelble MSS.

WIR DANKEN DIR, HERR JESU CHRIST.
Melody: "Herr Jesu Christ, wahr Mensch und Gott"
Anon. 1597

1. We bless Thee, Jesus Christ our Lord;
For ever be Thy name adored:
For Thou, the sinless One, hast died
That sinners might be justified.

ii. O very Man, and very God,
Redeem us with Thy precious blood;
From death eternal set us free,
And make us one with God in Thee.

iii. From sin and shame defend us still,
And work in us Thy stedfast will,
The Cross with patience to sustain,
And bravely bear its utmost pain.

iv. In Thee we trust, in Thee alone;
For Thou forsakest not Thine own:
To all the meek Thy strength is given,
Who by Thy Cross ascend to heaven.

Christoph Fischer (1520–97)   Tr. *Benjamin Hall Kennedy*[1].

Christoph Fischer's Passiontide hymn, "Wir danken dir, Herr Jesu Christ," is found in the Dresden *Gesangbuch* of 1597. Fischer was born at Joachimsthal, in Bohemia, in 1520. He graduated at Wittenberg in 1544, held pastoral charges at Halberstadt and elsewhere, and died at Celle in 1597. Though he was a voluminous writer, this is the only hymn known to be his.

The melody (*supra*), which is sung to several hymns, was published first in Johann Eccard's *Geistliche Lieder, Auff den Choral oder gemeine Kirchen Melodey durchauss gerichtet* (Part II, Königsberg, 1597). The tune is attributed by Winterfeld to Eccard himself. But the many and divergent texts of it found about the year 1597 prove the

[1] *Hymnologia Christiana*, No. 622. The original hymn has four stanzas.

melody of greater antiquity. The tune was set in 1597 to Paul Eber's hymn, " Herr Jesu Christ, wahr Mensch und Gott." Bach has not used it elsewhere than in the *Orgelbüchlein*. Witt's (No. 135) text, like Bach's, is true to the original form of the melody.

[138]

N. xv. 73. The movement is among the Passiontide Chorals of the *Orgelbüchlein*. The hymn is a thanksgiving for the Atonement. Hence the characteristic " Joy " formula in the Pedal part.

WIR GLAUBEN ALL' AN EINEN GOTT,
SCHÖPFER.

Melody: " *Wir glauben all' an einen Gott* "   Anon. 1524

WIR GLAUBEN ALL' AN EINEN GOTT 337

i. We all believe in One true God,
   Maker of the earth and heaven ;
   The Father Who to us in love
   Hath the claim of children given.
   He in soul and body feeds us,
   All we want His hand provides us,
   Through all snares and perils leads us,
   Watches that no harm betides us ;
   He cares for us by day and night,
   All things are governed by His might.

ii. And we believe in Jesus Christ,
    His Only Son, our Lord, possessing
    An equal Godhead, throne and might,
    Through Whom descends the Father's blessing;
    Conceivèd of the Holy Spirit,
    Born of Mary, virgin mother,
    That lost man might life inherit ;
    Made true man, our Elder Brother,
    Was crucified for sinful men,
    And raised by God to life again.

iii. And we confess the Holy Ghost,
     Who from Son and Father floweth,
     The Comforter of fearful hearts,
     Who all precious gifts bestoweth ;

338 MELODIES

> In Whom all the Church hath union,
> Who maintains the Saints' Communion;
> We believe our sins forgiven,
> And that life with God in heaven,
> When we are raised again, shall be
> Our portion in eternity.
>
> Martin Luther (1483-1546) Tr. *Catherine Winkworth*[1].

Luther's "Wir glauben all' an einen Gott," a free version of the Nicene Creed, was first published, with the melody (*supra*), in Johann Walther's Hymnbook (Wittenberg, 1524). The hymn was sung at the funeral of Luther's patron, Frederick the Wise of Saxony, in 1525, and was used as a funeral hymn in later times. During the Reformation it was generally sung after the sermon. The tune, no doubt, is derived from the plainsong of the Creed and was adapted by Walther. Bach uses it in the Organ works *infra* and *Choralgesänge*, No. 382. His text conforms closely to the original and Witt (No. 226).

[139]

N. xvi. 49. This and the following movement stand for the Creed among the Catechism hymns of the *Clavierübung*. To this, the longer of the two, English use attaches the popular name, the "Giant's Fugue," on account of its Pedal passages. They symbolize the impregnable foundation on which the

---

[1] *Chorale Book for England*, App. VI. The original hymn has three stanzas.

WIR GLAUBEN ALL' AN EINEN GOTT

Church's faith rests and may be compared with the structure of Pedal crotchets on which Bach builds the "Credo in Unum Deum" and "Confiteor" of the B minor Mass. Above this foundation the first phrase of the melody

          We all believe in One true God

is reiterated.

[140]

N. xvi. 52. The shorter movement in the *Clavierübung* is a Fughetta, for manuals only, upon the first line of the melody.

B.G. xl. 187 (P. ix. 40) prints a movement on the melody which Naumann holds to be "recht gut von Seb. Bach herrühren." It is quite different in style from the *Clavierübung* movements and treats the melody without interludes. The MS. of it is in Krebs' *Sammelbuch*.

WIR GLAUBEN ALL' AN EINEN GOTT, VATER

Melody: "Wir glauben all' an einen Gott"   Anon. 1699

i. We all believe in One true God,
Father, Son, and Holy Ghost,
Strong Deliverer in our need,
Praised by all the heavenly host,
By Whose mighty power alone
All is made, and wrought, and done.

ii. And we believe in Jesus Christ,
Son of man and Son of God;
Who, to raise us up to heaven,
Left His throne and bore our load;
By Whose Cross and death are we
Rescued from our misery.

iii. And we confess the Holy Ghost,
Who from both for ever flows;
Who upholds and comforts us
In the midst of fears and woes.
Blest and holy Trinity,
Praise shall aye be brought to Thee.

Tobias Clausnitzer (1618–84)   Tr. *Catherine Winkworth*[1].

Tobias Clausnitzer's Trinity hymn, "Wir glauben all' an einen Gott, Vater," was first published in the *Neu-Vollständigers Marggräfl. Brandenburgisches Gesang-Buch* (Bayreuth, 1668). The melody (*supra*) was set to it in the *Neu verfertigtes Darmstädtisches Gesangbuch* (Darmstadt, 1699). Bach uses it only in the Organ movement *infra*. Witt's (No. 228) text is uniform, excepting that he writes C for E as the fourth note of the second part of the tune.

[1] *Chorale Book for England*, No. 75. The original hymn has three stanzas.

WIR GLAUBEN ALL' AN EINEN GOTT 341

[141]

N. xix. 30. Schweitzer[1] places the movement among Bach's "admittedly youthful works," and Spitta[2] finds the concluding arabesque "an unmistakeable Buxtehude coda." But the Prelude is not juvenile in feeling. The MS. of it is in the Schelble-Gleichauf Collection. With alterations Krebs included it in his Organ *Tonstücke*[3].

WO SOLL ICH FLIEHEN HIN.

Melody: "Auf meinen lieben Gott"   J. H. Schein 1627

   i. O whither shall I flee,
      Depressed with misery?
      Who is it that can ease me,
      And from my sins release me?
      Man's help I vain have proved,
      Sin's load remains unmoved.
  ii. O Jesus, Source of Grace,
      I seek Thy loving face,
      Upon Thy invitation,
      With deep humiliation;
      O let Thy blood me cover,
      And wash my soul all over.

[1] Vol. I. 293.   [2] Vol. 1. 609.   [3] B.G. xl. Pref. xxxvi.

iii. I, Thy unworthy child,
    Corrupt throughout and spoiled,
    Beseech Thee to relieve me,
    And graciously forgive me
    My sins, which have abounded,
    And my poor soul confounded.

iv. Through Thy atoning blood,
    That precious healing flood,
    Purge off all sin and sadness,
    And fill my heart with gladness :
    Lord, hear Thou my confession,
    And blot out my transgression.

v. Thou shalt my comfort be,
    Since Thou hast died for me ;
    I am by Thee acquitted
    Of all I e'er committed :
    My sins by Thee were carried,
    And in Thy tomb interred.

* * *

vii. I know my poverty ;
    But ne'ertheless, for me
    Are all good gifts procured,
    Since Thou hast death endured :
    Thus strengthened, I may banish
    All fears ; my foes must vanish.

* * *

ix. Christ, Thy atoning blood,
    The sinner's highest good,
    Is powerful to deliver
    And free the soul for ever
    From all claim of the devil,
    And cleanse it from all evil.

x. Lord Jesus Christ, in Thee
   I trust eternally:
   I know I shall not perish,
   But in Thy kingdom flourish:
   Since Thou hast death sustained,
   Life is for me obtained.

xi. Lord, strengthen Thou my heart;
   To me such grace impart,
   That nought which may await me
   From Thee may separate me.
   Let me with Thee, my Saviour,
   United be for ever.

Johann Heermann (1585-1647)   Tr. *Moravian Hymn-book*[1].

AUF MEINEN LIEBEN GOTT.

i. In God, my faithful God,
   I trust when dark my road;
   Though many woes o'ertake me,
   Yet He will not forsake me;
   His love it is doth send them,
   And when 'tis best will end them.

ii. My sins assail me sore,
   But I despair no more;
   I build on Christ Who loves me,
   From this Rock nothing moves me,
   Since I can all surrender
   To Him, my soul's Defender.

---

[1] Ed. 1877, No. 286. The original hymn has eleven stanzas, of which vi and viii are omitted in the translation.

iii. If death my portion be,
    Then death is gain to me,
    And Christ my life for ever,
    From Whom death cannot sever;
    Come when it may, He'll shield me,
    To Him I'll wholly yield me.

iv. Ah, Jesus Christ, my Lord,
    So meek in deed and word,
    Thou diedst once to save us,
    Because Thou fain wouldst have us
    After earth's life of sadness
    Heirs of Thy heavenly gladness.

v. "So be it," then I say,
    With all my heart each day;
    Guide us while here we wander
    Till, safely landed yonder,
    We too, dear Lord, adore Thee,
    And sing for joy before Thee.

? Sigismund Weingärtner (1607) Tr. *Catherine Winkworth*[1].

Johann Heermann's "Wo soll ich fliehen hin" was published in 1630. The melody associated with it from the outset had been sung, since 1609, to Sigismund Weingärtner's (?) "Auf meinen lieben Gott," which was published in 1607. The tune is of secular origin, and as attached to "Auf meinen lieben Gott" largely retained the form of the original[2]. The version in later use (*supra*) is found in Johann H. Schein's Leipzig *Cantional* (1627).

[1] *Chorale Book for England*, No. 147. The original hymn has five stanzas.
[2] See *Bach's Chorals*, Part II. 142, for the secular and 1609 forms.

Bach uses the melody in Cantatas 5, 89, 136, 148, 188 (c. 1725–35), and the Organ movements *infra*. His text is invariable, with one exception: in the Organ movements his second phrase of the melody follows Schein; elsewhere he writes G for F as the fifth note (*supra*) of it. Of this and other variations of Schein's text (A for E as the first note of bar 4 *supra*; A for F as the fifth note of bar 5 *supra*) Witt's text (No. 695) seems to afford the earliest example.

There are two Organ movements on the melody:

[142]

N. xvi. 4. The movement is the second of the *Schübler Chorals*. That it is among them indicates it as the arrangement of a movement in one of the lost Cantatas. The titles of Heermann's and Weingärtner's (?) hymns are both attached to it. There is no doubt, however, that it was inspired by the first stanza of "Wo soll ich fliehen hin." Its constantly recurring "genial little figure," as Sir Hubert Parry calls it[1], was suggested by the word "fliehen":

O whither shall I flee?

[143]

N. xix. 32. The movement also is based upon the first stanza of Heermann's hymn and exhibits

[1] *J. S. Bach*, p. 504.

similar treatment of the word "fliehen." Copies of it are in the Kirnberger, Voss, Forkel, and Schicht MSS.

In Krebs' *Sammelbuch*, in the Berlin Royal Library, is the MS. of a movement on the melody, printed in B.G. xl. 170 (P. ix. 39) among the "doubtful" compositions of Bach[1].

[1] Besides the 143 authentic compositions considered in this volume, there are six others of doubtful authority (see *supra*, p. 11): (1) ACH GOTT, VOM HIMMEL SIEH' DAREIN. The melody of Luther's hymn is also treated in Cantata 2 and elsewhere (see Part II. 132). (2) ACH, WAS SOLL ICH SÜNDER MACHEN. Johann Flittner's adaptation of this secular tune is treated by Bach in the *Choralgesänge*, No. 10. (3) AUS DER TIEFE RUFE ICH. The familiar tune (*Hymns A. and M.* No. 92) is not used by Bach elsewhere. (4) GOTT DER VATER WOHN' UNS BEI (N. xiii. 153). The melody of Luther's hymn is treated in the *Choralgesänge*, No. 113, but not elsewhere by Bach. (5) O VATER, ALLMÄCHTIGER GOTT. This sixteenth century (1531) melody to Johann Spangenberg's hymn is not used by Bach elsewhere. (6) JESU LEIDEN, PEIN UND TOD. Bach uses Vulpius' tune in Cantata 159 and elsewhere (see Part II. 431).

INDEX

NOTE. The titles of Bach's Organ Choral Preludes are printed in capitals.
Where biographical information is afforded in Parts i or ii the place is indicated in a square bracket.
Where other versions of the melodies are given in Parts i or ii the place is shown.
Bibliographical details of hymns and melodies provided in Parts i and ii are not repeated fully in Part iii. A single or a double asterisk indicates that additional information is available in Parts i or ii respectively.

**A solis ortus cardine, 128, 310
**ACH BLEIB' BEI UNS, HERR JESU CHRIST, 2, 74, 83 f.: melody, 83; hymn text, 84
Ach Gott, erhör' mein Seufzen und Wehklagen, 51
Ach Gott, thu' dich erbarmen, 58
**ACH GOTT UND HERR, 2, 86: melody, 86, ii. 237; hymn text, 86
**Ach Gott und Herr, 43
**ACH GOTT, VOM HIMMEL SIEH' DAREIN, 11: melody, ii. 132; hymn text, ii. 499
**Ach Gott, vom Himmel sieh' darein, 53, 346
**Ach Gott, wie manches Herzeleid, 51, 57
**Ach Herr, mich armen Sünder, 43, 196
Ach lieben Christen, seid getrost, 51
Ach, was ist doch unser Leben, 61
ACH, WAS SOLL ICH SÜNDER MACHEN, 11, 346
Ach, was soll ich Sünder machen, 60
**ACH WIE FLÜCHTIG, 2, 23, 25, 61, 89: melody, 89, ii. 193; hymn text, 90
Ach wir armen Sünder, 35
"Achtzehn Choräle," see "Eighteen Chorals"
**" Agnus Dei," the, 125, 282
Agricola, Johannes (1492–1566), 210 [ii. 451]
Ahle, Johann Rodolph (1625–73), 252 [ii. 254]
Albert, Heinrich (1604–51), 58 [i. 57]
Alberus, Erasmus (d. 1553), 37, 40, 58, 59, 110
Albinus, Johann Georg (1624–79), 56, 94 [ii. 198]

INDEX

**ALLE MENSCHEN MÜSSEN STERBEN, 2, 24, 25, 56, 93, 171, 227, 302: melody, 93, ii. 434; hymn text, 93
**Alle Menschen müssen sterben, 56
**ALLEIN GOTT IN DER HÖH' SEI EHR', 3, 67, 68, 69, 81, 96, 194, 261 : melody, 96, ii. 305; hymn text, 96
**Allein Gott in der Höh' sei Ehr', 39, 46
Allein nach dir, Herr Jesu Christ, 35
**Allein zu dir, Herr Jesu Christ, 43
Allenthalben, wo ich gehe, 61
Altenburg, Johann Michael (1584-1640), 32, 52, 189 [ii. 225]
Altnikol, Johann Christoph (d. 1759), 79, 236, 322
Amalienbibliothek, the, 14, 15, 79, 261
AN WASSERFLÜSSEN BABYLON, 3, 80, 101 : melody, 101; hymn text, 101
An Wasserflüssen Babylon, 50
Anhalt-Cöthen, Prince Leopold of, 19
"Art of Fugue," the, 12, 72, 79
**AUF MEINEN LIEBEN GOTT, 11, 74, 341 : melody, 341; hymn text, 343
**Auf meinen lieben Gott, 44, 57
**AUS DER TIEFE RUFE ICH, 11, 346
Aus meines Herzens Grunde, 59
**AUS TIEFER NOTH SCHREI ICH ZU DIR, 3, 67, 70, 106 : melody, 106; hymn text, 106
**Aus tiefer Noth schrei ich zu dir, 42, 158
Autographs, Bach's, 12, 13, 14, 18, 22, 25, 80, 99, 112, 132, 205, 242, 275, 308, 327, 331, 332
Ave ierarchia, 175

Bach, Andreas (1713-79?), 18, 177
—— Anna Magdalena (1700-60), 14, 239, 327
—— Bernhard (1700-43), 99
—— Carl Philipp Emmanuel (1714-88), 18, 71, 75, 78
—— Johann Christoph (1645-93), 17, 145
—— Wilhelm Friedemann (1710-84), 14, 28, 71, 226, 327
Bachgesellschaft Edition, the, 2 f., 13
Becker, Carl Ferdinand (1804-77), 16, 177, 296
Behm, Martin (1557-1622), 57 [ii. 250]
Berlin Royal Library, 12, 14, 17, 23, 71, 76, 78, 80, 100, 120, 153, 172, 194, 195, 213, 224, 239, 257, 271, 275, 299, 308, 328, 331, 332, 340, 346
Blaurer, Ambrosius (1492-1564), 50
Bodenschatz, Erhart (1608), 139
Böhm, Georg (1661-? 1734), 9, 104, 105, 111, 157, 279, 304, 328

INDEX 349

Böschenstein, Johann (1472-1539?), 134
Böttiger, Johann (1613-72), 46
Bolandus, Peter, 135
Bonn, Hermann (d. 1548), 35
Bourgeois, Louis (fl. 1541-61), 41, 53, 56, 316 [ii. 166]
Bowring, Sir John, 91
Brandenburg, Luise Henriette of (1627-67), 238
Brandenburg-Culmbach, Albrecht Margrave of (1522-57), 49 [i. 13]
Breitkopf and Haertel Edition, the, 2 f., 13, 17
Burck, Joachim von (1541?-1610), 41, 42
Burmeister, Franz Joachim (? 1633-72), 252 [ii. 254]
Buxtehude, Dietrich (1637-1707), 104, 105, 236, 245, 274

Calvisius, Seth (1556-1615), 6, 49, 50, 85, 214 [i. 17]
Camerarius, Joachim, 320
CHRIST, DER DU BIST DER HELLE TAG, 3, 109, 158, 296: melody, 109; hymn text, 109
Christ, der du bist der helle Tag, 59
**CHRIST IST ERSTANDEN, 3, 24, 26, 36, 113, 117 : melody, 113; hymn text, 113, 114
**Christ ist erstanden, 213
**CHRIST LAG IN TODESBANDEN, 3, 23, 26, 36, 115 : melody, 115, ii. 138; hymn text, 115
**CHRIST UNSER HERR ZUM JORDAN KAM, 4, 67, 70, 120: melody, 120; hymn text, 121
**Christ unser Herr zum Jordan kam, 42, 157
CHRISTE, ALLER WELT TROST, 69, 249: melody, 249; hymn text, 249
Christe, der du bist Tag und Licht, 59
Christe, du bist der helle Tag, 110
**CHRISTE, DU LAMM GOTTES, 4, 24, 25, 34, 124 : melody, 124; hymn text, 125, ii. 189
Christe, qui lux es et dies, 110
**CHRISTUM WIR SOLLEN LOBEN SCHON, 4, 24, 32, 126: melody, 126, ii. 368; hymn text, 126
**Christus, der ist mein Leben, 57
*CHRISTUS, DER UNS SELIG MACHT, 4, 24, 25, 34, 128, 140: melody, 129, i. 30, ii. 491 ; hymn text, 130
Christus ist erstanden, 213
Clausnitzer, Tobias (1618-84), 42, 252, 340
"Clavierübung" (Part III), 1, 12, 40, 66 f.
Coelos ascendit hodie, 37
Conditor alme siderum, 255
Coverdale, Bishop Myles, 102, 113, 157, 170, 183, 244

INDEX

Cruciger, Elisabethe (d. 1535), 183 [ii. 187]
Crüger, Johann (1598–1662), 35, 87, 91, 204, 224, 236, 241, 264, 291, 331 [i. 4]

DA JESUS AN DEM KREUZE STUND, 4, 25, 34, 133, 280: melody, 133; hymn text, 133
Dachstein, Wolfgang (d. *c.* 1561), 50, 101, 103
Danket dem Herrn, denn er ist sehr freundlich, 60
Danket dem Herrn, heut' und allzeit, 2, 85
DAS ALTE JAHR VERGANGEN IST, 4, 23, 25, 33, 65, 137: melody, 137; hymn text, 137
DAS JESULEIN SOLL DOCH MEIN TROST, 4, 140: melody, 140; hymn text, 141
Das walt' mein Gott, 59
Decius, Nikolaus (d. 1541), 39, 46, 97, 282 [i. 2]
Dehn, Professor S. W. (1799–1858), 17, 71, 281
Der du bist Drei in Einigkeit, 39
**Der Herr ist mein getreuer Hirt, 46
DER TAG, DER IST SO FREUDENREICH, 4, 24, 32, 143: melody, 143; hymn text, 143
Des heil'gen Geistes reiche Gnad', 38
Dies est laetitiae, 144
**DIES SIND DIE HEIL'GEN ZEHN GEBOT', 4, 25, 26, 41, 67, 69, 146, 181: melody, 146, ii. 287; hymn text, 146
Drese, Johann Samuel (d. 1716), 19
Dröbs, Herr, 16, 25, 254, 260, 299, 308
**Du Friedefürst, Herr Jesu Christ, 55
**Du sollst Gott, deinen Herren, lieben, 149
Duetti for Cembalo, the, 68, 70
**DURCH ADAMS FALL IST GANZ VERDERBT, 4, 23, 26, 44, 150: melody, 150; hymn text, 150
**Durch Adams Fall ist ganz verderbt, 55

Eber, Paul (1511–69), 41, 56, 179, 312, 317, 336 [ii. 174]
Ebert, Jakob (1549–1614), 55, 198 [ii. 268]
Eccard, Johann (1553–1611), 56, 335.
"Eighteen Chorals," the, 1, 12, 13, 78 f.
**EIN' FESTE BURG IST UNSER GOTT, 4, 153: melody, 153; hymn text, 153
**Ein' feste Burg ist unser Gott, 53
**EIN KIND GEBORN ZU BETHLEHEM, 9, 286: melody, 286; hymn text, 286
Eler, Franz (1588), 320
England, Paul, 117
Er denket der Barmherzigkeit, 74

Er kent die rechten Freudenstunden, 74
ERBARM' DICH MEIN, O HERRE GOTT, 5, 155 : melody,
    155 ; hymn text, 156
Erbarm' dich mein, O Herre Gott, 43
**Erhalt' uns, Herr, bei deinem Wort, 54
**ERSCHIENEN IST DER HERRLICHE TAG, 5, 25, 26, 36, 145,
    158 : melody, 158 ; hymn text, 159
ERSTANDEN IST DER HEIL'GE CHRIST, 5, 24, 26, 36, 160,
    168 : melody, 160 ; hymn text, 161
Erstanden ist der Herre Christ, 164
Erstanden ist uns Jesus Christ, 211, 214
**ES IST DAS HEIL UNS KOMMEN HER, 5, 23, 24, 26, 44, 166 :
    melody, 166 ; hymn text, 166
*ES IST GEWISSLICH AN DER ZEIT, 8, 266, 269 : melody, 266 ;
    hymn text, 269
*Es ist gewisslich an der Zeit, 269
*Es sind doch selig alle, 9, 284
Es spricht der Unweisen Mund wohl, 53
Es steh'n vor Gottes Throne, 41
**Es woll' uns Gott genädig sein, 53, 135, 157
Eya der grossen Liebe, 35

Fabricius, Werner (1633–79), 295 [ii. 163]
Figulus, Wolfgang (c. 1520–91), 177 [i. 64]
Fischer, Christoph (1520–97), 335
—— Michael Gotthardt (1793), 17
Fischhof, Professor, 14, 227, 271, 327
Flittner, Johann (1618–78), 60, 61, 62, 346
Förtsch, Basilius, 59, 199
Forkel, Johann Nikolaus (1749–1818), 2, 14, 71, 112, 115,
    129, 142, 187, 257, 281, 296, 308, 327, 346
Fowler, Rodney, 285
Franck, Johann (1618–77), 61, 226, 291 [i. 58]
—— Melchior (d. 1639), 34, 37, 56 [ii. 233]
—— Michael (1609–67), 61, 91 [ii. 193]
Frankenberger, Herr, 17, 24
**Freu' dich sehr, O meine Seele, 54, 58
Frisch auf, mein' Seel', verzage nicht, 51
Fritsch, Ahashuerus (1629–1701), 61 [ii. 248]
Fuger, Caspar (1593), 332 [i. 51]
—— Caspar (d. c. 1592), 333 [i. 52]

Gambold, John, 256
Gastoldi, Giovanni Giacomo (d. 1622), 217
Gelobet sei der Herr, der Gott Israel, 40

352 INDEX

**GELOBET SEIST DU, JESU CHRIST, 5, 23, 24, 25, 32, 95, 169,
194 : melody, 169 ; hymn text, 169
Gen Himmel aufgefahren ist, 37
Gerhardt, Paul (1607–76), 59, 196 [i. 7]
Gesius, Bartholomäus (c. 1555–1614), 52, 55, 199 [ii. 268]
Gieb Fried', O frommer, treuer Gott, 55
Gigas, Johannes G. (1514–81), 51 [ii. 357]
Gleichauf, Herr, 16, 88, 98, 119, 120, 227, 275, 341
**Gloria in excelsis Deo, 39, 96
GOTT DER VATER WOHN' UNS BEI, 12, 346
Gott der Vater wohn' uns bei, 38
*Gott des Himmels und der Erden, 58
GOTT, DURCH DEINE GÜTE, 5, 31, 174 : melody, 173 ; hymn text, 174
Gott hat das Evangelium, 58
Gott ist mein Heil, mein' Hülf' und Trost, 52
Gott sei gelobet und gebenedeiet, 46
Gott Vater, der du deine Sonn, 60, 137, 139
GOTTES SOHN IST KOMMEN, 5, 18, 23, 24, 31, 173, 222, 304 :
melody, 173 ; hymn text, 173
Gotthold Bequest, the, 16
Grasnick, Herr (d. 1877), 15
**Grates nunc omnes reddamus, 169
Graumann, Johann (1487–1541), 47 [ii. 177]
Greitter, Matthäus (d. c. 1550), 285 [i. 15]
Grell, Herr, 261
Griepenkerl, Friedrich Conrad, 13, 16, 25, 28, 71, 103, 172, 177, 261, 281, 296
**Gross ist, O grosser Gott, 275, 278
Grüenwald, Georg (d. 1530), 49 [ii. 309]
Guhr, Capellmeister, 112

Handel, Georg Friedrich, 76
Harsdörffer, Georg Philipp (1607–58), 43
Hassler, Hans Leo (1564–1612), 195 [i. 8]
**Hast du denn, Jesu, dein Angesicht, 61, 246
Hauser, Franz (1794–1870), 16
—— Joseph, 16, 24, 72, 79, 88, 112, 115, 153, 172, 292, 303
Heermann, Johann (1585–1647), 35, 44, 50, 278, 343 [i. 4]
Hegenwalt, Erhart (1524), 43, 157
Helder, Bartholomäus (d. 1635), 142
*HELFT MIR GOTT'S GÜTE PREISEN, 5, 25, 33, 177, 312 :
melody, 177, i. 63 ; hymn text, 178
Helmbold, Ludwig (1532–98), 41, 42, 49, 60, 312 [ii. 282]
Henssberg, Paul von (d. 1652), 94

INDEX 353

Herberger, Valerius (1562–1627), 56, 298 [i. 35]
Herman, Nikolaus (c. 1485–1561), 56, 60, 139, 159, 258 [ii. 171]
**HERR CHRIST, DER EIN'GE GOTTES-SOHN, 5, 23, 24, 25, 31, 95, 171, 182, 227, 281: melody, 182, ii. 186; hymn text, 182
**Herr Gott, dich loben alle wir, 41
**HERR GOTT DICH LOBEN WIR, 5, 185, 194: hymn text, 185
**Herr Gott, dich loben wir, 41
Herr Gott, erhalt' uns für und für, 42
HERR GOTT, NUN SCHLEUSS DEN HIMMEL AUF, 5, 24, 26, 33, 65, 136, 187, 280: melody, 187; hymn text, 188
HERR GOTT, NUN SEI GEPREISET, 5, 31, 183: melody, 182, ii. 186; hymn text, 183
HERR JESU CHRIST, DICH ZU UNS WEND', 6, 24, 26, 38, 81, 191: melody, 191; hymn text, 191
**Herr Jesu Christ, du höchstes Gut, 43, 46, 57
**Herr Jesu Christ, ich weiss gar wohl, 57
**Herr Jesu Christ, mein's Lebens Licht, 57
**Herr Jesu Christ, wahr Mensch und Gott, 35, 56, 334
*Herzlich lieb hab' ich dich, O Herr, 57
Herzlich thut mich erfreuen, 59
*HERZLICH THUT MICH VERLANGEN, 6, 195: melody, 195; hymn text, 195
*Herzlich thut mich verlangen, 43, 196
*Herzliebster Jesu, was hast du verbrochen, 35
HEUT' TRIUMPHIRET GOTTES SOHN, 6, 24, 26, 36, 198: melody, 198; hymn text, 198
Heyden, Sebald (1494–1561), 285 [i. 15]
HILF GOTT, DASS MIR'S GELINGE, 6, 24, 26, 34, 136, 201: melody, 201; hymn text, 202
Hintze, Jakob (1622–1702), 56
Hodenberg, Bodo von (1604–50), 319, 323
Hörnigk, Ludwig von (d. 1667), 58
Homilius, Gottfried August (1714–85), 9, 292
Horn, Johann (d. 1547), 60
Hostis Herodes impie, 129
Huber, Christian (1682), 315

**Ich dank' dir, lieber Herre, 54, 58
Ich dank' dir schon durch deinen Sohn, 59
Ich freu' mich in dem Herren, 54
*Ich ging einmal spazieren, 180, 312
**ICH HAB' MEIN SACH' GOTT HEIMGESTELLT, 6, 205: melody, 205, ii. 344; hymn text, 206

T. B. C. 23

INDEX

**Ich hab' mein Sach' Gott heimgestellt, 46
**Ich hört ein Fräulein klagen, 184
Ich komm jetzt als ein armer Gast, 46
**ICH RUF' ZU DIR, HERR JESU CHRIST, 6, 23, 25, 26, 49, 209: melody, 209; hymn text, 209
**Ich weiss ein Blümlein hübsch und fein, 46
**Ich weiss mir ein Röslein hübsch und fein, 205
*IN DICH HAB' ICH GEHOFFET, HERR, 6, 24, 25, 26, 50, 145, 211, 313, 326: melody, 211, 212; hymn text, 212
*In dich hab' ich gehoffet, Herr, 50, 135, 214
IN DIR IST FREUDE, 6, 24, 25, 33, 65, 215: melody, 215; hymn text, 216
IN DULCI JUBILO, 6, 24, 32, 176, 194, 220: melody, 220; hymn text, 220
**In Gottes Namen fahren wir, 148

Ja, er ists, das Heil der Welt, 251
Jacobi, John Christian, 131, 151, 167, 179, 191, 270
Jauchzet dem Herren, alle Land, 329
**Jesu, der du meine Seele, 43
*JESU LEIDEN, PEIN UND TOD, 12, 346: melody, i. 27, ii. 431; hymn text, ii. 532
**JESU, MEINE FREUDE, 7, 23, 24, 25, 32, 95, 224, 302: melody, 224; hymn text, 224
Jesu, meines Herzens Freud', 60
Jesu, wollst uns weisen, 218
Jesus Christus, nostra salus, 231
JESUS CHRISTUS, UNSER HEILAND, DER DEN TOD, 7, 25, 26, 36, 227: melody, 227; hymn text, 228
JESUS CHRISTUS, UNSER HEILAND, DER VON UNS, 7, 25, 67, 70, 81, 230: melody, 230; hymn text, 230
Jesus Christus, unser Heiland, Der von uns, 45
**JESUS, MEINE ZUVERSICHT, 7, 236: melody, 236, ii. 412; hymn text, 236
Jetzt komm ich als ein armer Gast, 46
Joachimsthal Gymnasium, the, 14, 15, 79
Jonas, Justus (1493-1555), 53 [ii. 453]

Kegel, Cantor, 172
Keimann, Christian (1607-62), 61, 294 [ii. 221]
Keinen hat Gott verlassen, 51
Kellner, Johann Peter, 15, 99, 195
Kennedy, Benjamin Hall, 84, 335
Kiel, Tobias (1584-1626), 189
Kinchen, C., 127

INDEX 355

Kirnberger, Johann Philipp (1721-83), 15, 22, 25, 79, 80, 87, 118, 129, 142, 153, 155, 172, 177, 193, 208, 215, 227, 254, 257, 275, 304, 307, 327, 334, 346
Kittel, Johann Christian (1732-1809), 15, 16, 129, 172, 185, 224, 254, 308
Knoll, Christoph (1563-1650), 196 [ii. 433]
Königsberg University Library, the, 14, 16, 25, 80, 88
Kolross, Johann (d. 1558?), 49, 58 [ii. 212]
**KOMM, GOTT, SCHÖPFER, HEILIGER GEIST, 7, 23, 24, 26, 37, 81, 239: melody, 239, 240, ii. 479; hymn text, 240
Komm, heiliger Geist, erfüll' die Herzen, 37
**KOMM, HEILIGER GEIST, HERRE GOTT, 7, 80, 242: melody, 242; hymn text, 243
**Komm, heiliger Geist, Herre Gott, 37
**KOMMST DU NUN, JESU, VOM HIMMEL HERUNTER, 7, 61, 74, 246: melody, 246; hymn text, 246
**Kommt her zu mir, spricht Gottes Sohn, 49, 52
Krebs, Johann Ludwig (1713-80), 15, 23, 79, 80, 87, 88, 99, 100, 103, 105, 155, 158, 172, 194, 198, 224, 235, 245, 254, 260, 275, 281, 284, 296, 308, 313, 339, 341, 346
Kugelmann, Johann (d. c. 1556), 47
Kuhnau, Johann (d. 1722), 158
"Kunst der Fuge," see "Art of Fugue"
KYRIE, GOTT HEILIGER GEIST, 69, 249: melody, 249; hymn text, 250
KYRIE, GOTT VATER IN EWIGKEIT, 7, 69, 248: melody, 248; hymn text, 249
Kyrie summum bonum, 250

Lass' mich dein sein und bleiben, 54
Leipzig Municipal Library, the, 14, 16
Leon, Johannes (d. 1597), 207
**Leve le cœur, ouvre l'oreille, 10, 316
LIEBSTER JESU, WIR SIND HIER, 8, 23, 25, 26, 38, 40, 251: melody, 251; hymn text, 251
Lindemann, Johann (c. 1550-1634), 217
"Little Organ-book," see "Orgelbüchlein"
LOB SEI DEM ALLMÄCHTIGEN GOTT, 8, 23, 24, 25, 31, 95, 255, 281: melody, 255; hymn text, 255
Lob sei Gott in des Himmels Thron, 32
**Lobe den Herren, den mächtigen König der Ehren, 7, 248
Lobe den Herren, der Alles so herrlich regieret, 74
Lobet den Herrn, denn er ist sehr freundlich, 60
**LOBT GOTT, IHR CHRISTEN, ALLE GLEICH [ALLZUGLEICH], 8, 24, 25, 32, 194, 258: melody, 258; hymn text, 258

Lobwasser, Ambrosius (1515–85), 53
Luther, Martin (1483–1546), 37, 38, 39, 41, 42, 45, 46, 47, 48,
    53, 54, 55, 56, 106, 110, 117, 122, 127, 129, 148, 152, 153,
    170, 186, 203, 229, 230, 241, 244, 263, 268, 273, 301, 304,
    309, 338, 346

Macdonald, George, 122, 127, 148, 186, 229, 231, 241, 268,
    273, 301, 309
MacGill, Hamilton M., 287
*Mach's mit mir, Gott, nach deiner Güt', 57
Mag ich Unglück nicht wiederstahn, 50
Magdeburg, Joachim (c. 1525–83), 49 [i. 13]
Major, Johann (1564–1654), 87 [ii. 238]
Marenzio, Luca, 265
Mathesius, Johannes (1504–65), 59
Media vita in morte sumus, 56
*Mein G'mut ist mir verwirret, 196
Mein' Wallfahrt ich vollendet hab', 58
**MEINE SEELE ERHEBT DEN HERREN, 8, 74, 260
**Meine Seel' erhebt den Herren, 40
Melanchthon, Philipp (1497–1560), 84, 110, 135
Mendelssohn Bartholdy, Felix, 16, 22, 25, 132, 205, 242, 292
Mensch, willst du leben seliglich, 41
Menschenkind, merk eben, 175
Merk auf, merk auf, du schöne, 270
Meusel, Wolfgang (1497–1563), 46, 59 [ii. 351]
**MIT FRIED' UND FREUD' ICH FAHR' DAHIN, 8, 24, 25, 33,
    262: melody, 262; hymn text, 262
Mitten wir im Leben sind, 56
Mizler, Lorenz Christoph (1711–78), 76
Moller, Martin (1547–1606), 51 [ii. 134]
Mozartstiftung, the, 14, 15
Müller, Heinrich (1527), 203
Müntzer, M. R., 58
"Musical Offering," the, 12, 72
"Musikalisches Opfer," see "Musical Offering"

Nachtenhöfer, Caspar Friedrich (1624–85), 247
Naumann, Ernst, 13
Neander, Joachim (1650–80), 248 [ii. 399]
"Neues Cantional," Witt's, 29
Neumark, Georg (1621–81), 52, 324, 325 [ii. 184]
Nicolai, Philipp (1556–1608), 51, 53, 315, 328 [ii. 130]
Niedling, Johann (1602–68), 38
Novello Edition, the, 2 f., 13, 23

INDEX

Nun bitten wir den heil'gen Geist, 37
**NUN DANKET ALLE GOTT, 8, 81, 264: melody, 264; hymn text, 264
Nun freut euch, Gottes Kinder, all, 37
*NUN FREUT EUCH, LIEBEN CHRISTEN G'MEIN, 8, 266: melody, 266; hymn text, 266
*Nun freut euch, lieben Christen g'mein, 46
Nun giebt mein Jesus gute Nacht, 35
**NUN KOMM, DER HEIDEN HEILAND, 8, 24, 31, 81, 272: melody, 272, ii. 208; hymn text, 272
Nun lasst uns den Leib begraben, 57
**Nun lasst uns Gott, dem Herren, 60
**Nun lob', mein' Seel', den Herren, 47
*Nun ruhen alle Wälder, 59
Nyberg, L. T., 298

**O GOTT, DU FROMMER GOTT, 9, 95, 140, 275, 296: melody, 275; hymn text, 276
**O Gott, du frommer Gott, 50
O Gott, mein Herre, 215, 218
**O grosser Gott von Macht, 56
*O Haupt voll Blut und Wunden, 6, 196
O heil'ger Geist, du göttlich's Feu'r, 38
O heiliger Geist, O heiliger Gott, 38
**O Herre Gott, dein göttlich Wort, 41
**O Jesu Christ, mein's Lebens Licht, 57
O Jesu, du edle Gabe, 46
O Jesu, wie ist dein' Gestalt, 34
*O LAMM GOTTES UNSCHULDIG, 9, 25, 34, 81, 234, 281. melody, 281, i. 1, ii. 495; hymn text, 282
*O Lamm Gottes unschuldig, 315
O lux beata trinitas, 39
*O MENSCH, BEWEIN' DEIN' SÜNDE GROSS, 9, 23, 24, 25, 34, 140, 284: melody, 284; hymn text, 285
O Traurigkeit, O Herzeleid, 27, 34
O VATER, ALLMÄCHTIGER GOTT, 12, 346
*O Welt, ich muss dich lassen, 59
O wir armen Sünder, 35
**"Old Hundredth," the, 41
Oley, Johann Christoph (d. 1789), 16, 24, 25, 79, 100, 194, 208, 215, 271, 327, 334
**Or sus, serviteurs du Seigneur, 41
"Orgelbüchlein," the, 1; Autograph of, 12, 14, 18; date of, 19 f.; MSS. of, 22 f.; Mendelssohn's MS. of, 25; plan of, 26 f.; modelled on Witt's Hymn-book, 29 f.; reveals

23—3

Bach's favourite hymns and tunes, 64; his probable use of the Gotha " Cantional," 65

Pachelbel, Johann (1653-1706), 194, 250, 265
*Patris Sapientia, 129, 132
Pavier Tone, the, 152
Peters Edition, the, 2 f., 13
" Psalmodia sacra, Oder : Andächtige und schöne Gesänge," 29
**PUER NATUS IN BETHLEHEM, 9, 24, 32, 165, 171, 286: melody, 286, 308; hymn text, 286
**Puer natus in Bethlehem, 145, 308
Puer nobis nascitur, 310

Reichardt, Court Organist (1846), 23
Reinken, Johann Adam (1623-1722), 105
Reissner, Adam (d. c. 1575), 50, 213 [i. 17]
Resonet in laudibus, 331
Ringwaldt, Bartholomäus (1532-c. 1600), 43, 57, 270 [ii. 353]
Rinkart, Martin (1586-1649), 265 [ii. 294]
Rist, Johann (1607-67), 27, 34, 35, 43, 44, 59 [i. 20]
Rodigast, Samuel (1649-1708), 52 [ii. 164]
Roh, Johann (d. 1547), 175
Roitzsch, Ferdinand, 13, 23, 281
" Rolandslied," the, 51
Rosenmüller, Johann (1619-84), 94 [ii. 197]
Rosenthal, Johann (1615-90), 61
Russell, Arthur T., 159, 250, 258
Rust, Friedrich Wilhelm (1739-96), 17, 23
—— Wilhelm, 21, 23, 29, 72, 80
Rutilius, Martin (1550-1618), 87 [ii. 238]

Sachs, Hans (1494-1576), 50
Sachse, Michael (1542-1618), 32
" St Anne's " Fugue, 68, 70
Salve Jesu, summe bonum, 294
Saxe-Weimar, William Duke of (1598-1662), 191
Schalling, Martin (1532-1608), 57 [i. 39]
Schechs, Jakob Peter (1607-59), 51
Schein, Johann H. (1586-1630), 38, 57, 66, 180, 214, 341 [i. 32]
Schelble, Johann Nepomuk (1789-1837), 16, 25, 88, 98, 99, 119, 120, 172, 227, 271, 275, 292, 307, 308, 327, 328, 334, 341
Schicht, Johann Gottfried (1753-1823), 17, 99, 172, 307, 308, 334, 346
Schmidt, Balthasar (1746), 75
—— Johann (1746), 15, 72

INDEX 359

Schmidt, Johann Christoph (1746), 73
Schmucker, Caspar, 51
**SCHMÜCKE DICH, O LIEBE SEELE, 9, 80, 289: melody, 289
    hymn text, 289
**Schmücke dich, O liebe Seele, 61
Schneegass, Cyriacus (1546–97), 43, 55, 196 [ii. 370]
Schneesing, Johannes (d. 1567), 43, 44 [ii. 206]
Schnurr, Balthasar (1572–1644), 56
Schübler, Johann Georg (c. 1746), 72
—— Chorals, the, 1, 12, 70 f. ; date of, 71 ; arrangements
    of Cantata movements, 73, 85
Schumann, Clara, 26
—— Richard, 292
Schwenke, Christian Friedrich (1767–1822), 17
Sedulius, Coelius, 128
SEI GEGRÜSSET, JESU GÜTIG, 9, 292 : melody, 292, 293;
    hymn text, 293
Sei gegrüsset, Jesu gütig, 61
Selnecker, Nikolaus (1532–92), 35, 46, 54, 84 [ii. 146]
Sieber, Justus (1628–95), 46
**Singen wir aus Herzensgrund, 60
So wünsch' ich nun ein' gute Nacht, 51
Spangenberg, Cyriacus (1568), 111
—— Johann (1484–1550), 175, 346
Spengler, Lazarus (1479–1534), 45, 151 [ii. 179]
Speratus, Paul (1484–1551), 45, 167 [ii. 154]
Spiritus Sancti gratia, 38
Spitta, Philipp, 17
Stabat ad lignum Crucis, 135
Steurlein, Johannes (1546–1613), 138
Stieler, Caspar (1679), 44 [ii. 439]
Stolshagius, Caspar (1591), 199
**Surrexit Christus hodie, 161, 164

Tapp, Jakob (d. 1630), 138
Telemann, Georg Philipp (1681–1767), 190, 226
Terry, C. Sanford, 110, 125, 141, 143, 174, 183, 196, 247, 294, 319
Teschner, Melchior (1614), 56, 297 [i. 34]
Tonus Peregrinus, 40

*VALET WILL ICH DIR GEBEN, 9, 297 : melody, 297 ; hymn
    text, 297
*Valet will ich dir geben, 56
*VATER UNSER IM HIMMELREICH, 9, 23, 26, 42, 69, 95, 177,
    300 : melody, 300 ; hymn text, 300

*Vater unser im Himmelreich, 51, 157
**Veni Redemptor gentium, 272
**Veni Sancte Spiritus reple tuorum, 37
**Vespera jam venit, nobiscum Christe maneto, 84
Vetter, Daniel (d. 1721), 66, 254 [ii. 152]
Vitam quae faciunt beatiorem, 60
*VOM HIMMEL HOCH DA KOMM ICH HER, 10, 12, 13, 14, 23, 24, 32, 72, 75 f., 194, 304: melody, 304; hymn text, 304
**VOM HIMMEL KAM DER ENGEL SCHAAR, 10, 12, 25, 32, 288, 308 : melody, 308; hymn text, 308
*VON GOTT WILL ICH NICHT LASSEN, 10, 81, 145, 310, 326 : melody, 310; hymn text, 311
*Von Gott will ich nicht lassen, 49, 180
Vopelius, Gottfried (1645–1715), 61, 292, 331
VOR DEINEN THRON TRET' ICH HIEMIT, 10, 79, 82, 318 : melody, 316; hymn text, 318
Voss, Count, 14, 129, 142, 177, 193, 208, 215, 227, 296, 327, 346
Vulpius, Melchior (c. 1560–1615), 38, 346 [i. 28]

Wach, Frau (1880), 26
**Wach auf, mein Herz, und singe, 60
Wach auf, wach auf, du schöne, 266
**WACHET AUF, RUFT UNS DIE STIMME, 10, 73, 314 : melody, 314, ii. 495 ; hymn text, 314
**Wachet doch, erwacht, ihr Schläfer, 43
**Wär' Gott nicht mit uns diese Zeit, 53
Wagener, Professor (1878), 22
Walther, Johann (1496–1570), 43, 53, 117, 120, 122, 128, 135, 148, 152, 157, 171, 184, 229, 232, 273, 338 [i. 42]
—— Johann Gottfried (1684–1748), 12, 16, 17, 23, 24, 80, 88, 155, 172, 177, 198, 208, 274, 275, 299, 304
**Warum betrübst du dich, mein Herz, 50
WAS FÜRCHT'ST DU, FEIND HERODES, SEHR, 4, 127, 129 : melody, 126; hymn text, 127
**Was Gott thut, das ist wohlgethan, Es bleibt, 52
Was Gott thut, das ist wohlgethan, Kein einig, 52
*Was mein Gott will, das g'scheh' allzeit, 49, 50, 51, 58
Weingärtner, Sigismund (1607), 57, 344 [ii. 468]
Weisse, Michael (c. 1480–1534), 49, 57, 131, 164, 175, 256 [i. 30]
Weltlich Ehr' und zeitlich Gut, 49
Wenn dich Unglück thut greifen an, 51
**Wenn mein Stündlein vorhanden ist, 43, 56
WENN WIR IN HÖCHSTEN NÖTHEN SEIN, 10, 23, 24, 50, 82, 316, 327 : melody, 316; hymn text, 317
Wer Gott vertraut, 49

INDEX 361

**WER NUR DEN LIEBEN GOTT LÄSST WALTEN, 10, 13, 23, 52, 74, 324: melody, 324; hymn text, 324
*Werde munter, mein Gemüthe, 59
Westphal, Rudolf, 14, 296, 308, 327
Wie nach einem Wasserquelle, 53
**WIE SCHÖN LEUCHTET DER MORGENSTERN, 10, 13, 328: melody, 328; hymn text, 329
**Wie schön leuchtet der Morgenstern, 34, 53, 315
Wie soll ich doch die Güte dein', 57
Wie's Gott gefällt, 50
Wildenfels, Anark Herr zu (d. 1539), 41 [ii. 462]
Winkworth, Catherine, 87, 94, 107, 138, 154, 174, 189, 195, 206, 210, 213, 216, 226, 237, 252, 263, 265, 278, 282, 291, 298, 306, 312, 315, 317, 325, 330, 333, 338, 340, 344
*WIR CHRISTENLEUT', 10, 24, 25, 32, 332: melody, 332; hymn text, 332
WIR DANKEN DIR, HERR JESU CHRIST, 11, 24, 26, 34, 145, 334: melody, 334; hymn text, 334
Wir danken dir, Herr Jesu Christ, 46
WIR GLAUBEN ALL' AN EINEN GOTT, SCHÖPFER, 11, 67, 69, 336: melody, 336; hymn text, 337
WIR GLAUBEN ALL' AN EINEN GOTT, VATER, 11, 339: melody, 339; hymn text, 340
Wir glauben all' an einen Gott, Vater, 42
Wir haben schwerlich, 44
Witt, Christian Friedrich (d. 1716), 29 f.; collation of his Hymn-book with the "Orgelbüchlein," 31 f.; his melodic texts, 85, 87, 91, 95, 104, 107, 111, 114, 117, 123, 125, 128, 129, 132, 135, 139, 142, 145, 149, 152, 155, 157, 160, 165, 167, 171, 176, 180, 184, 188, 197, 200, 204, 207, 210, 213, 214, 215, 221, 226, 229, 232, 238, 241, 245, 250, 253, 257, 259, 263, 265, 271, 273, 278, 283, 285, 288, 291, 293, 295, 298, 302, 307, 310, 313, 320, 326, 331, 333, 336, 338, 340
**Wo Gott der Herr nicht bei uns hält, 51, 53
Wo Gott zum Haus nicht giebt sein' Gunst, 48, 49
**WO SOLL ICH FLIEHEN HIN, 11, 74, 341: melody, 341; hymn text, 341
**Wo soll ich fliehen hin, 44, 57
Wohl dem der in Gottes Furcht steht, 48, 49
Wohlauf, ihr Musicanten, 218
Woodward, Rev. G. R., 199

**Zion hört die Wächter singen, 73
Zwingli, Huldreich, 135, 233

CAMBRIDGE: PRINTED BY
J. B. PEACE, M.A.,
AT THE UNIVERSITY PRESS

BY THE SAME AUTHOR

JOHANN SEBASTIAN BACH: HIS LIFE, ART, AND WORK. Translated from the German of JOHANN NIKOLAUS FORKEL, with Notes and Appendices. Pp. xxxii+321. With seven illustrations. 21s net.

[LONDON: CONSTABLE AND CO., LTD.]

"A complete guide to Bach's noble contribution to music."—*Today.*

"The first adequate translation of this work...The appendices are probably to the student the most valuable part of the present volume."—*Musical Opinion.*

"A valuable addition to the Bach literature."—*Spectator.*

"Dr Terry's copious footnotes and appendices add enormously to the value of the book."—*Music Student.*

"Indispensable to all Bach students."—Mr Ernest Newman in *Sunday Times.*

"Two-thirds of what Dr Terry magnanimously describes as 'Bach by Forkel' is Bach by Terry. My only complaint is that there is not still more Terry."—*New Statesman.*

"Should be in every musician's library."—*Glasgow Herald.*

"One of the most valuable contributions possible to Bach literature."—*Queen.*

"Contains materials for a history of Bach criticism from the beginning of the nineteenth century until the present day."—*Times.*

"An extremely valuable collection of learned information."
Athenaeum.

"A model of historical research; should prove indispensable to the student of Bach."—*Aberdeen Journal.*

"Professor Terry has added appendices that altogether more than double the size of the original, so that Forkel has ceased to be a merely interesting survival and has become a necessity."
Musical Times.

"Of the first importance to all interested in searching below the surface of the subject."—*Oxford Magazine.*

"Extremely useful as a work of reference."—*Scotsman.*

"What an admirable storehouse of facts this volume is."
Yorkshire Post.

BACH'S MASS IN B MINOR. A Study. Pp. 37. 2s 6d net.

[J. MACLEHOSE AND SONS]

"Brimful of information."—*Musical News.*

"Should be read for something more than its comment upon technical details, since there is something more in it—a spirit of enthusiastic reverence which illumines its sound scholarship."—*Times.*

"As handy and stimulating a guide as the student or the man in the street could wish to have...No one, we imagine, could read this little book without being forthwith fired with a desire to hear a performance of the Mass."—Mr Ernest Newman in *Birmingham Post.*

"Of genuine value to musical expository literature."—*Scotsman.*

CPSIA information can be obtained
at www.ICGtesting.com
Printed in the USA
LVHW101517011122
732097LV00005B/262